THE GREAT MAGDALENS

"*And behold a woman that was in the city, a sinner, when she knew that he sat at meat in the Pharisee's house, brought an alabaster box of ointment; and standing behind at his feet, she began to wash his feet, with tears, and wiped them with the hairs of her head, and kissed his feet, and anointed them with the ointment.*"

—Luke 7:37-38

St. Mary Magdalen,
the penitent woman of the Gospels.

THE GREAT MAGDALENS

Famous Women Who Returned to God after Lives of Sin

By

Msgr. Hugh Francis Blunt, LL.D.

"Many sins are forgiven her, because she hath loved much. But to whom less is forgiven, he loveth less. And he said to her: Thy sins are forgiven thee."   —Luke 7:47-48

TAN BOOKS AND PUBLISHERS, INC.
Rockford, Illinois 61105

Nihil Obstat: Arthur J. Scanlan, S.T.D.
                  Censor Librorum

Imprimatur: ✠ Patrick Cardinal Hayes
                  Archbishop of New York
                  New York
                  September 29, 1927

ISBN 0-89555-837-8

Printed and bound in the United States of America.

TAN BOOKS AND PUBLISHERS, INC.
P.O. Box 424
Rockford, Illinois 61105
2006

"And he said to the woman: thy faith hath made thee safe, go in peace."
—*Luke* 7:50

PREFACE

I ONCE heard a very learned and very pious bishop say that he found Tennyson's *Idylls of the King* one of the finest books of spiritual reading. And, indeed, the *Morte d'Arthur,* which the non-Catholic mind of Tennyson somehow could not successfully cope with, is essentially a spiritual book, for the story of the Knights of the Round Table is nothing more than a commentary on the folly of sin. It was sin which destroyed the work of King Arthur and his noble knights, the sin of Launcelot and Queen Guinevere. It is sin, and then at the end above it all rises the Magdalen Queen in the glory of her penitence. "And when Queen Guinevere," says the old book, "understood that King Arthur was slain, and all the noble knights, Sir Mordred and all the remnant, then the Queen stole away, and five ladies with her, and so she went to Almesbury; and then she let make herself a nun, and wore white clothes and black, and great penance she took, as ever did sinful lady in this land, and never creature could make her merry; but lived in fasting, prayers and almsdeeds, that all manner of people marveled how virtuously she was changed."

And so she wore out, as Tennyson makes her say,

> in almsdeed and in prayer
> The sombre close of that voluptuous day
> Which wrought the ruin of my lord the King.

When later Launcelot found her there in her abode of penance, she said to him, "Therefore Sir Launcelot, wit thou well I am set in such a plight to get my soul heal; and yet I trust through God's grace that after my death to have a sight of the blessed face of Christ, and at domesday to sit on his right side, for as sinful as ever I was are saints in Heaven." Whether or not the story of Guinevere be mostly legend, there is truth in what the old writer puts upon her lips to say that even greater sinners than she were now saints in Heaven. That is the message of hope which runs through all the ages. It is in the heart of Guinevere; it is in the heart of Anne Boleyn.

I have always felt pity for poor Anne Boleyn. A heartless, scheming woman she was, indeed. She may have been guilty of all the horrible crimes of which she was accused and convicted. But at least she went before her God with a contrite heart. The day before her execution she invited one of her attendant ladies to be seated in the chair of state. The horrified lady replied that it would ill become her to take the seat of the Queen. "Ah, madame," replied Anne, "that title is gone. I am a condemned person, and by law have no estate left me in this life, but for clearing of my conscience." Most of that night she spent in prayer with her almoner. She had made her confession with true penitence. She had cleared her conscience well. As she prepared her head for the block, she said, "Alas, poor head! in a very brief space thou wilt roll in the dust on the scaffold; and as in life thou didst not merit

to wear the crown of a queen, so in death thou deserv-
est not better doom than this." Then as she took leave
of her weeping ladies, she said, "Esteem your honor
far beyond your life; and in your prayers to the Lord
Jesu forget not to pray for my soul."

At the end, all of Anne's queenly glories were gone;
she was then but a poor, sinful woman anxious only
about the clearing of her conscience.

Anne had but little time for repentance, no more
than had the Good Thief. Some of her penitent sisters, like La Vallière, like Montespan, measured their
contrition by the austerities of the years. But they were
all essentially the same—all sisters under the skin, all
earnest, whether for the day that was left or the years
that were left, to clear their conscience. A mighty
task, indeed. It was a holy pope who said that it is a
greater miracle to convert a sinner than to restore a
dead man to life. A mighty task, but not a hopeless
one. Lady Macbeth might despair of cleansing her
hand of the "damnèd spot": "Here's the smell of the
blood still: all the perfumes of Arabia will not sweeten
this little hand."

But her sisters in crime knew better. There was no
indelible spot to Him Who said, "If your sins be as
scarlet, they shall be made as white as snow; and if
they be as red as crimson, they shall be as white as
wool." The penitent women took those words as a
personal message to themselves. Therein was their
hope for the "clearing of their conscience." And in the
repentance of these women who are witnesses to the

folly of sin, we have examples unto our sanctification. St. Teresa found it so, at any rate. One of her favorite saints was St. Mary Magdalen, Magdalen who had sinned much, but who, more than all else, had loved much. "Albert the Great," says Father Sicard in his *Life of St. Mary Magdalen,* "holds it true that God made two great luminaries, the Mother of the Lord, and the sister of Lazarus; a greater luminary to preside over the day, and a lesser luminary to watch over the night in serving as an example to sinners."

Even lesser luminaries still are these penitent women whose stories I beg to tell, but luminaries nevertheless, shining lights of God's good mercy. Many of them are heroines of penance. It is so easy to imitate their sins, so hard to compete with their tears, so easy to condemn their wickedness, so hard to follow them in their zeal to atone for that wickedness. "David sinned, as kings are wont to do," says St. Ambrose, "but he did penance; he wept and he groaned, as kings are not wont to do." Somehow it takes the saint to appreciate the worth of the penitent. "Sanctity to sin is kind," sings Father Tabb, in one of his unpublished poems. There is nothing more beautiful than St. Jerome's description of Asella, the penitent: "Nothing can be milder than her severity, nothing more severe than her mildness; nothing more melancholy than her sweetness, nothing sweeter than her melancholy. Her figure denotes mortification without the least pride; her words are like silence, and her silence has words; her exterior is always the same; her dress exhibits nothing refined or curious; her ornaments consist in their plainness. The good speak of her with admiration, and the wicked dare not attack her. Let the priests of the Lord on beholding her be filled with profound veneration."

Veneration, indeed, for these women who sacrificed the sweetness of sin for the salt of tears. "There but for the grace of God go I," said the good man watching the condemned criminal going to execution; but better still, and truer still, we may say, as we watch these once abandoned women taking the Kingdom of God by the violence of their penitential love, "There *with* the grace of God go I."

CONTENTS

THE GREAT MAGDALENS

"Mary therefore took a pound of ointment of right spikenard, of great price, and anointed the feet of Jesus, and wiped his feet with her hair; and the house was filled with the odour of the ointment." —John 12:13

Chapter 1

PENITENTS OF THE STAGE

THE church from the very beginning was suspicious of the theater. She had good reason for her suspicions. Her fight was against paganism, its false worship, its immorality; and the stage, body and soul, was bound up with paganism. Those who know the theater of the present time, who know that in a great many cases its drama is uplifting, its amusement wholly innocent, its players beyond reproach, cannot understand, even while they recognize the many evils in present-day theatrical performances, why there was for centuries such a wholesale condemnation of theaters and actors. Why was no distinction made between the good and the bad? Simply because there was no such thing as the good theater in those days. Understanding that, it is easy to appreciate what would otherwise seem to be puritanical severity on the part of such men as St. John Chrysostom, who with his amazing eloquence thundered against the stage, expressing his gratitude to God that he had escaped the perils which had threatened his soul in his fondness as a youth for the theater.

To the early Christians the theater was one of the allurements of the devil. Running through the works of the early Fathers is the condemnation of "spec-

1

tacles," a word that included the public games as well as theatrical exhibitions. St. Clement of Alexandria in his *Instructions* lashes the theater. He writes: "The Instructor will not then bring us to public spectacles; not inappropriately might one call the racecourse and the theater, 'the seat of plagues'; for there is evil counsel as against the Just One, and therefore the assembly against Him is execrated. These assemblies, indeed, are full of confusion and iniquity; and these pretexts for assembling are the cause of disorder—men and women assembling promiscuously for the sight of one another. In this respect the assembly has already shown itself bad; for when the eye is lascivious, the desires grow warm; and the eyes that are accustomed to look impudently at one's neighbors during the leisure granted to them inflame the amatory desires. Let spectacles therefore and plays that are full of scurrility and of abundant gossip be forbidden. For what base action is it that is not exhibited in the theaters? And what shameless saying is it that is not brought forward by the buffoons? And those who enjoy the evil that is in them stamp the clear images of it at home. And on the other hand those that are proof against these things and unimpressible will never make a stumble in regard to luxurious pleasures."

Tertullian is even stronger. He forbids the theater to the Christian both on the grounds of idolatry and immodesty. He shows how the whole theater is a part of the worship of false gods. That of itself was with him enough to make it forbidden ground. But he also scores it for its immorality. "Are we not," says he, "in like manner enjoined to put away from us all immodesty? On this ground again we are excluded from the theater, which is immodesty's own peculiar abode, where nothing is in repute but what elsewhere is disreputable." And after telling in very plain words some of the moral evils of the theater of his day, he concludes: "I say nothing about other matters, which it were good to hide away in their own darkness and their own gloomy caves lest they should stain the light of day."

In a word, the theater was, as St. Chrysostom called it, the reign of vice and iniquity, and the ruin of cities. The stage being so regarded, it followed that the actor was considered a public sinner. Thus in the Theodosian Code it was decreed that the sacraments should be administered to actors only in imminent danger of death, and then only if the actor promised to renounce his calling if he recovered. We have a letter which was written by St. Cyprian concerning an actor who had himself given up the stage but continued to teach the art of acting to others. He is not to be permitted to communicate in the Church if he continues his instructing, says St. Cyprian, for it is not befitting the Divine Majesty nor the discipline of the Gospel that the modesty and credit of the Church "should be so polluted by so disgraceful and infamous a contagion." If the actor alleges that he has no other means of support, then, says St. Cyprian, let the Church support him as the other needy poor.

To Cyprian, Scripture plainly condemned the stage when it condemned idolatry—"the mother of all public amusements." He regarded all these things as the inventions of demons, not of God. "Thus the devil who is their original contriver, because he knew that naked idolatry would by itself excite repugnance, associated it with public exhibitions that for the sake of their attraction it might be loved." And as to the morality of the stage, he says: "I am ashamed to tell what things are said; I am ashamed to denounce the things that are done—the tricks of arguments, the cheatings of adulterers, the immodesties of women, the scurrilous jokes, the sordid parasites, even the toga'd fathers of families themselves, sometimes stupid, sometimes obscene, but in all cases dull, in all cases immodest. And though no individual or family, or profession is spared by the discourses of these reprobates, yet every one flocks to the play. The general infamy is delightful to see or to recognize; it is a pleasure, nay, even to learn it. People flock thither to the public disgrace of the brothel for the teaching of obscenity, that nothing less may be done in secret than what is learnt in public; and in the midst of the laws themselves is taught everything that the laws forbid. What does a faithful Christian do among these things, since he may not even think upon wickedness? Why does he find pleasure in the representation of lust so as among them to lay aside his modesty and become more daring in crimes?"

The stage being so regarded as a hotbed of crime, the

actor as an abandoned being, who had no social standing even in the empire, it is plain to be seen that it was considered a great victory for Christianity to convert such a professional idolater as the play-actor.

One of the most beautiful stories we have in hagiology is the history of the conversion of the actor Genesius who died a martyr's death for the faith, and is venerated as St. Genesius. True, the details of the "Acts" of Genesius are considered by Delehaye an "imaginative romance," but the essentials are historical, and however much of the merely legendary is mixed with the facts, the story is as instructive as it is beautiful.

Genesius was a comedian in Rome. His popularity is evidenced by the fact that he was one of the players chosen to take part in the performance specially arranged to greet the Emperor Diocletian, who after a great military victory had come to visit Rome. There was great rejoicing on the occasion, and entertainments of all kinds were prepared; but the chief celebration was the one to take place in the amphitheater. It was surely a red-letter day for the popular Genesius, and we can imagine that he gave great care to the preparation of the comedy to be presented. He would choose, of course, something up to date for his buffoonery. Nothing in those days offered such a chance for burlesque as the new religion—Christianity. The "Christian" was generally the clown, exciting the laughter of the audience by burlesquing the sacred ceremonies of that ignominious sect. Such burlesquing being common enough, that was sufficient reason for the Fathers of the early Church to keep their people away from the sacrilegious mocking of all that they held dear.

On this occasion of the Emperor's visit, Genesius had prepared a very laughable farce in which he was to make fun of the ceremonies of Baptism. It strikes us today as rather cheap and pointless humor, but in those days it was a sure hit.

The amphitheater was crowded at the gala performance. Genesius in his rôle of Christian came upon the stage. He pretended to be very ill, and stretched himself on the floor.

"Ah, my friends," he moaned, "I find a great weight upon me and I would gladly be eased."

The other players answered: "What can we do to give thee ease? Wouldst thou have us plane thee to make thee lighter?"

"Ye senseless creatures," cried out Genesius in mock heroics, "I am resolved to die a Christian, that God may receive me on this day of my death, as one who seeks his salvation by flying from idolatry and superstition."

At these words there advanced on the stage two characters, one representing a Christian priest, the other an exorcist. They sat down beside Genesius and proceeded with the burlesque.

"Well, my child," they said, "why did you send for us?"

In that instant, as the story of the Saint goes, Genesius was converted miraculously to belief in Jesus

Christ, and he replied—no more in burlesque, but in sincere faith—"Because I desire to receive the grace of Jesus Christ and to be born again that I may be delivered from my sins."

No one of course suspected even then that Genesius had come out of his character of comedian, and the other players proceeded in what to them was the tomfoolery of Baptism. They went through the ceremonies, asking him the necessary questions, every one of which was greeted with great laughter on the part of the audience—this Christianity was such a good joke —and then poured water on his head, and clothed him in a white garment. At the conclusion of the ceremony other actors representing soldiers seized him, as was the custom when Christians were led to martyrdom, and dragged him before the box of the Emperor, who had entered into the playful spirit of the affair. But at once Genesius, now dead in earnest as he stood before the ruler, burst forth in a profession of faith and a defense of Christianity.

"Hear, O Emperor," he cried out, "and all you that are here present, officers of the army, philosophers, senators, and people, what I am going to say. I never yet so much as heard the name of Christian but I was struck with horror, and I detested my very relations because they professed that religion. I informed myself exactly concerning its rites and mysteries, only that I might the more heartily despise it, and inspire you with the utmost contempt for the same. But whilst I was washed with the water and examined, I had no sooner

answered sincerely that I believed than I saw a company of bright angels over my head who recited out
of a book all the sins I had committed from my childhood; and having afterward plunged the book into the
water which had been poured upon me in your presence
they showed me the book whiter than snow. Wherefore, I advise you, O great and mighty Emperor, and
all you people here present, who have ridiculed these
mysteries, to believe with me that Jesus Christ is the
true Lord; that He is the light and the truth; and that
it is through Him you may obtain the forgiveness of
your sins."

At last the Emperor and the people realized from the
sincerity of Genesius that it was no longer a burlesque
they were witnessing. Here was one of the hated
Christians. Bad enough was the profession of the
faith at any time, but to fool the audience by pretending a comedy belittling the despised religion and using
the occasion to make an apology for it was to add insult
to injury.

Diocletian was beside himself with rage. How dare
this comedian fool him? How dare he stand before
him and glory in being a Christian? He would soon
show him the folly of his heroics. So he ordered forthwith that Genesius be beaten with clubs and after that
be given over to Plautian, the prefect of the praetorium,
to be forced to offer sacrifice to the gods.

Poor Genesius! The play had begun with comedy;
it was to end with tragedy. But after all Genesius
wanted no pity. His was the most blessed lot he could

imagine—to be persecuted for the new faith with which God had blessed him. Tortures were little when they could purchase Heaven. And gladly he suffered the awful tortures which he was now made to endure. Refusing to offer sacrifice he was put on the rack, his limbs torn from the joints. This punishment failing to break his courage, his flesh was torn with hooks and burned with torches. But he did not flinch. The punishments, so terrible in their intensity, thrilled him to a new glorying in his religion, that faith which a short time ago he had despised. He cried out while they tortured him: "There is no other Lord of the universe besides Him Whom I have seen. Him I adore and serve, and to Him will I adhere though I should suffer a thousand deaths for His sake. No torments shall remove Jesus Christ from my heart or mouth. I regret exceedingly my former errors, and that I once detested His Holy Name, and came so late to His service."

The words enraged the prefect still more. He was sick of this profession of faith on the part of one who seemed to despise his cruelty; and to end it all he gave command that the head of the comedian be struck off.

Thus ended the strange drama; Genesius had played his last part. He had made his supreme act of contrition for his sins and had sealed his penitence with his blood. A few hours before and he was the popular actor, the idol of the public craving amusement; now a headless corpse, a thing of wounds and blood, carried away to be buried by a few Christians who must have been stirred to newer desires for martyrdom by this wonderful example of God's goodness.

The martyred comedian, the patron of actors and musicians, has been venerated in the church since the day of his death. Even as early as the fourth century we find him venerated in Rome with a church built in his honor.

A case very similar to that of Genesius is the martyrdom of St. Gelasinus; so similar that some authorities regard the story of Genesius as merely a variant of that of Gelasinus. There seems to be no reason to identify the two, similar as their lives were, for Butler quotes Theodoret to the effect that it was no unheard of thing to find some on the stage who had passed from the worship of devils to the rank of martyrs. The case was common enough to generalize about it.

Gelasinus was a comedian who lived at Heliopolis in Phoenicia. Like Genesius, he had in one of his comedies a burlesque of the ceremony of Baptism, making a lot of foolery in a warm bath on the stage. It was comedy of the lowest slapstick kind, and it is easy to imagine how far he pushed the pantomime, which was always such an indecent thing on the Roman stage. But in the midst of the buffoonery the grace of God came to him. He was converted miraculously, and as he came forth from the bath he declared that he was a Christian. So infuriated was the mob, both on account of this deception and the fact that their idol had professed the despised religion, that they immediately stoned him to death. This was in the year 297, eleven years after Genesius had died the death of a martyr.

Here and there through the early history of the Church we find many a beautiful story of the strange workings of the grace of God in the hearts of sinners. One such story relates to Babylas, the actor. He was a comedian and lived in the great city of Tarsus, immortal as the place where St. Paul was born and where he received most of his education.

Babylas was one upon whom the world smiled. He was talented, popular, and by means of his great talents had made a considerable fortune. But he was saturated with paganism and was a slave to pagan immorality. His life was one of open wickedness, as is evident from the fact that he kept two concubines. The story gives us their names as Cometa and Nicosa. One day he happened to be in a Christian church. Why he was there we cannot guess, for a public sinner of his type that openly defied the laws of God was hardly a welcome visitor in the Christian assemblies. It may have been that he had come to the church seeking material for his pantomimes, looking for some dainty bit to burlesque. If he had come to scoff, he remained to pray. In the reading of the Scriptures, or in the sermon of the priest, these words alone sounded in his ears: "Do penance, for the Kingdom of Heaven is at hand." The grace of God came to him. He saw himself in all his wickedness, his sins unnumbered, his life a scandal to the city, himself the cause of the destruction of others both in his private life and in his public profession. He was filled with great sorrow for his past, and threw himself upon his knees, begging God to have mercy upon him. Then and there he took the resolution to abandon his sinful profession, get away entirely from the world of sin, and spend the rest of his days in prayer and works of penance. He was a changed man as he left the church and returned home. At once he told the women, his partners in crime, of the wonderful change that had come into his soul and how he had determined that he must separate from them, leave his profession and go into penitential retirement. As for them, they could have his property to divide between them.

But the women would not have it so. The grace of conversion came to them also. Why should he choose the better path, they asked, and leave them in the lurch? They had been partners in his sin, they would also be partners in his conversion; they, too, would consecrate themselves to God in a life of sacrifice.

Babylas at once left his home and shut himself up in one of the towers of the walls of the city where he set about doing penance for his past sins. The idol of the public who had so loved applause became a humble penitent, treating his own body with rigor, while at the same time he devoted himself untiringly to the poor of the city. As to the women, they disposed of all their worldly goods and gave the price to the poor. Then they made for themselves in the neighborhood a cell, where till the day of their death they devoted themselves to a life of penance.

The writer of the life of St. Pachomius, one of the greatest of the fathers of the desert, gives us a very interesting and edifying account of the conversion of a young actor. The player, touched by the grace of God, had quit his profession, and had entered the monastery founded by Pachomius—Pachomius, indeed, was the founder of the cenobitical life, that is, of monks living in community in contradistinction to the life of the hermit or solitary, which up to his time had prevailed with those who wished to live apart from the world. Pachomius had taken the youth under his care and sought to train him to the life of perfection. But the young actor, converted though he was from the life of sin, was a very sorry kind of monk. He was very careless in his duties, did not scruple to break the rules of the monastery, and, with the old instinct for acting still strong in him, delighted in entertaining some of his companions with the tricks of his trade. The monastery was hardly the place for a buffoon, and the elder monks, scandalized by such exhibitions of foolery, came to the abbot and begged him to dismiss from the monastery this half-converted comedian. Pachomius, however, knowing that there must be a lot of good in a youth who had fled from the allurements of the stage to a life of penance, set aside their protests and undertook to advise the young monk. But it was wasted advice; the actor was still the lukewarm penitent. Pachomius, seeing that his good words fell on deaf ears, resorted to other measures. He prayed and fasted and wept for the soul of his young charge; and after having persevered in this course for some time he took the actor aside one day and spoke to him so earnestly of the need of doing penance, of the dangers that threatened his soul, of eternity and Hell, that Silvanus, as the actor was named, was so filled with fear at having led such a lax life, even after the grace of conversion had come to him, that he now became thoroughly converted and determined to be a real penitent. He was now filled with sorrow for his past sins and sought every means to atone for them. Such a sincere penitent did he become that he was never seen without tears in his eyes. He sobbed and mourned even at his meals, so much so that the sight of his grief became distressing even to the brethren who a short time before had been scandalized at his indifference. They complained to Silvanus that he distressed them, and begged him in plain words to keep his grief to himself. Silvanus in his deep humility promised them that he would try to obey their wishes; but it was useless for him to try to conceal his sorrow, for his heart was breaking as he thought of the terrible crimes he had committed and the little return he had made to God for the grace of being saved from the world. Again the brethren remonstrated. What was the need of all these tears and groans, they asked.

"Ah," said Silvanus, "how can I help weeping when I see so many holy brethren, the dust of whose feet I ought to venerate, so charitable as to take notice of me. When I see a wretch that is come from the playhouse, quite laden with sins, receive so many good offices.

Alas, I have reason to fear lest the earth should open under my feet and swallow me down as it did Dathan and Abiron in punishment of my having profaned all that was sacred after so clear a knowledge and experience of divine grace by leading so slothful and wicked a life. Wonder not at my weeping. Oh, my brethren, I have just reason to labor to expiate my innumerable sins with ever-flowing fountains of tears; and if I could even pour forth this wretched soul of mine in mourning it would be all too little to punish my crimes."

So Silvanus was allowed to follow his own course of penance, to the edification of the brethren. He became such a model of penance and virtue that even Pachomius, saint that he was, was edified by him. He often proposed Silvanus to his monks as a pattern of humility, telling them that even the most holy of them were in greater danger of losing their souls through pride than the converted actor whom they had once regarded as a buffoon.

Eight years passed in this manner, long years of tears and penance, and Silvanus at the end of that time died the death of a saint. Old Pachomius assured his brethren that a multitude of heavenly spirits had carried to God the soul of the young comedian as a choice sacrifice.

In this same period of the Fathers of the Desert we have the story of another conversion related in the life of Serapion, of whom it was said so beautifully that he "had no other hermitage for many years but his love of God." Serapion determined to leave his cell and live the life of an anchorite in the midst of other men for the one purpose of saving souls. So he came to live in the licentious city of Corinth, where the theater was popular and where there was consequently an abundance of singers and actors. Among these was a heathen juggler who with his family gained a livelihood from the stage. His house of licentiousness seemed to the holy Serapion just the place to begin his work of saving souls. In order to gain an entrance into the luxurious home he sold himself as a slave to the juggler, who had no suspicion of the designs of the new servant. He was a poor slave, nothing more. Serapion gave himself whole-heartedly to his menial tasks, washed the feet of his master and did promptly whatever he was commanded to do. Soon he was found to be an invaluable servant, and the juggler must have flattered himself that he had bought the man at so cheap a price. But Serapion bided his time. He spoke rarely, but when opportunity presented itself he dropped an occasional remark about the things of God. The juggler was at first surprised and amused; then he became interested. He delighted in listening to the words of wisdom that fell from Serapion's lips, and he came to ask more and more about the religion of which his slave spoke so beautifully. It all ended in the conversion of the juggler and his family to Christianity and their abandonment of their sinful profession. They were moved to tears when they discovered what sacrifices Serapion had made to save their souls, and they begged him to remain with them always. But Serapion went on his way to bring to other souls the knowledge of the faith he loved so much.

But the most celebrated conversion of a player we have in the case of St. Pelagia, who lived in the early fifth century. Her history as given by James, the Deacon, a contemporary of hers, has always been popular in the Christian church. St. John Chrysostom, in his sixty-seventh Homily on St. Matthew, tells of a celebrated actress who came to Antioch from one of the most corrupt cities of Phoenicia. She was notorious for her wickedness as far as Cilicia and Cappadocia. Her evil example was the cause of the moral ruination of many; it was said that she had led to ruin even the sister of the Emperor. Being converted, however, the once popular actress led a life of austerity, wearing a hair shirt and shutting herself up in prison, where she allowed no one to see her. Delehaye considers the story of St. Pelagia an adaptation of this. However that may be, there is a wealth of legendary lore about the saint. But the story as told by James has always been the most popular.

According to this story Pelagia, who was also called Margaret on account of her wonderful pearls, was a noted actress or dancing girl living at Antioch, at that time the capital of Syria and of the whole east. She had professed herself a Christian and for a time had been numbered among the catechumens receiving instruction preparatory to Baptism. She gave up attending church, however, lured from the hard road of the Christian life by the glory and wealth which came to her as a popular favorite. The extraordinary beauty and talents of the girl were her destruction. Many a lover she ensnared, all of them eager to shower their wealth upon her, so that very soon she became the lowest of the low, selling herself, soul and body, to a life of sin. Her very life as an actress branded her in those days as a public sinner, and her very shamelessness in vice made her presence a stench to decent people, in spite of the remarkable beauty that made all in Antioch turn to look at her as she passed by in regal magnificence, adorned with fine clothes and priceless jewels, the price of sin. But Pelagia cared not how the Christians regarded her; she was rich, beautiful, flattered, happy. What more could she ask?

One day, however, it happened that several bishops and many other clergy had assembled at Antioch, being called thither by the Patriarch of Antioch, the metropolitan See, to consider certain ecclesiastical matters. Among them was the bishop of Heliopolis, St. Nonnus. He was a very holy and very wise man who before his elevation to the episcopacy had been a monk. All were assembled in the church of St. Julian the Martyr—or rather before the church—listening to a spiritual conference from Bishop Nonnus which followed the discussion of the affairs for which the assembly had been called. In the midst of the conference Pelagia, chief singer and dancer, passed by. She was in all her glory, dressed in magnificent raiment, her shoulders bare, her head uncovered, her hair flowing, priceless jewels twined about her neck and in her hair, and flashing from her gown.   It was an exhibition of diamonds and pearls and fine scents of Arabia, a brazen display of wealth and power as she sat on her mule with its gold-embroidered trappings.   With her went her women companions, a throng of admiring, lustful youths following her.   It was, indeed, a great honor to be considered a friend of the noted actress.   On they went laughing, chatting, ridiculing no doubt the assembly of ecclesiastics who knew so little about the pleasures of the world!   What a poor fool this Bishop Nonnus must have seemed to the woman who had the city at her feet.

Many in the vast congregation who had been listening to the Bishop's sermon were distracted by the parade of magnificence, and they turned to follow with their eyes the gorgeous spectacle.   Nonnus and his brother ecclesiastics turned away in disgust, horrified at the flaunted immodesty of the woman.   But then Nonnus turned again and looked attentively and pityingly after her.   When the merrymakers had passed and the sound of their revelry had died away, he turned to his brethren and said to them with tears in his eyes, "The Almighty in His infinite goodness will show mercy even to this woman, the work of His hands.

"But," he continued, "I fear God will one day bring this woman to confront us before the throne of justice, in order to condemn our negligence and tepidity in His service, and in the discharge of the duty He has committed to our care.   For how many hours do you think she has employed this very day in her chamber in washing and cleansing herself, in dressing, adorning, and embellishing her whole person to the best advantage, with a view to exhibiting her beauty to please the eyes of the world, and particularly her unhappy lovers, who, though alive today, may possibly be dead tomorrow? Whereas we who have an Almighty Father, an immortal Spouse in Heaven, to whose love and service we have consecrated ourselves; we, to whom the immense and eternal treasures of Heaven are promised as the reward of our short labors on earth, are far from taking as much pains to wash and purify our souls from their stains, and procure for them those bright ornaments of virtue and sanctity, which alone can render them truly agreeable in the eyes of God."

Having given these words of advice to his brethren, Nonnus returned to his room near the church, and there threw himself upon the floor and wept bitterly to think that this sinful woman had shown more zeal in the service of the devil than he had shown in the service of God, and he begged God to pardon his coldness of heart. So he spent that day and night weeping and praying, doing penance for himself and for the heedless actress who little knew and little cared that a saint was storming Heaven in her behalf.

The following day was Sunday, and all the ecclesiastics with a great crowd of people were assembled in the chief church of Antioch where Mass was being celebrated by the Patriarch. At the end of the Gospel he requested Nonnus to preach. Nonnus assented, and preached a thrilling sermon on the judgment and eternity. He was thinking perhaps of the sinful woman

whom he had seen the day before, going the way of
eternal destruction. Anyway, Pelagia happened to be
in the church that day, drawn thither no doubt by
curiosity to witness the great celebration. Call it
curiosity or what you will, it was in reality the grace
of God. For the heart of the actress was touched by
the words of the preacher. She saw herself in all her
vileness, saw the many graces she had neglected, and
the eternity of Hell she had merited by her wicked
career. In that instant she became an ardent penitent,
astonishing those nearby with her deep sighs and tears
of contrition. We can hear now the raillery of her
companions as she came from the church, the tears
still in her eyes; perhaps some of her admirers con-
gratulated her on this new exhibition of her fine talents
as an actress. They must have been amazed as she
passed on to her home leaving them there to discuss
such a strange thing as the seeming conversion of their
former companion in sin. Pelagia in her first fervor
sat down and wrote this letter to Nonnus:

"To the holy disciple of Jesus Christ, from a sinful
wretch, a scholar of the devil:

"I have learned that the God Whom you worship
came down from Heaven to earth, not for the sake of
the just, but to save poor sinners, and that He humbled
Himself so far as to suffer publicans to come to Him,
and did not disdain to speak with the sinful Samaritan
woman at the well; wherefore, as I understand, that
though you never have seen Him with your mortal
eyes, you are nevertheless a follower of His, and have

served Him faithfully for many years, I conjure you, for His sake, to show yourself to be His true disciple, by suffering a poor sinner to come to you, and not despise the extreme desire I have to approach to Him through your assistance."

The conversion of any sinner, even of this woman, was no surprise to the holy Bishop; still he wished to make sure that she had the proper dispositions, and he wrote to her in reply that if she was in earnest she should come to him at the church of St. Julian, where in the presence of the other bishops he would talk to her about the affairs of her soul.

Pelagia, as soon as she received this message, hurried to the place of meeting, threw herself at the feet of the Bishop, and begged him to receive her, the greatest of sinners, and cleanse her of her iniquities by baptizing her. Nonnus had no doubt about the sincerity of her conversion, but the discipline of the church required that a public sinner should be well tried before being admitted into the Church, lest, weak in purpose, such a one might return to the life of sin and so bring scandal to the faithful. He told Pelagia that she must give sure proof of her reform and that when that was done to the satisfaction of those in authority she would be baptized. But the poor penitent, loathing the sins that weighted her down to the earth, fearing the punishment that must be hers if she should die in that condition, was inconsolable at the thought of delay. Bitterly she wept, and again and again begged him to baptize her, assuring

him that never more would she commit the crimes for
which she was notorious. So impressed were the
bishops by these extraordinary signs of repentance that
they decided an exception might be made in this case.
They placed the matter before the Patriarch, and the
holy man, impressed as they had been, gave his permission for her to be baptized immediately, sending one
of the widows who served the church, the lady Romana,
superioress of the deaconesses, to be godmother for the
new convert. Romana found Pelagia still at the feet of
Nonnus, breaking her heart crying over her past life.
Gently she lifted her up, folded her in her arms and
led her to the font where, after a public confession of
her sins, she was baptized by Nonnus. Nonnus asked
her what her name was. She answered, "My parents
called me Pelagia; but now also I am known by the
name of Margaret, because I loved to be adorned with
pearls, and because my miserable beauty, that snare of
Satan, was compared to the beauty of pearls." After
baptism Nonnus confirmed her and gave her Holy
Communion.

The soul of the woman was filled with joy, such joy
as she never had known even in the days of her triumph
as the beautiful actress when all the world was at her
feet. She was now converted to God, yet her struggles
were not ended. Temptations came back, seeking to
lure her away from her course of penance to the old life
which had been so pleasant. It was in those days of
trial that the Bishop stood by her, and with his advice

and sympathy armed her against the powers of Hell which she had defeated.

Three days after her Baptism she came to Nonnus and gave him the list of all that she owned in the world —the jewels, the rich garments, the furniture of her magnificent home—and begged him to dispose of the criminally gotten goods now that she never more would use the fruits of sin. "My Lord," said she, "here is the whole of the goods I have acquired from the devil; I give them all up to your disposal; give such orders concerning them as you judge to be best. As for my part, I desire no riches for the time to come but those of my Savior, Jesus Christ."

Nonnus ordered that all the goods be sold and the proceeds given to the poor. That same day Pelagia freed all her slaves, exhorting them as they left her service to free themselves also from the bonds of sin, and follow her into the freedom of the service of Jesus Christ.

During the entire week, as was the custom with the newly baptized, the convert wore the white garment. It was a strange sight, the once richly adorned woman now in the simple garb which declared her to be a follower of the Lamb. When it came time for her to lay it aside, she arose in the middle of the night, put on a garment of haircloth, and then wrapping herself in an old cloak which Nonnus had given her, she went out secretly from her home, telling no one whither she was going except Nonnus, who had assented to her plans and had given her a man's tunic to wear to prevent her from being molested on her journey, and walked until she reached the Holy Land.

In those days Mt. Olivet, and in fact all the hills of Palestine, were the abodes of the ascetics. The hills were all pierced by caverns and clefts formed by nature in the soft limestone and easily multiplied by digging. Mt. Olivet was especially dear because the Passion had begun there, and because it was also the scene of the Ascension. We are told that on one of the three peaks of the Mount of the Ascension there once stood a church in honor of St. Pelagia.

To Mt. Olivet, then, she at once repaired, and shut herself up in one of these narrow cells which had but a small window through which she received the few necessities of life. There she determined to spend the rest of her life in fasting and prayer, continually serving God and begging him to forgive her sins. So retired a life did she lead that even the other anchorets on the mountain knew nothing of her antecedents, knew not even that she was a woman, since she had called herself Pelagius instead of Pelagia. But though none knew anything of her history, all soon knew that here was a holy servant of God on the sure way to sanctity. There she lived four years, all the while growing weaker and weaker, paler and paler.

The story goes that James, the Deacon, who afterwards wrote the life of Pelagia, came on a pilgrimage to the holy places. When he was leaving Edessa, the bishop of that place, none other than the holy Nonnus, told him to make inquiries about a certain hermit named

Pelagius, the reputation of whose sanctity was spread through all Christendom. Nonnus knew very well, or at least suspected, that this penitent hermit was the actress whom he had baptized.

No one in Jerusalem, however, seemed to know anything about the case. But James persevered and at last found the cell of the penitent. He spoke to her through the little window, and was amazed to see how emaciated she was from her severe penances. He told her that Bishop Nonnus had sent him to speak to her. "Nonnus," said she, "is a great saint, and I beg that he will pray for me." That was all. She shut the window and returned to her devotions, leaving the Deacon to kneel outside, thrilled with joy as he listened to a saint at prayer. To him it sounded like the singing of angelic choirs.

As James went from monastery to monastery in the Holy Land all he could hear was the story of the great sanctity of the holy hermit, Pelagius. When the time came for him to return to Edessa he determined to visit the saint again. He came to the humble cell and knocked at the window. No answer. He knocked again and again, but still received no answer, and feeling that something strange had happened, he forced the window, and looking in saw the hermit lying dead upon the floor. He acquainted the other hermits with his discovery, and they all hastened to the little cell eager to have part in paying the final honors to one who had been such an example of heroic penance. It was then discovered that the holy hermit was a woman, and the nuns came forth from their convents with lighted tapers in their hands to carry into their church the relics of the once notorious actress now to be invoked as a saint of God.

The drama of Pelagia had the happiest of endings.

Chapter 2

VOICES FROM THE DESERT

SOME time before St. John Climacus wrote his famous *Climax* (or *Ladder*) he made a visit to a celebrated monastery in Egypt, and while there lived for thirty days in the "prison of the penitents," situated about a mile from the abbey. In the fifth chapter of the book he writes of penitence, and to exemplify what true penance consists in he narrates the things he had seen.

"Being come into this monastery of the penitents," he writes, "I beheld things which the eye of the slothful has never seen, the ear of the negligent has never heard, and which have never entered into the heart of the sluggard—things and words capable of doing violence, if I may use the expression, to the Almighty. I saw some of these penitents standing whole nights upright, without allowing themselves any sleep or rest whatsoever; others, in a pitiful manner, looking up towards Heaven, and calling for help from thence with groans, sighs, and prayers; others, who whilst at prayer, had their hands bound behind them like criminals, bowing down their pale countenances towards the ground, declaring aloud that they were unworthy to lift up their eyes to Heaven, and that they durst not presume to speak to God. . . . I saw some sitting on the floor covered with haircloth and ashes, hiding their faces between their knees, and striking their foreheads against the earth; others beating their breasts with inexpressible contrition of heart, some of whom watered the ground about them with their tears, others grievously lamenting that they could not weep, several mourning with a loud cry over their own souls, as we moan over the dead corpse of a dear friend, others ready to roar out for grief, eagerly struggling to stifle the noise of their complaints, till being no longer able to repress them, they were forced to let them break forth with greater violence; others appeared so astonished, that one would have supposed them to be statues of brass, so insensible of all things had the excess of their sorrow rendered them. Their heart was plunged in an abyss of humility, and their scorching grief had dried up all their tears. . . . No other words could be heard amongst them but such as these: 'Woe, woe to me, a miserable sinner!' ' 'Tis with justice, O Lord, 'tis with justice!' 'Spare us, O Lord, spare us!' 'Have mercy on us!' Some of them afflicted themselves by standing parching in the most violent heat of the sun; others, on the contrary, exposed themselves to suffer no less violently from extremity of the cold. Some, in the violence of their thirst, taking a small quantity of water, contented themselves with only tasting of it, whilst others, after eating a morsel of bread, cast the rest away, saying they were not worthy to eat the food of men, who had acted more like irrational creatures. There was no room for laughter, none for idle talk, none for resentment, anger or contradiction, none for mirth, the care of the body, for good cheer, or for the pleasures of eating or drinking; none for the least spark of vainglory. No earthly cares distracted them, nor did they know what it was to judge or condemn any man but themselves. Their whole employment, day and night, was to cry to our Lord, and no voice was heard amongst them but that of prayer. Some there were who, beating their breasts with all their might, as if they were knocking for admittance at the gate of Heaven, said to the Lord: 'Open to us, through Thy mercy, the gate which we have shut against ourselves by our sins.'

" 'Let us neglect nothing that depends on us,' they continued; 'let us continue to knock at the door of His mercy, even till the end of our lives; perhaps He will yield to our importunity and perseverance; for He is good and merciful. Let us run, brethren, let us run, for we have need to run, and to run with all our speed, that we may recover what we have lost. Let us run and not spare this filthy flesh; let us make it suffer in time, because it has exposed us to the danger of suffering for eternity.' Thus said these holy criminals, and they were as good as their words. Their knees were hardened by incessant kneeling; their eyes appeared sunk into their sockets; the hair of their eyelids was fallen off by their continual weeping; their cheeks were shrivelled, and, as it were, parched with the scalding brine of their tears; their breasts bruised with blows."

Out of the desert, out of the far distant past, come the cries of penitence of these "holy criminals." The severity of the penance with which the anchorites afflicted themselves, even when their past lives had not been stained by grievous sin, is enough to strike terror into our hearts. St. Paul of Thebes, a youth of refinement, leaving his place in the world for the desert, subsisting on a few dates and a little water, clothing himself with palm leaves plaited together; St. Anthony, praying most of the night, fasting from food for several days and then eating but a bit of bread and salt, his couch a mat of rushes, when he did not sleep on the bare earth, his clothing a hair-shirt, his dwelling the limestone caves of the desert; St. Hilarion, who was but a lad of fourteen when he left the world to become an anchorite and put on the sackcloth; St. Simon Stylites, doing penance at the top of his pillar; no wonder the world has marveled at these heroes of the penitential life. It was the story of St. Anthony's penances that put the finishing touch to the conversion of St. Augustine. "What is this?" he cried. "What have we heard? The simple rise up and bear Heaven away with violence, and we, the learned, the wise, the educated, we faint-hearted dastards wallow in flesh and blood."

All through these penitential ages there is case after case of the reclaimed sinner atoning for his past crimes with extraordinary penitence; but somehow there is a special appeal in the lives of the great women penitents of those days, such as Pelagia, Thais, Mary of

Egypt—courtesans all, brazen in their immoralities, but when the grace of God purified their foul hearts, stopping at nothing in their zeal to prove their love to Him they had once rejected.

In the history of women penitents the story of St. Mary of Egypt has been second in importance to that of St. Mary Magdalen. Many a soul has been converted to God by reading of her heroic atonement. It was by reading her life the day that he was fuming because he had to wait for his dinner that John Colombini, the founder of the Jesuates, became a great penitent and a great saint. Even the unbelieving Renan says somewhere that he would give all that he owned to have seen her pacing the desert in ecstasy, that woman half starved and turned to the semblance of Nabuchadonosor.

There lived in Palestine in the fifth century a holy monk and priest by the name of Zosimus. He had lived in the one religious house for more than fifty years, had acquired a great reputation for sanctity and was resorted to by multitudes for spiritual direction. The thought came to him that he knew all there was to be known about the spiritual life, and God, seeing that in this great servant of His there was the danger of falling into spiritual pride, directed him to leave his monastery and enter another one which was near the Jordan. As soon as he was installed in the new house of religion he saw from watching the lives of the occupants that he was not as near to perfection as he had imagined. For their penance was greater than that which he had thought so wonderful in his own life. Here the members of the community had no association one with the other. They labored hard all day long, and even at their labors prayed continually. They sang psalms all night, one relieving the other while a little sleep was taken; and their food consisted of bread and water. Great, indeed, was their penance all the year round, but they led a life of special mortification during the holy season of Lent. On the first Sunday of Lent, after having received Holy Communion, they all crossed the Jordan and dispersed in the great desert, where they remained in perfect retreat until Palm Sunday, when they returned to the monastery for Holy Week. During that Lenten penance their life was hidden with Christ in God. They never told their companions what their experiences had been.

When Lent came around again Zosimus decided to go with the other monks. Alone he proceeded farther and farther into the great desert, praying with fervor, and looking for even more perfect examples of the religious life. When he had journeyed for twenty days, he stopped one noon to rest and to recite his psalter. Suddenly there appeared to him something that looked like a human body. It made him tremble, for he felt it must be a diabolical apparition, and instinctively he made the sign of the Cross and began to pray. It was a naked body, burnt by the sun, the hair short and white. Suddenly it began to run away, and Zosimus thinking that it must be one of the hermits who had buried themselves in the desert gave chase. He called upon the other to come and bless him, and the other replied, "Abbot Zosimus, I am a woman; throw me your mantle to cover me, that you may come near me."

Zosimus, astounded, knowing that it was only by a revelation that she could know his name, threw her his cloak and soon she came to him. So they talked and prayed together, and Zosimus asked her in the name of Jesus who she was and how long she had lived in the desert. It was then that Mary of Egypt told the holy monk her history. "I ought to die with confusion and shame in telling you what I am," she said; "so horrible is the very mention of it, that you will fly from me as a serpent; your ears will not be able to bear the recital of the crimes of which I have been guilty. I will, however, relate to you my ignominy, begging of you to pray for me, that God may show me mercy in the day of His terrible judgment.

"My country is Egypt," she continued. "When my father and mother were still living, at twelve years of age I went without their consent to Alexandria: I cannot think without trembling on the first steps by which I fell into sin, nor my disorders which followed." For the next seventeen years, she told him, she had lived as a public prostitute, not for gain but from lust. "I continued my wicked course," she went on, "till the twenty-ninth year of my age, when perceiving several persons making toward the sea, I inquired whither they were going, and was told that they were about to embark for the Holy Land to celebrate at Jerusalem the feast of the Exaltation of the glorious Cross of our Savior. I embarked with them, looking only for fresh opportunities to continue my debauches, which I repeated often during the voyage and after my arrival at Jerusalem. On the day appointed for the festival, all going to church, I mixed with the crowd to get into the church where the holy Cross was shown and exposed to the veneration of the faithful; but found myself withheld from entering the place by some secret but invisible force. This happening to me three or four times, I retired into a corner of the court and began to consider with myself what this might proceed from, and seriously reflecting that my criminal life might be the cause, I melted into tears. Beating, therefore, my sinful breast with sighs and groans, I perceived above me a picture of the Mother of God. Fixing my eyes upon it, I addressed myself to that Holy Virgin, begging of her by her incomparable purity to succor me, defiled with such a load of abominations, and to render my repentance the more acceptable to God. I besought her I might be suffered to enter the church doors, to behold the sacred wood of my redemption, promising from that moment to consecrate myself to God by a life of penance, taking her for my surety in this change of heart. After this ardent prayer, I perceived in my soul a secret consolation under my grief; and attempting again to enter the church, I went up with ease into the very middle of it, and had the comfort to venerate the precious wood of the glorious Cross which brings life to man. Considering therefore the incomprehensible mercy of God, and His readiness to receive sinners to repentance, I cast myself on the ground, and after having kissed the pavement with tears, I arose and went to the picture of the Mother of God whom I made the witness and surety of my engagements and resolutions. Falling there on my knees before her image, I addressed my prayers to her, begging her intercession and that she would be my guide. After my prayer, I seemed to hear this voice: 'If thou goest beyond the Jordan, thou shalt there find rest and comfort.' Then weeping and looking at the image I begged of the Holy Queen of the world that she would never abandon me. After these words I went out in haste, bought three loaves, and asking the baker which was the gate of the city which led to the Jordan, I immediately took that road, and walked all the rest of the day, and at night arrived at the church of St. John the Baptist on the banks of the river. There I paid my devotions to God, and received the precious Body of Our Savior Jesus Christ. Having eaten the half of one of my loaves, I slept all night on the ground. Next morning, recommending myself to the Holy Virgin, I passed the Jordan, and from that time I have carefully shunned the meeting of any human creatures."

When Zosimus met the woman she had been living in the desert forty-seven years, her food the wild herbs which the desert supplied, her clothing long since fallen to shreds, so that her body, unprotected from the heat and the cold, suffered every agony.

These were the sufferings of the poor body, but to them was added an affliction of soul all the harder to bear, for when Zosimus asked her if she had passed all these years without suffering in her soul, she replied: "Your question makes me tremble, by the very remembrance of my past dangers and conflicts through the perverseness of my heart. Seventeen years I passed in most violent temptations and almost perpetual conflicts with my inordinate desires. I was tempted to regret the flesh and fish of Egypt and the wines which I drank to excess in the world; whereas here I often could not come at a drop of water to quench my thirst. Other desires made assaults on my mind; but weeping and striking my breast on those occasions, I called to mind the vows I had made under the protection of the Blessed Virgin, and begged her to obtain my deliverance from the affliction and danger of such thoughts. After long weeping and bruising my body with blows, I found myself suddenly enlightened, and my mind restored to a perfect calm. Often the tyranny of my old passions seemed to drag me out of my desert; at those times I threw myself on the ground and watered it with my tears, raising my heart constantly to the Blessed Virgin till she procured me comfort; and she has never failed to show herself my faithful protectress."

Thus Mary told her story. She could not read, and for forty-seven years she had spoken to no one, yet Zosimus found that God had taught this penitent child of His, and that the unlettered woman knew the Holy Scriptures. After finishing her story she begged the monk to keep the secret as long as she lived, and to pray for her. She begged him then that the following Lent he should not return to the monastery on Palm Sunday but should bring her Holy Communion on Holy Thursday. Then she left him, and Zosimus, amazed at the wonderful sanctity of the woman, bent and kissed the ground where she had stood.

The following Lent, on Holy Thursday, Zosimus took with him the Blessed Sacrament, also a basket of figs and dates and lentils, and went to the banks of the Jordan. At night she came to him, and after praying and receiving Holy Communion she lifted her hands to Heaven and cried out, "Now Thou dost dismiss Thy servant, O Lord, according to Thy word in peace; because my eyes have seen my Savior."

Mary then bade adieu to Zosimus, begging him to return the following Lent, and returned across the river as she had come.

The next Lent the holy monk returned as he had promised. He found her dead body, with an inscription saying her name was Mary and stating the time of her death as that very day on which she had received the Bread of Life at his hands. There in the desert he buried her, the poor corpse of an abandoned woman who had sounded the depths of iniquity and then by penitence rose to the heights of sanctity.

A story that has grown in popularity in recent times is that of the converted courtesan, St. Thais. Anatole France with his perverted realism has popularized her in a book that in many places is wonderfully beautiful with its compelling description of the life of her times, but woefully inadequate in its failure to comprehend the spiritual sense of the history of her reclamation. He perverts history in making the monk Paphnutius, who reclaimed Thais to God, fall a victim to her charms and seek to win her back to her sinful life for his own gratification. The fall of Paphnutius is with France very dramatic—the opera "Thais" follows the story as conceived by France—but it is a libel on the holy monk whose one desire in life was the salvation of souls. The simple story of Thais does not need the imaginings of Anatole France to make it a compelling narrative. So compelling is it that it has always been a favorite with the old writers of the Church.

Thais was a contemporary of St. Mary of Egypt and also lived in Egypt. She had been brought up as a Christian, but to the girl who was extraordinarily beautiful, of a quick and witty mind, lover of the gay, sensual life which paganism, not yet dead, flaunted before her eyes, the restrictions of Christianity became unbearable. She threw aside her religion and brazenly gave herself to a life of sin, till in a short time she was notorious everywhere for her immoral life. She was the glorified courtesan. The story of her shamefulness reached even to the caves of the anchorites in the desert. One of the holy monks, the abbot Paphnutius, was so horrified by the tales he had heard of the many souls she had lured to Hell by her bodily charms, and full of pity, too, for the woman who was lost to all sense of decency, that he determined with the grace of

God to leave his safe retreat in the desert and go forth into the licentious world to redeem her.

Paphnutius put aside his penitential garments and dressed himself as a man of the world in order that he might gain access to her. In this manner he came to her luxurious home where Thais and her friends were making revel. Thais, thinking that it was a new gallant who had succumbed to her wiles, gave orders to the servants to admit him. She must have been struck at once by the ascetic appearance of the man whom no gay garments could disguise. Perhaps she thrilled at this new tribute to her charms. Paphnutius told her that he would like to talk to her privately and for that reason asked to be admitted to an apartment more private.

"What are you afraid of?" asked Thais. "If you fear men, no one can see us here. But if you are afraid of God, no place can hide us from that all piercing eye."

"What!" exclaimed the monk, "do you then believe there is a God?" "Yes," replied the woman of sin, "and I moreover know that a Heaven will be the portion of the good, and that everlasting torments are reserved in Hell for the punishment of the wicked."

"Is it possible then," said Paphnutius, "that you know these great truths, and yet dare to sin in the eyes of Him who knows and will judge all things?"

The eyes of Thais were opened at these words; she saw that here was no gallant who desired to be the partner of her crimes, but a holy man who sought to save her soul. The earnestness of the man, the holiness that seemed to glow about him, touched her heart. She compared his holiness with her own wasted life of sin; she saw the misery in which she was plunged, and bursting into tears she threw herself at his feet.

"Father," she cried, "enjoin me what course of penance you think proper. Pray for me that God may vouchsafe to show me mercy. I desire only three hours to settle my affairs, and then I will be ready to comply with all you shall counsel me to do."

Paphnutius, seeing that she was in earnest, already a humbled penitent, appointed the place of their future meeting and then went back to his cell.

Thais had been a public sinner; she had been the cause of the destruction of many; her life was a perpetual scandal. Filled with the spirit of heroic penance, she resolved by a public act to undo, insofar as she could, the evil she had committed. Quickly she gathered together all her fine clothes and jewels, all the price of her lost virtue, and to the consternation of her friends and the passers she threw all the finery into the fire which she had made in the public street, and as the flames consumed these relics of sin she begged all who had been her accomplices in crime to share now in her penance.

Thais was insane, the public must have thought. It is easy to picture how the old discarded friends tried to break down her resolution, but, swept on by the grace of God, she closed her ears to the alluring voices and went secretly to join the monk who was to initiate her into the penitential life.

Paphnutius silently brought her to a monastery for women, shut her up in a cell and then sealed the door as if to enclose her in a living tomb. He gave orders to the sisters to give her but a little bread and water every day, and told Thais ever to beg God's mercy and pardon. When she asked him to teach her how to pray he answered: "You are not worthy to call upon God by pronouncing His Holy Name, because your lips have been filled with iniquity; nor to lift up your hands to Heaven, because they are defiled with impurities; but turn yourself to the east and repeat these words, 'Thou who hast created me, have pity on me.'"

In this penitential cell, in perpetual prayer and tears, Thais continued for three years. At the end of that time Paphnutius wished to know if her penance had been sufficient and he consulted the great St. Anthony to find out if God had forgiven her sins. Anthony called his monks together and bade them watch and pray during the coming night, each by himself, in order to obtain from God some answer to the question of Paphnutius. While they were all engaged in prayer Paul the Simple, the greatest of Anthony's disciples, saw in Heaven a bed adorned with precious curtains and ornaments guarded by four virgins. Paul, seeing such a beautiful place, thought to himself that this must be the reward waiting for the great St. Anthony, but while he meditated in this wise a voice came to him from Heaven, "This bed is not for thy father Anthony, but for Thais, the sinner."

It was then that Paphnutius, hearing the story of
Paul the Simple, decided to release the woman from
her awful penance. Thais, however, did not wish to
have this kindness shown to her, in her own eyes the
most miserable of sinners; and she begged to be allowed
to continue as she had done for the past three years,
saying that she had always bewailed her sins and must
continue to bewail them.

"It is on that account," said Paphnutius, "that God
has blotted them out."

So the penitent woman, much against her wishes, was
released from her penitential prison. But this new
freedom to her poor body brought no joy of heart.
Hers might have been the motto of St. Theresa, "To
suffer or to die." Now that her beloved suffering was
taken away, she had no longing but for the coming of
the great Releaser, Death. Soon was heard her eager
prayer of those atoning years, "Thou who hast created
me, have pity on me." Fifteen days after her release
from her penitential prison her soul went to God.

It is there the biographer stops. He tells us nothing
of the gay world from which the courtesan disappeared
so suddenly. Perhaps one day the story of her penance
and death was brought back to the gay Egyptian capital
and whispered to her old companions in the days of
sin. But we can fancy with what merriment it was
greeted. Poor Thais! What a fool! The beauty of
Egypt to end her days in sackcloth and ashes. Poor
Thais, indeed, to the smart ones of the world who think
the pleasures of the flesh and the pride of life the only

things worth seeking. But how the wisdom of the world is mocked by the desert silence of the penitent soul! Gone on the wind, blown with the sands of the desert are the names even of the boon companions of Thais, the courtesan; but the name of Thais, the penitent, is written in letters of gold on the roster of the saints of God, and her gentle prayer reëchoes forever in world-weary hearts that yearn to follow her in her penance as they followed her in her sin: "Thou who hast created me, have pity on me."

Chapter 3

MAGDALENS OF THE AGES OF PENANCE

"Do you see this woman?" asked St. Peter Chrysologus concerning Mary Magdalen. "When she came to the feet of Jesus, she was a sinner, impure, accursed of God and man; when she departed, she was pure, holy, radiant with the glory of virgins. Her crimes and her scandals had made her a dishonored, despicable creature; her lively repentance and her love wrought such a change in her that she merited to bear the name of the purest of virgins—that of Mary. *Venit mulier, sed rediit Maria.* "She came a woman, but returned Mary."

Magdalen, the great penitent, indeed, but not the sole one. She has had many a sister, many a brother, through the ages, but especially in those ages of penance, the fourth and fifth centuries, when the Fathers of the Desert were so pitiless to themselves and so pitiful to poor sinners.

St. Anthony, St. Pachomius, St. Mary of Egypt, St. Pelagia—the life of every one of them makes a thrilling story. The name of Antony, indeed, was one to conjure with even among his contemporaries. To imitate Antony was the inspiration that came to many a one seeking perfection. St. Augustine tells us of two courtiers in the service of the emperor who chanced to read the life of St. Antony and thereupon gave up their high positions and left the world, becoming very fervent monks.

It was in these days of glorified penance that many of these "Other Magdalens" lived and sinned and sorrowed, and won the crown of eternal life. Their stories have been tenderly cherished in the history of the Church as a proof of the democracy of sanctity, that even those who have fallen the lowest may hope for the glory of the saints.

The persecution of the Christians under the Emperor Diocletian gave many martyrs to the Church. It was the last persecution, the last attempt to destroy Christianity. It aimed at the complete annihilation of the new religion by making everybody offer sacrifice to the gods; the penalty for refusing was death. The persecution extended even to the remote provinces, including even the province of Rhaetia, at that time an important Roman colony.

In the city of Augsburg in that province lived a woman by the name of Afra. From the authentic "Acts" of her martyrdom we learn that she had been a woman of evil life. We know little of her antecedents, but there is an old legend to the effect that her family belonged originally to Cyprus, and that her grandparents had moved thence to Augsburg, bringing Afra with them and initiating her into the vile worship of Venus. The legend even states that the young girl had been given over by her own mother to the service of the vile goddess. It seems unthinkable today that such a crime could be committed in the name of religion, but there was no limit to the degradation of paganism. It was the glory of Christianity that it could redeem even from such loathsomeness. For the story goes that a Christian bishop by the name of Narcissus, of Spain, fled from his persecutors and by some strange chance found a refuge and protection in the house of Afra's mother, Hilaria. The holy man so impressed that house of sin that all the members of the family were converted, and that, too, in the face of inevitable persecution. Dionysius, a brother of Hilaria, was so sincere in his conversion that the bishop ordained him deacon. Sincere, too, was a girl who up to that time had been a woman of sin. Her hatred for her past life had made her more zealous in the profession of her new faith. She was arrested on the charge that she was a Christian and brought before the judge, Gaius by name, for trial. He put her to the first test by ordering her to sacrifice to the gods. "Sacrifice to the gods," said he; "it is better to live than to die in torments."

But the threat of punishment had little effect on the iron will of the new convert. "I was a great sinner before I knew God," she replied simply, "but I will not add new crimes, nor do what you command me." The judge could not understand such stubbornness about a little matter of throwing a few grains of incense on the fire when the simple action would mean freedom. "Go to the capitol and offer sacrifice," he said brusquely, as if anxious to end this silly matter. But Afra answered calmly: "My capitol is Jesus Christ Whom I have always before my eyes. I every day confess my sins, and because I am unworthy to offer Him any sacrifice, I desire to sacrifice myself for His Name, that this body in which I have sinned may be purified and sacrificed to Him by torments."

Seeing that no commands could weaken her resolve, Gaius resorted to other methods. He sought to humiliate her by sneering at the new virtue of this notorious woman. "I am informed," said he, "that you are a woman of evil life. Sacrifice, therefore, as you are a stranger to the God of the Christians, and cannot be accepted by Him." But the sneer was unheeded by the young penitent. "Our Lord Jesus Christ," said she, "hath said that He came down from Heaven to save sinners. The Gospels testify that an abandoned woman washed His feet with her tears, and obtained pardon, and that He never rejected the publicans, but permitted them to eat with Him." It was not the answer the judge expected, and he was nonplussed for a moment. "Sacrifice," said he, "that your gallants may follow you and enrich you." But Afra answered: "I will have no more of that execrable gain. I have thrown away as so much filth what I had gained by it. Even our poor brethren would not accept of it till I had overcome their reluctance by my entreaties, that they might pray for my sins."

Gaius returned to his old sneer. "Jesus Christ will have nothing to do with you. It is in vain for you to acknowledge Him for your God; a common woman can never be called a Christian."

"It is true," said she humbly, "I am unworthy to bear the name of Christian; but Christ hath admitted me to be one."

"Sacrifice to the gods and they will save you," continued Gaius.

"My Savior," she replied, "is Jesus Christ Who upon the cross promised Paradise to the thief that confessed Him."

"Sacrifice," he thundered, "lest I order you to be whipped in the presence of your lovers."

"The only subject of my confusion and grief are my sins," she answered..

Gaius was losing his temper.

"I am ashamed," said he, "that I have disputed so long with you. If you do not comply, you shall die."

"That is what I desire," said she, "if I am not unworthy to find rest by this confession."

The judge made a last appeal.

"Sacrifice," said he, "or I will order you to be tormented and afterward burned alive."

"Very well," said she, "let that body which hath sinned undergo torments; but as to my soul I will not taint it by sacrificing to demons."

The judge rose in all his majesty. He was angry at the coolness with which this girl had defied all his threats. He would waste no more time in seeking to reclaim her. He pronounced the sentence of death. "We condemn Afra, a woman of evil life who hath declared herself a Christian to be burned alive because she hath refused to offer sacrifice to the gods."

At these words of condemnation the executioners seized the unprotesting girl and dragged her away. They brought her to an island in the river Lech and there stripped her and tied her to a stake. She did not resist. She rejoiced that she had been called to die for her Lord. Lifting her eyes to Heaven, she prayed: "O Lord Jesus Christ, Omnipotent God, Who camest to call not the righteous but sinners to repentance, accept now the sacrifice of my sufferings, and by this temporal fire deliver me from the everlasting fire which torments both body and soul."

The gloating murderers piled the pine branches about her and, as they lighted the fire, she prayed again: "I return Thee thanks, O Lord Jesus Christ, for the honor Thou hast done me in receiving me a holocaust for Thy Name's sake; Thou who hast vouchsafed to offer Thyself upon the altar of the cross a sacrifice for the sins of the whole world, the just for the unjust and for sinners. I offer myself a victim to Thee, O my God, Who livest and reignest with the Father and the Holy Ghost, world without end. Amen."

She could speak no more, for the smoke suffocated her. And thus she died, a victim of the brutality of men in the name of religion. It was such a death as even the first Magdalen might have envied.

Historically that is all that we know of the beautiful Afra. But the legend goes on to tell that the awful scene of her martyrdom was witnessed by three of her maids, Digna, Eunomia and Eutropia, who had once been women of sin as Afra herself, but had been converted with the rest of the household and had been baptized by Bishop Narcissus. They stood on the banks of the river watching the agony of their beloved mistress. When the executioners had departed to give to their master the final report of the crime against womanhood, they, accompanied by a man servant, went over to the island to recover the remains. What was their joy to find the poor body untouched by the flames. Immediately the man returned to the city with the sad yet glorious news to Afra's mother, Hilaria. What a joyful message to the mother who had once consecrated her child to sin, that now this same child was a martyr for the faith! She ran at once to tell the priests, and that night they came secretly with her to take away the holy relics. Hilaria had a sepulcher made two miles outside the city of Augsburg and there the martyr was buried. Augsburg still cherishes those sacred relics.

Meanwhile, Gaius was told of what had been done by the mother and the priests. Filled with rage he sent soldiers to seize all who had participated in the action and to put them to the test. If they refused to offer sacrifice to the gods they were to be put to death in the same manner as Afra had been executed.

The soldiers came upon the band of Christians as they were laying to rest the holy remains of Afra. Obeying the orders of the judge they sought to persuade the new prisoners to sacrifice and by that deny their religion. But the Christians, strengthened by the example of Afra, refused. Thereupon the soldiers filled the tomb with dry branches which they set on fire. Then they shut the door, leaving their victims to suffer and die. So ended this glorious martyrdom on August seventh, in the year 304. St. Afra is the patroness of Augsburg, an object of love and veneration where once her life had been a scandal.

The poor material out of which God can make saints is seen in the story of the Roman lady, Aglae, and her paramour, now enrolled on the list of martyrs as St. Boniface.

Aglae was a pet of fortune. Born to one of the great families of Rome in the early fourth century she had an assured position in the world. Her youth and beauty alone would have made her a favorite in her own social set, but in addition to that she was immensely wealthy, so rich that it is told in her life that three times she personally paid the expenses of shows to entertain the public. That was a sure way to popularity, and Aglae loved to be in the eye of the public as much as any modern social butterfly. She knew her beauty, her wealth, her power, and gloried in them.

But vanity and love of popularity were not the only failings of the girl. She was no better than the pagan times in which she lived, though she seems to have been a nominal Christian. Boniface was her chief steward and with him she lived in sin for several years, the world of society little suspecting the moral corruption of their favorite. Boniface was addicted to drink and morally rotten, but as sometimes happens in such characters he had certain good qualities. He was especially kind to the poor and would even go about the city at night seeking cases that needed relief. These many acts of kindness brought their blessings to Boniface as well as to Aglae, who very likely had furnished the funds which he distributed as alms. Anyway the day came when the woman realized the miserable condition of her soul, and desired to put away her iniquities. "You know," she said to her lover, "how deep we are plunged in vice, without reflecting that we must appear before God to give an account of all our actions. I have heard it said that those who honor those who suffer for the sake of Jesus Christ shall have a share in their glory. In the East the servants of Jesus Christ every day suffer torments, and lay down their lives for His sake. Go thither then and bring the relics of some of those conquerors, that we may honor their memories and be saved by their assistance."

Boniface, eager as she to break the bonds of sin that enslaved them, assented to the proposal, and after collecting a large sum of money with which to buy the bodies of the martyrs and to help the poor was ready for the pilgrimage. "I won't fail to bring back with me," said he, "the relics of martyrs, if I find any. But," he continued laughing, "what if my own body should be brought to you for a martyr?" Aglae reproached him for jesting about such a serious matter.

But events proved that the seeming joke of Boniface was in reality a prophecy of his own martyrdom. Poor material for a martyr, indeed! The lustful *bon vivant*

Boniface! But as he set out on his journey the grace of God came into his heart. He saw his sins in all their enormity, saw himself as a hypocrite, and despised himself as he knew all good men would despise him if they knew the low life he had been leading. Sorrow filled his soul as he thought of his wasted life. His one aim now was to redeem himself, to atone for his sins by a life of mortification. During that journey from Rome to the East he lived on the humblest fare, to mortify the appetite which so often had led him into sin, and all his time was given to prayer for God's mercy, to bitter tears for the past and to bodily austerities. He had set out with the purpose of buying the bodies of martyrs; he was now filled with the hope that he himself might suffer death for the faith which up to now had meant so little to him.

In those days the Christians in the East were being persecuted, though the West was now at peace after having endured every manner of torment for centuries. As soon as Boniface arrived at Tarsus, the capital city of Cilicia, where the persecution was the most severe, he sent his servants with the horses to an inn while he proceeded immediately to the governor of the province. He found him seated on his tribunal watching with fiendish glee the suffering martyrs who had been brought to judgment that day. It was a pitiful sight. One was hanged by his feet over a fire, one stretched on stakes, one sawn asunder, one with his hands cut off, one fixed to the ground with a stake through his neck, one with his hands and feet tied behind him while he was beaten with clubs, and others afflicted with such punishments as the human devils could invent. The patience of the sufferers thrilled Boniface as it astonished all the bystanders. Boniface with his new zeal for the faith came forward and saluted his brethren in religion. "Great is the God of the Christians," said he, "great is the God of the holy martyrs. I beseech you the servants of Jesus Christ to pray for me that I may join with you in fighting against the devil."

The governor, indignant at this interruption of his pleasure, wanted to know who this fellow was. Boniface answered calmly that he was a Christian, and that he feared nothing the governor could do to him to seek to make him renounce Jesus, his Master. That was enough for the governor. He would spend no time in trying to convert the stranger. He ordered that a sharpened reed be thrust under the nails of the fellow and that boiling lead be poured into his mouth. Boniface was not dismayed. He submitted cheerfully, as he called on the name of Jesus for help and committed himself to the prayers of his brother martyrs. The cruelty shocked the onlookers, and, filled with admiration at the bravery of this newcomer, they shouted out, "Great is the God of the Christians," a cry that so alarmed the governor that he quickly withdrew, fearing harm to himself. Boniface suffered no more that day, but on the day following he was haled again before the governor for the final test. He was thrown into a caldron of boiling oil, but came forth unharmed. The governor then, to end the matter speedily, commanded that his head be struck off, and thus while praying to God to forgive him his own sins and to pardon his murderers he was given the glorious honor of sealing his faith with his blood.

It was all done so quickly that the servants who remained at the inn had not heard even of the arrest and the trial. They wondered why their master did not return, and going out to search the city for him they learned that a stranger had that day been put to death on the charge of being a Christian. When they came to the place of execution and recognized the remains as those of their master they begged the authorities that they might be allowed to take them away; but they obtained the sacred treasure only when they paid five hundred pieces in gold, the very money which poor Boniface had collected among his friends in Rome to bring back the relics of other martyrs. He little knew that he had been collecting the price of his own headless corpse. They embalmed the body, and then glorifying God for the great honor He had given to Boniface they set out for Rome. A messenger went in advance to break the news to Aglae. The jesting prophecy had come true. His own body was being brought back to her as a martyr. Yet it was not a time for grief; it was a time of holy joy that they who had sinned and repented had received this mark of God's love. Hastily summoning several priests, she went forth with them with lighted tapers and perfumes and met the holy relics half a mile outside the city, all the while singing hymns of praise to God. In that very place where she met her former lover the penitent woman had a tomb built and therein laid the sacred remains. Some years afterwards out of her great fortune she built a chapel in honor of him. She was no longer the frivolous, pleasure-loving, notoriety-seeking pet of society; she was now the Magdalen, the penance-loving, suffering woman, who had been a sinner. Fifteen long years she served God after her conversion, finding her consolation in invoking as St. Boniface him who had once been her partner in crime. When she died she was buried close to the relics which she had rejoiced in honoring.

The story of St. Theodota is in many respects similar to that of St. Afra. She had been a woman of sin, but the career of vice had not killed all the faith in her. She lived at Philippi in Thrace. It was at the time the persecution of the Christians was raging, under Licinius. The prefect Agrippa, following instructions, had commanded that on the feast of Apollo everybody in the city should offer sacrifice to the gods. This was the sure method of discovering who were Christians, in the effort to destroy entirely the hated religion. Theodota, though a bad woman, though she had sold her soul for money, could not bring herself to deny her faith. She refused to sacrifice to the gods and for that refusal was dragged before the prefect. She admitted that she had been a woman of loose morals, but she declared that she would not add to her sins and defile herself by denying her God. So courageous was she in the face of the authorities, such a defense did she make of her faith, that her biographer tells us that seven hundred and fifty men—very likely from the soldiers gathered there—professed themselves Christians and refused to offer the sacrifice.

In the effort to break her spirit Theodota was kept in prison for twenty days. But the imprisonment served only to strengthen her in her determination to be true to her faith. All the while she prayed and wept, begging God to forgive her the terrible sins she had committed, and to send her the needed strength to endure the torments she knew she would have to suffer.

When she was brought to trial she confessed that she had been a wicked woman, but that she was a Christian, however unworthy to bear that holy name. Agrippa commanded that she be scourged. Calmly she submitted while the onlookers begged her to spare herself and comply with the simple request to sacrifice. "Never," she exclaimed; "I will never abandon the true God, nor sacrifice to lifeless statues." When the lashing did not break her will, the prefect ordered that she be placed on the rack and torn with an iron comb. But during these torments she did not flinch. "I adore Thee, O Christ," she cried out, "and thank Thee because Thou hast made me worthy to suffer this for Thy Name."

The prefect was beside himself with anger at the steadfastness of the weak woman, and he ordered that again she be torn with the iron comb, and vinegar and salt poured into the wounds. Theodota, however,

craved such sufferings. "So little do I fear your torments," said she, "that I entreat you to increase them
to the utmost, that I may find mercy and attain to the
greater crown." They plucked out her teeth one by
one with pincers, and finding that she still lived after
all these horrible cruelties they led her outside the city
to be stoned to death. "O Christ," she prayed as she
went this last journey, "as Thou didst show favor to
Rahab the harlot and didst receive the good thief, so
turn not Thy mercy from me." Thus died this fair
Magdalen, happy to come home, even by the way of
the cross, to the God she had once so grievously
offended.

In reading the lives of the Fathers of the Desert,
no matter how thrilling the deeds related, the heroic
penance, one feels that here is essential truth. The
life led by these holy men and women was a tremendous
warfare against the very powers of darkness. There is
no minimizing temptation. They knew that it was possible for even the cedars of Lebanon to fall. The story
of those who had sinned was held up as a warning, and
the story of those who had repented was told as a
message of hope.

In the life of the great St. Abraham, one of the
Fathers of the Desert, we read of such a fall and such
a redemption. Abraham's brother when dying had left
an only daughter, Mary, then seven years of age, to the
care of the monk. The little girl was brought to the
desert and committed to the protection of her uncle
who, wishing to bring her up in the religious life, had

a cell built for her next to his own with a small window through which he instructed her in spiritual things. Under his loving care she grew up a model of piety and penance, living this life of holiness for twenty years. One day she was led into sin by a man who had come to her cell on the pretext of consulting her uncle. The good of twenty years of penance was undone. So filled with remorse was she as she realized her folly that she despaired of God's mercy, quitted her cell and fled back to the world, where she gave herself up to a life of sin.

When the holy monk discovered the terrible calamity that had come upon the lamb he had so tenderly guarded, he was inconsolable. He knew not where to look for her. All he could do was to weep and pray and afflict himself to atone for her sin, trusting that God would one day bring her back to him. Not until two years after she had fled did he find any trace of her. Then someone told him that she was living in a certain city where her life was a scandal. Abraham lost no time; he determined to go to her. By the aid of a friend he procured a horse, dressed himself as a soldier, with a hat that concealed his identity, and borrowed enough money to help him in his plans to recover the lost sheep. He went to the city, found the inn where Mary was living and, still playing his part of soldier, gave orders for a fine supper. He told the innkeeper that he had heard a great deal about the beauty of a young woman named Mary living at the inn, and he begged him to get her to eat with him.

The young woman came as requested, thinking it was another gallant smitten by her. Not until the supper was over and the waiters had withdrawn did Abraham tell who he was. She was struck with shame when she discovered who her companion was. He was the last man in the world that she wished to see. But there was no reproach in the old man's words; only sorrow and yearning for her to come back to God.

"My child," said he, "don't you know me? My child, did I not bring you up? What has befallen you? Who is the murderer that has killed your soul? Where is that angelical habit that you formerly wore? Where that admirable purity? Where are those tears which you poured out in the presence of God? Where those watchings employed in singing the divine praises? Where that holy austerity that made you take pleasure in lying on the bare ground? Why did you not after your first fall come presently to acquaint me with it, since I certainly should have done penance for you? Why had you so little confidence in me? Alas, who is there without sin but God alone?"

The tender appeal of the broken-hearted man filled the woman with confusion. Despair still ruled her soul as she thought of the wonderful years of innocence she had so quickly thrown away. But the more she despaired, the more the monk pleaded. He would have her soul, even against all the powers of Hell. He spoke to her of the great mercy of God. He even promised to her that he would take all her sins upon his own head and do penance for them, and at last the despair was lifted from her. She threw herself in grief and penance at his feet and remained there the night long, a converted Magdalen. In the morning the monk placed her on his horse and led her back to the cell which she had quitted two years before.

So austere was the life of Mary from that time on, so unceasing were her tears and prayers, so holy did she become that the biographer of St. Abraham tells us that within three years after her return to her cell God was pleased to give the woman that had been a sinner the grace to work miracles on the sick. Thus for fifteen years she lived a life of the most severe penance, as she sought to atone for her many iniquities. She died five years after Abraham had gone to his reward, and the biographer testifies simply that at the hour of her death a certain extraordinary brightness was observed on her countenance, which gave all that were present occasion to glorify God. Another "woman of sin" had entered the Kingdom of Heaven.

There is the story of another Mary in these same ages of penance. One day two old monks traveling to Tarsus stepped into an inn on the way to rest from the extreme heat of the day. Nearby there sat three young men and with them this same Mary, who was a woman of evil character. Ignoring their companions, the monks sat down, and to pass the time in prayer one of them began to read aloud the Gospels. Mary, perhaps with old memories stirring in her heart, left her rollicking companions and came over to the monks and sat down beside them to listen to the reading. The monk, who was reading, thinking that she sought to insult him ordered her to go away, asking her how she dared, she whose profession was so evident, to come near them.

"I am a wretched sinner, it is true," said she in all humility, "but as our God and Savior, Jesus Christ, did not prevent a sinful woman from coming to Him, why should you cast me off?"

"Yes," answered the monk, "but the woman that came to our Savior renounced her wicked way of life and was no longer a harlot."

"And I," she returned humbly, "trust in Jesus Christ that from this very instant by His divine grace I shall quit this sinful way and never more be guilty of like sins."

She was as good as her word. She gave away all that she owned and entered a house of penance to which the good monks directed her. There she lived to a great age, doing penance for her sins. The glorious example of Mary Magdalen had brought back another soul to God.

There are many beautiful examples in the ages of penance of the peace of soul that comes to those who forsake their sins for the love of Christ. One of these monks who had left the world to come into the desert had a sister who was leading a wicked life and bringing ruin on the souls of many others. His brother monks who had heard of the scandalous woman persuaded the monk that it was his duty to seek her out and reclaim her, both for her own sake and for the sake of her victims. He set out for the city where she lived. Meanwhile, the news was brought to her that her brother was coming to see her. She was delighted at the prospect of seeing him and ran forth to meet him. She, unmindful of her sins that had disgraced him as well as herself, was astonished that he ignored her joyful greeting and forbade her to come near him. He stood at a distance from her and lectured her upon her disgraceful life, threatening her with the torments of the damned, and then his heart overflowing with love for her he tearfully begged her to take pity on her own poor soul and change her life.

Filled with confusion, she asked him if there was any hope for one who had fallen so low; was it too late for her to return to God? The brother, seeing that the victory was already won, assured her that it was still possible for her to redeem herself if she was willing to practice true penance. Immediately she threw herself at his feet and begged him to take her with him to the desert where she might be free from her old life and find the means of atoning for her sins. The brother told her to go back and get a covering for her head, since it was a disgrace for a woman to pass through the streets with head uncovered, "O brother," said she, "let us not make this delay; is it not better for me to suffer the disgrace of going bareheaded than to enter any more into a house that has been the shop of my iniquities?"

The monk agreed with her that this was wise, and they hurried off in the direction of the desert, he all the while speaking to her of the necessity of doing penance. As they approached the desert and the monk saw some of his brethren approaching, he urged her to keep at a distance from him for fear the others, not knowing she was his sister, might be scandalized at seeing him in the presence of a woman. As soon as they had gone on he went to look for her to continue the journey in directing her conscience. When at last he found her she was lying dead, her feet all bloody from walking barefoot all those weary miles. Hers was a short penance, so short that the monks to whom the brother related the story wondered if she had had time to save her soul. The old chronicle relates that the doubts were set at rest by a revelation to one of the monks that her renunciation of the world and her wicked life had been so complete, her grief so sincere and intense, that God had been merciful to her. It was the old story of the short penitence of the repentant thief—"This day shalt thou be with Me in Paradise."

One could compile a litany of penitents from these old stories of sorrowing women who, after having drunk the cup of shame to the bitter dregs, braved the ridicule of the world they had so long served and put off the soft garments for the sackcloth and ashes. One story varies little from the other; a difference in the minor details; but all are the beautiful story over and over again of Magdalen, the woman who was a sinner, suffered even to behold face to face her risen Master.

Chapter 4

THE WOMAN AUGUSTINE LOVED

FOR centuries the Christian world has thrilled at the story of St. Augustine. He is not only the learned Doctor of the Church, the great bishop, the keen philosopher, the spiritual soldier who fought against all the enemies of the Church and the Empire, but he is—and this more than anything else is the secret of his everlasting appeal to the souls of men—the great penitent, the great exemplar of the mercy of God to sinners. Never to be separated from him, either in life or in eternity, is St. Monica, the doting mother who, in spite of every rebuff, in spite of the apparent hopelessness of the case, pursued him like a veritable hound of Heaven till she succeeded in reclaiming him to God. "Where you are he will be," said the angel that came to her in her dream. We never get tired of meditating upon this beautiful example of mother love. One name brings up the other. Say Monica and you visualize Augustine; say Augustine and you visualize Monica, joined in life, in sorrow; joined in death, in glory.

But there is another great character in this story of love and sacrifice and penance, a character of whom we know much and at the same time very little. Those who write the story of Augustine or Monica dismiss this other woman in a very few lines, dismiss her as summarily as she was dismissed out of the life of Augustine. That is not strange, for large as she looms in the life of the man, so large that during the central years of his life she may be considered as the very essence of it, she comes from nowhere and in like manner goes to nowhere, leaving but the memory of love destroyed and sacrifice triumphant. We do not even know her name, that name which the poetic Augustine in the delirium of his love must have spoken countless times to the stars of the African night; yet we can never think of Augustine without thinking of this nameless woman, the partner of his sin, the mother of his son, who sacrificed herself for love and penance and in a great way made it possible for Augustine the sinner to become Augustine the saint.

Augustine was about nineteen years old when she came into his life and took possession of him body and soul.

To say that is by no means to say that she was a scheming woman who had led an unsuspecting youth astray. It was presumably a chance encounter, a "wayward passion," as he himself calls it, merely one more event in the endless lists of the young student's falls, a passing love to be rid of in a day, but one that somehow continued for more than ten years, and in many ways made a lasting impression on the life of Augustine. It was during the Carthage student days that the sinful union began, and to say Carthage is to get the background of an iniquity that only the prayers of a St. Monica could cope with.

When Augustine had come to study at Carthage he had already been drunk with corruption, young as he was. It is a question if his mind from boyhood to the time of his conversion had ever been clean. It was not so much the fault of the boy himself as of his surroundings. Tagaste, where he was born, in 354, was a town of passage, a town of traffic, a great market place where all the roads of the pagan world met. And such a world as it was! Africa then as always was sensual and pleasure-loving. The growing boy had ever before his eyes the allurements of vice. Add to this the fact that his father was a pagan who knew little of the restraints of Christian modesty and you will know what a handicap it all was even to a lad that had such a mother as Monica was. He did not have even the grace of Baptism, through the strange conviction prevailing at the time that since a man was sure to commit sin it was advisable to defer Baptism so that all actual sin as well as original sin would be wiped away when one was sick of sinning and ready to give himself to God. A strange way to reason, indeed, but such was the consideration in depriving Augustine of Baptism and bringing him up as a mere catechumen for many years. And he suffered from that deprivation almost to the loss of his soul.

So the unregenerate boy lived his heedless life, eager for play like a real boy, perfecting himself in the game of "nuts," like the modern shell-game, snaring birds, and in every way living a rough, wild boyhood, a precocious boyhood in which he picked up on the streets of Tagaste a lot of moral dirt. As the schools in Tagaste were inadequate, he was sent to Madaura, thirty miles away, to continue his education. It was a city almost entirely pagan, and that means chiefly pagan morality. Amid such surroundings, where pleasure and lust were regarded as the whole of life, and where he was brought up wholly on a diet of pagan classics with their romance-coated pills of iniquity, it is no wonder that the boy of fifteen soon forgot all the lessons of Monica and became thoroughly pagan at heart, with a knowledge of unmentionable things that had already tarnished his innocence. He returned home when he was sixteen, as it was decided that he should complete his education at Carthage, but as his father found it hard to raise the money right away for that purpose the boy was permitted to spend the following year in rank idleness. As usual the period of idleness did him no good. Thrown in with idle companions as bad as himself and as worldly-wise, he soon sacrificed whatever virtue had remained to him after the school days in Madaura. From that time on Augustine was morally rotten. And of course with the loss of morality there was also the loss of faith. As Bertrand says, "It is not reason which turns the young man from God; it is the flesh. Scepticism but provides him with the excuses for the new life he is living."

And not content with corruption, the ambitious youth wanted to have the reputation of being the most corrupt of all his fellows. For Augustine was above all ambitious, ambitious in everything, even in vice. His father was determined to see him a great man, and in his scheme of greatness moral rectitude or Christian purity had no place. As Augustine wrote later on in his *Confessions,* "My father gave himself no concern how I grew towards Thee, or how chaste I was, provided only that I became a man of culture, however destitute of Thy culture, O God."

Finally his father, Patricius, succeeded in getting together the necessary money, and at once Augustine was despatched to Carthage. "To Carthage I came," he writes, "where there sang all around me in my ears a cauldron of unholy loves." Carthage naturally made a deep impression on the mind of a boy just up from the country. It was one of the five great capitals of the Empire and was consequently a voluptuous city, a city of pleasure and laziness, all contained in the name it enjoyed—Carthage of Venus. The sentimental, romantic, poetic Augustine fell an easy prey to its seductions. The theater, hardly a school for saints in those days, made him its slave. Poetry and music and romantic literature filled his thoughts to the exclusion of everything Christian, and one can easily guess the consequences to a moral weakling like Augustine. "For the space of nine years then," he writes "(from my nineteenth year to my eight and twentieth), we lived seduced and seducing, deceived and deceiving, in divers lusts; openly by sciences which they call liberal; secretly with a false-named religion; here proud, there superstitious, everywhere vain! Here hunting after the emptiness of popular praise, down even to theatrical

applause, and poetic prizes, and strifes for grassy gar-
lands, and the follies of shows, and the intemperance
of desires."

In spite of all this fast living, Augustine was an
earnest student. He knew that his future depended on
himself, and he worked hard, burning the candle at
both ends. He was thrown on his own resources now,
for his father had died and he could expect but little
help from home. But hard as he worked at his studies
he still found plenty of time for his degrading pleasures, and he confesses that he was so full of lust that
he did not scruple to arrange his love affairs in the
churches. Not strange, for the Christian churches
meant little to him now since, in his pride of intellect
and his rebellion against Catholic doctrine, but more
against Catholic morals, he had given himself over to
the errors of Manicheism. Again and again he found
himself in love, or rather in love with love, a period
which Augustine passes over lightly with a burning
blush upon his face even after all the years of penance.
But it is all expressive of the degradation into which
the youth, then about twenty, had fallen.

It was at this impressionable, romantic period of his
life that he first met the girl who was to play such
an important part in his life for many years, and who
was to give him the son he idolized, Adeodatus, the
"son of my sin."

"In those years," he writes, "I had one, not in that
which is called lawful marriage, but whom I had found
in a wayward passion, void of understanding; yet, but

one, remaining faithful even to her; in whom I in my own case experienced what difference there is between the self-restraint of the marriage covenant, for the sake of issue, and the bargain of a lustful love where children are born against their parents' will, although once born they constrain love."

It was, indeed, evidently a "wayward passion," only another incident in the life of the riotous student. That is evident from the fact that scarcely had he met the girl when he decided to return to his native town in order to open a school there. He came to Tagaste, leaving his latest love at Carthage, perhaps glad to be rid of her. Augustine had come back to Monica, but so changed was he that it broke her heart. She knew of his moral lapses, no doubt, and prayed over them. But when this her son boasted openly and brazenly of being a Manichean, of rejecting the faith that was all to her, she became so indignant that she ordered him out of her house.

Augustine did not remain long at Tagaste. He was not a prophet in his own country; there was little hope of speedy advancement, and so he decided to return to Carthage. It is not hard to believe that there was a more urgent reason for cutting short his stay at home. The woman he loved was calling him. No doubt she was in distress, for shortly after his return to Carthage a child was born to them, a son to whom by some strange feeling he gave the name Adeodatus, the Gift of God. Adeodatus was anything but a gift of God according to Augustine's way of thinking at that time;

he did not want the child and he very likely rebelled against his fate to be so encumbered just when he was trying to make his way in the world, but as soon as he looked into the face of the child his heart softened and he was filled with joy at this veritable Gift of God.

For Augustine now there seemed to be no way of turning back, even if he had wished to do so. But there is no sign that he did wish to be relieved of his burden. On the contrary, he was madly in love with the mother of his child. She fascinated him, whether by her beauty or by her charm of disposition no one can say; so fascinated him that he became a slave to her for more than ten years. And just there is the mystery of it all. Since he loved her as he unquestionably did, the question arises why did he not marry her, if only for the good name of his son. A mystery it will ever be. Even when Monica, to reclaim Augustine to a decent life, sought to arrange a marriage for him, it never seemed to enter her mind that he should marry this girl, but she chose a prospective wife for him elsewhere, a girl who was not yet of marriageable age. It is no good to try to answer the problem, for all is hid in secrecy. Various writers have suggested in the attempt to solve the problem that the girl was of a very humble or lowly class, perhaps even of the slave class, at any rate of a lower social caste, a thing that in those days would have been a great barrier to such a curial family as that to which Monica and Augustine belonged. Whatever the cause, it is certain that there was some insurmountable barrier which made the marriage of these two impossible to consider. Knowing Augustine, it is hard to believe that he would have refused to marry the mother of his child, a girl, too, with whom he was deeply in love, just for the sake of class distinction. The one thing that we can be sure of is that there could be none other than a sinful union there, and that is why Monica in season and out of season sought to separate the lovers, who were damning each other's soul. To Monica it was all a horrible scandal and it could be remedied only by the departure of the girl.

But the heart of Augustine was unquiet. Carthage was palling on him, for he was not advancing in the world as one of his great talents should advance. He decided to try his luck at Rome, and no sooner had he decided than he set out for the great capital of the world. The girl agreed to remain for the time being in Carthage with the child. Monica was terrified at the thought of Augustine's going to Rome, which she regarded as the center of all iniquities, and she followed him, determined to accompany him on his travels. He resented her watchfulness over him, and, evading her, set out for Rome, leaving her to mourn for his deceit and his lack of filial love.

He remained at Rome but a short time, and not finding things as promising as he had expected, he went to Milan. Still was he dissatisfied, still on the quest for something indefinable, not knowing that all the while he was questing God.

Augustine was thirty years old when he came to Milan. As soon as he was settled he sent for his mistress and their son, and rented an apartment in a large house which boasted of a garden, that famous garden wherein his conversion took place. But there was no thought of conversion yet. It was a happy life, an easy one, and yet he felt that something was lacking. He did not want to realize that the lack was due to his sinful life. Sin it was, and he knew it, but he flattered himself that a life of continency was impossible. "And Ambrose himself," he writes, "as the world counts happy, I esteemed a happy man, whom personages so great held in such honor; only his celibacy seemed to me a painful course." If painful to Ambrose, it was unthinkable to Augustine. And so he writes, "I was entangled in the life of this world, clinging to dull hopes of a beauteous wife, the pomp of riches, the emptiness of honors, and the other hurtful and destructive pleasures."

His mother and brother and some of his friends soon joined him at Milan and all together formed a friendly, united household under the direction of the motherly Monica. But the new associations at Milan put new ideas of social ambition into Augustine's head. His contact with fashionable people gave him the desire to be of their number, in wealth and in worldly power. But as the first condition to that it was necessary that he should put his house in order. His reputation was bound to be injured by his living with a woman to whom he was not married. Even for his worldly advancement it was necessary for him to be respectable. It was then that he began to think seriously of marriage, but for some unaccountable reason not with the mother of Adeodatus. His friends, seeing what way the wind was blowing, urged him to separate from her, to dismiss her. They, as well as Monica, thought that this was the psychological moment. Monica's reasons were doubtless different from the reasons of the friends. More than all else she regarded the welfare of Augustine's soul. This woman, whom she must have looked upon as an intruder, was the one thing that delayed her son's conversion, and it was his salvation that she desired more than anything else in the world. This woman had enslaved him in sin for more than ten years, she had fettered him body and soul, and Monica was convinced that since it was impossible for him to marry her she must go from him forever. Monica then interested herself even so far as to pick out the bride she wanted him to marry.

Did Monica use her persuasion on Augustine's mistress? Did she represent to her that she was an incumbrance to him, that she was destroying his life, his prospects and the future of Adeodatus? Doubtless she did; but more than all she prayed. Monica's prayers succeeded in converting the woman as well as Augustine. Whatever the method of persuasion, and we would like to believe that it was essentially spiritual, the woman decided that it was her duty to go out of the life of Augustine. It was all, indeed, the act of a heroine. Must she leave him whom she so dearly loved, must she leave forever this little son who was the apple of her eye? It was a terrible lot to endure, but she had more of the Christian fortitude than they gave her credit for. The grace of God touched her; Monica's prayers had conquered her. Perhaps in her heart of hearts she had some prophetic vision of the Divine mission which God was saving for Augustine. She knew his longings better than anyone else knew them, she knew his capabilities, and she was willing to prove her love by sacrificing it. The die was cast. Hiding her anguish, she took leave of Augustine, took leave of her little son, and went back to Carthage, a broken-hearted woman no doubt, but a truly repentant one filled with the grace of God for her mastery over self.

Even though Augustine well knew that this woman was the shame of his life it broke his heart to have her go. All the thoughts of worldly position did not balance the affection he had for her. So he writes in his *Confessions:* "Meanwhile my sins were being multiplied, and my concubine being torn from my side as a hindrance to my marriage, my heart which clave unto her was torn and wounded and bleeding. And she returned to Africa vowing unto Thee never to know any other man, leaving with me my son by her." And he regrets that he himself "could not imitate a very woman."

But that "very woman" had the soul of a martyr. The hint about her vowing never to know any other man gives some inkling of the earnestness of her conversion. It was not that she felt herself driven away! it was that she felt the will of God working in her. Stronger indeed, she was than Augustine, for scarcely had she gone when he went looking for others to take her place until the chosen bride would be of suitable age.

The woman went as she came, unknown. There is a tradition that back in Africa she entered a monastery and devoted the rest of her life to works of penance. There, a few years after, she heard of the death of Adeodatus, the boy "with the soul of an angel," and she must have rejoiced that he was in Heaven to plead for her; there, too, she heard of Augustine's conversion, and the news must have made her penances easier to bear. The tradition that she entered a monastery is easy to accept. The penance of the monastery was little compared with the great sacrifice of penance she made that day when she went out of the life of Augustine and Adeodatus. Nameless she may be, yet in all history there is no greater heroine of sacrifice, no truer Christian penitent. We would not rob St. Monica of her glory in converting Augustine by her prayers and tears, but who knows how much was contributed to his spiritual awakening by the prayers and penitential tears of the "very woman" whose heart like his own "was torn and wounded and bleeding"?

Chapter 5

ROSAMOND CLIFFORD

MISS STRICKLAND, in her *Lives of the Queens of England,* calls Rosamond Clifford "the Magdalen of the Middle Ages." Hence her story deserves retelling, not so much for the romance connected with her name as for the prosaic penance that made her seek through twenty years to atone for her wicked life as mistress of Henry II, King of England. The romantic story of the Fair Rosamond has always appealed to the poets and the dramatists. It is strange that Shakespeare did not make her the heroine of a tragedy. It may be because he had never heard, at any rate never accepted, the false tradition that Rosamond had been put to death by Queen Eleanor. Nevertheless, from Shakespeare's time, when Daniel wrote his drama, the *Complaint of Rosamond,* in 1619, three years after the death of the great bard, the poets have found Rosamond a very enticing subject. No need to recall all of them. It may be noted that Addison in 1706 wrote an opera on the subject, and that Tennyson wrote his *Becket,* in which the chief character after the martyred St. Thomas is Rosamond Clifford.

But the tragedies, as is the way of all tragedies, do not show the happy ending of the life that is hidden with Christ in God. They stress the end of the romance and give no hint of the higher romance that succeeded to the loss of the love of an earthly king. They weep for Rosamond the Fair; they cannot vision her as the weeping Magdalen. But still across the ages we catch the scent of the Rose of the World, a rose that had many a thorn, a rose that was crushed by the spurred heel of the king, but in its crushed and withered state still fragrant with the memory of tears. Upon her tomb this epitaph was carved:

> Hic jacet in tumba Rosa Mundi, non Rosa munda;
> Non redolet, sed olet, quae redolere solet;

which has been Englished thus:

> Here Rose the graced, not Rose the chaste, reposes;
> The smell that rises is no smell of roses.

A gruesome bit of verse, indeed. And untrue. For from the dust where the tomb of the penitent and her poor ashes are mingled there comes the scent of such roses as never die.

The Fair Rosamond's real name was Jane Clifford, the "fayr daughter of Walter, lord Clifford." As Dryden puts it in his Prologue to the drama *Henry II,*

> Jane Clifford was her name as books aver:
> "Fair Rosamond" was but her nom de guerre.

She was but a young girl, evidently, when she met for the first time the future King of England. No doubt she had just come from the convent school at

Godstow Nunnery, the place which she was to make famous in literature by her penance in later years. She almost found a throne, but she met with tragedy instead. Queen she might have been, or at least a happy wife, if it were not for the unsettled condition of the kingdom where love and marriage had to adapt themselves to political affairs of state.

It was not long after the time of the Conquest. Henry I, who had succeeded his father, William the Conqueror, on the throne, had married his daughter Matilda, then twelve years of age, to the Emperor, Henry V. When the Emperor died, Henry, who had despaired of a male heir when his son and heir was drowned in the terrible "white ship" disaster, brought Matilda back to England and declared her the heiress-presumptive to the throne of England. Even Henry's nephew Stephen, a grandson of the Conqueror, promised fealty to her. It was even hinted that Matilda was very much in love with this same Stephen. Anyway, when Henry, again for affairs of state, insisted that she should marry Geoffrey Plantagenet, Count of Anjou, her heart was not in the match. Whether she still clung to the hope of one day marrying Stephen, or whether she had a dislike for Geoffrey, the true reason of her antipathy to the marriage will never be known. She and Geoffrey made an ill-sorted pair, and there was little love lost between them. It is even hinted that her son, Henry II, born March 25, 1133, was the son not of her husband Geoffrey but of her lover Stephen.

Stephen, on the death of Henry I, in spite of the fact

that he had promised fealty to Matilda as heiress-presumptive, had himself proclaimed at once King of England. But Matilda was not the kind to see a throne wrested from her without a struggle. She decided to fight for her rights, and with one hundred and forty followers she landed in England and was received into Arundel Castle by her stepmother, her father's widow. With her she brought her young son Henry, then a lad of nine, and placed him under a tutor at Bristol; but shortly afterwards he returned to Normandy. Matilda succeeded in defeating Stephen and entered London in state, but Stephen's queen was a woman of such great character that she occasioned a reaction of the people in her favor, and the haughty Matilda was forced to flee. Then followed three years of civil strife between the rival claimants to the throne. The young Henry again came from Normandy in 1149, this time to seek the aid of the Scots and the English barons against Stephen. He was then a youth of sixteen, and was trained in the science of arms by his uncle Gloucester, his mother's brother.

It was during this sojourn in England, according to many writers, that Henry met his Fair Rosamond for the first time, and fell in love with her at once. But he was soon awakened from love's young dream. His father Geoffrey recalled him home to invest him with Normandy, and soon after that by the death of Geoffrey Henry became Count of Anjou. Meanwhile all of Matilda's hopes for England having died, she too returned to Normandy.

If Henry had already met and loved the fair daughter of the Cliffords, it did not take him long to forget her, for in 1152 when he was nineteen years of age he married Eleanor of Aquitaine, the divorced wife of Louis VII of France. It has been claimed, and Tennyson holds to it in *Becket,* that Henry had gone through a marriage ceremony with Rosamond and that he kept her hidden in the famous Labyrinth so that she did not know until long after the event of his marriage to Eleanor. Eleanor's grandfather, William, Duke of Aquitaine, had abdicated in her favor, and then he who had been the most powerful prince in Europe became a pilgrim and a penitent. At the time of his abdication he had married her to the heir-presumptive of France, the future Louis VII. They were married with great pomp at Bourdeaux and were crowned Duke and Duchess of Aquitaine, August 1, 1137. Shortly after, by the death of the King of France, they succeeded to that throne. It was not destined to be a happy marriage. Eleanor was very beautiful, a fine musician, learned in all the Provençal poetry of the day and a noted poet herself. But the court of Aquitaine was notorious for its licentiousness, whereas the court of France was one of rigid morality, thanks to the influence of such men as St. Bernard. St. Bernard had preached the Crusade, and the King felt obliged to go on it. The Queen, much against the wishes of Louis, fancied herself an Amazonian heroine and insisted on going too. But their armies met with an inglorious defeat, due chiefly to the stubborn self-will of Eleanor.

From that time, owing to the temper of the Queen, and principally to the fact that she had formed a criminal attachment with a young Saracen, all love ended between the royal pair. After an absence of two years and four months, they returned to France, and from that time on there was nothing but dissension.

In 1150 Geoffrey Plantagenet had visited the French court and had presented to Louis and the Queen his son Henry, then a youth of seventeen. Eleanor, who was always very much of a defender of free love, was much smitten with Geoffrey. Henry was then too much of a boy to win favor in her eyes; but when eighteen months later, after the death of his father, he visited Paris again, this time Eleanor, disgusted with her pious husband, proceeded to fall in love with him. Henry was then "a noble, martial-looking prince, full of energy, learned, valiant and enterprising," just the type of hero for Eleanor to make advances to. She succeeded too well, so well that again the suspicions of the King were aroused, and a hint was given to Henry to leave at once for home. Almost immediately Eleanor applied for the annulment of her marriage with Louis on the grounds that she was related to him within the forbidden degrees of consanguinity. Whatever the reason, the marriage was annulled March 18, 1152. Eleanor was not one to lose much time. She left Paris, retired to her own domain of Aquitaine, and six weeks later she and Henry were married. She was thirty-two; he was twenty. It was a scandalous affair, for four months later their son William was born.

Henry's honeymoon was soon interrupted by the league which had been formed by Stephen and Louis. Stephen on the death of his wife had sent his son, Prince Eustace, to France to enlist the aid of the French King in order to wrest the Duchy of Normandy from Henry. It was not hard to get the aid of Louis, for he was still chafing under the insult of Henry's marriage to Eleanor. Stephen then sought to prevail upon the Archbishop of Canterbury to crown Prince Eustace as heir to the throne of England. But as none of the prelates, fearing still further civil war, could be induced to this, Stephen had all of them imprisoned. Whereupon the Archbishop of Canterbury, having escaped, hastened to Normandy and persuaded Henry to try his luck once more in England. Henry needed little encouraging. Leaving his wife Eleanor and his little son in Normandy, he embarked from Harfleurs with thirty-six ships, in May, 1153. The result was that an agreement was made with Stephen by which Stephen was to enjoy the crown during his life, and Henry was to succeed him as king. Stephen could not have objected to the agreement if it be true, as has been hinted, that Henry was his own son.

It was during this time spent in England that, according to many—and it seems to be the more likely story—Henry first met Jane Clifford, and after having won her heart by a promise to marry her, returned to Normandy. He did not have to remain there long. Prince Eustace died in 1153, followed by Stephen in 1154, and thus Henry, October 25, 1154, became King Henry II of England, and Eleanor Queen of England, the coronation taking place with great splendor, December 19, 1154.

Everything would seem to indicate that the liaison between Henry and the Fair Rosamond had practically ended at the time of his coronation. Stripped of all the legend that has grown up about the romantic affair, the story would seem to run thus. Henry when but a little over sixteen made a short stay in England, before going to Scotland. It was at that time he met Jane, or Rosamond, a girl who was then the most celebrated beauty in all England, the daughter of Clifford, a baron of Herefordshire. It was not merely a boy and girl affair, for Rosamond's eldest son William was born in 1150, and the youngest in 1153, and as Henry did not come back to England until 1153 it is evident that they were lovers from their first meeting, and perhaps, as one of the traditions puts it, man and wife. Hollingshead makes note of the liaison. "He delighted," he says of Henry, "most in the company of a pleasant demoiselle whom he cleped the Rose of the World; the common people named her Rosamond, for her passing beauty, properness of person and pleasant wit; with other amiable qualities, being verily a rare and peerless Piece in those days." And in another old writer of 1493 (Pynam) we find the following: "We read that in England was a King that had a concubine whose name was Rose, and for her great beauty he cleped her his Rose a Mounde (Rosa Mundi), that is to say Rose of the World, for he thought that she passed all women in beauty."

There is an old novel or romance on the subject which says that Clifford had a seat at Oxfordshire, and that one day a courtier spoke in such glowing terms to Henry of the beauty of Rosamond Clifford that the King decided to visit the Cliffords and find out for himself how beautiful the girl was. He made believe that he was going to visit all the kingdom and started out with that avowed purpose. However, he got no farther than the home of Rosamond. He found her even more charming than the courtier had described her, and so he lingered there indefinitely. Clifford then, suspecting the evil intentions of the King, sent Rosamond to visit relatives in Cornwall, hoping to get her away from the covetous eyes of Henry. But all his efforts were in vain, and he was soon informed that Rosamond instead of being in Cornwall was in the palace of the King and the mistress of Henry.

Much of this romance may be discarded, but it is quite certain that when Henry returned to England in 1153-4 the liaison was resumed. That Henry was really married to Rosamond is indicated by the affair as related by Lingard. "Of the King's natural children," he writes, "the most celebrated were his sons by Rosamond, the daughter of Walter Clifford, a baron of Herefordshire. William, the elder, was born while Henry was Duke of Normandy; Geoffrey, the younger, about the time of his accession to the throne of Eng-

land. They were educated with the children of Eleanor,
and destined for the highest offices in the church and
state. William, who received the name of 'long-sword,'
married the heiress of another William, earl of Salis-
bury, and succeeded to the estates and titles of that
powerful nobleman. Geoffrey before he had attained
the age of twenty was named to the bishopric of Lincoln. It was at the time of the first rebellion, and the
prelate elect immediately assembled a body of armed
men and dispersed the northern insurgents. At the
head of one hundred and forty knights he met his
father, who embraced him, exclaiming, 'Thou alone art
my legitimate son; the rest are illegitimate.' It was
two years before he could obtain the confirmation of
his election on account of his youth; and seven years
afterwards, though he continued to receive the revenues
of the see, he was still a layman. At length the pope
insisted that he should take orders or resign the bishopric. He chose the latter, and attended his father in
the quality of Chancellor during the last war, and at
his decease."

But this union of Henry and Rosamond did not continue long after his marriage to Eleanor; perhaps two
years. He may really have married Rosamond privately, or at least given her to understand that she was
his wife. Somehow, at any rate, he kept her in ignorance of the fact that he had married Eleanor, and also
on the other hand hid the existence of the Fair Rosamond from his Queen. So goes the tradition, though
it is pretty hard to believe that Rosamond could be

ignorant of such a public event as the marriage of the King to Eleanor. The way it is explained is that Henry kept Rosamond practically a prisoner in the maze or labyrinth which he had built for her at Woodstock. Scott in his novel *Woodstock* refers to this secret abode of the Fair Rosamond—"Rosamond's Labyrinth, whose ruins together with her well, being paved with square stones in the bottom, and also her Tower, from which the Labyrinth did run, are yet remaining, being vaults arched and walled with stone and brick, almost inextricably wound within one another, by which if at any time her lodging were laid out by the Queen, she might easily avoid peril imminent, and, if need be, by secret issues take the air abroad, many furlongs about Woodstock in Oxfordshire."

But if these two women were ever in ignorance of each other's existence, such ignorance could not last very long. The story goes that the Queen one day noticed the King as he walked in the gardens of Woodstock, and that she perceived a silk thread clinging to his spurs. She waited until Henry had disappeared and then by following the clue of the thread she came to Rosamond's bower, where she discovered this lady of incomparable beauty engaged in embroidering. She proceeded to heap abuses on the girl, as only Eleanor could, and only then, it is said, did Rosamond discover that she was not alone in the affections of the King. And as the result of the discovery on the part of the Queen, Rosamond, fully penitent for her sins, retired to the nunnery at Godstow, where she had been educated as a child. But that was too tame an ending for the romanticists. And consequently the story came into being—although there is no trace of it till the fourteenth century—that Eleanor having discovered the secret dwelling of her rival was so filled with hate against her that she brought to her one day a cup of poison and made her drink it. Eleanor had enough sins without adding that one to her list.

Thomas Percy in his *Reliques* declares that most of the circumstances in the story are taken as facts by English historians, who are unable to account for Eleanor's unnatural conduct in stirring up her sons to rebellion against the King except that she was jealous of the King's attachment to Rosamond Clifford. All have followed the monk of Chester, Higden, whose acccount is thus given by Stow. "Rosamond, the fair daughter of Walter, lord Clifford, concubine to Henry II (poisoned by Queen Eleanor as some thought) died at Woodstock 1177, where King Henry had made for her a house of wonderful working; so that no man or woman might come to her, but he that was instructed by the King, or such as were right secret with him touching the matter. This house after some was named Labyrinthus, or Dedalus work, which was wrought like into a knot in a garden called a Maze; but it was commonly said that lastly the Queen came to her by a clue of thread or silk and so dealt with her that she lived not long after; but when she was dead, she was buried at Godstow in a house of nuns, beside Oxford." Hol-

lingshead tells the story thus, that it was "the common
report by the people that the Queen found her out by
a silken thread, which the King had drawn after him
out of her chamber with his foot, and dealt with
her in such sharp and cruel wise that she lived not
long after." Speed's history says that the jealous
Queen found her out, "by a clue of silk, fallen from
Rosamond's lap as she sat to take air, and suddenly
fleeing from the sight of the searcher, the end of her
silk fastened to her foot, and the clue still unwinding,
remained behind; which the Queen followed till she
had found what she sought, and upon Rosamond so
vented her spleen, as the lady lived not long after."
The old broadside ballad says that the Queen discovered the clue by accident, from the knight Sir Thomas,
who had been sent by Henry to guard the Maze during
his own absence in France. The ballad ends thus:

> And forth she calls this trusty knight
>   In an unhappy hour;
> Who with his clue of twinèd thread
>   Came from this famous bower.
>
> And when that they had wounded him,
>   The Queen this thread did get,
> And went where lady Rosamond
>   Was like an angel set.
>
> But when the Queen with steadfast eye
>   Beheld her beauteous face,
> She was amazèd in her mind
>   At her exceeding grace.

Cast off from thee, those robes, she said,
    That rich and costly be;
And drink thou of this deadly draught
    Which I have brought to thee.

Then presently upon her knees
    Sweet Rosamond did fall;
And pardon of the Queen she craved
    For her offences all.

Take pity on my youthful years,
    Fair Rosamond did cry;
And let me not with poison strong
    Enforcèd be to die.

I will renounce my sinful life,
    And in some cloister bide;
Or else be banished if you please
    To range the world so wide.

And for the fault which I have done,
    Though I was forced thereto,
Preserve my life and punish me
    As you think meet to do.

And with these words, her lily hands
    She wrung full often there;
And down along her lovely face
    Did trickle many a tear.

But nothing could this furious Queen
    Therewith appeasèd be;
The cup of deadly poison strong,
    As she knelt on her knee,

She gave this comely dame to drink;
  Who took it in her hand,
And from her bended knee arose,
  And on her feet did stand.

And casting up her eyes to Heaven
  She did for mercy call;
And drinking up the poison strong,
  Her life she lost withal.

And when that death through every limb
  Had showed its greater spite,
Her chiefest foes did plain confess
  She was a glorious wight.

Her body then they did entomb
  When life was fled away,
At Godstow, near to Oxford town,
  As may be seen this day.

The old writers, says Percy, do not attribute Rosamond's death to poison, but merely say that Eleanor treated her so harshly and menaced her so that she did not live long after. On her tomb there were many fine engravings, and among them a cup, perhaps meant to indicate a chalice, but the cup started the story of the poison, for when the stone was demolished at the time the nunnery was dissolved "the tombstone of Rosamond Clifford was taken up at Godstow and broken in pieces, and that upon it were interchangeable weavings drawn out and decked with weavings, roses red and green, and the picture of the cup out of which she drank the poison given her by the Queen, carved in stone."

Most of the modern writers have held to the legend of the poison. Swinburne in his tragedy of Rosamond follows it. Addison in his opera on the subject makes Eleanor give Rosamond a sleeping potion rather than real poison, so that when the victim wakes up she will find herself in a nunnery. Whereupon Henry and Eleanor are reconciled and sing a love duet. The tragedy, or comedy, it may be added, does not increase the reputation of Addison. Barnett in his grand opera (1837) has Rosamond rescued by her father just as she is about to drink the fatal draught. Michael Field— the penname of those two fine poets, Katherine Bradley and Edith Cooper, aunt and niece respectively, who became Catholic in 1907—has the Queen bring both poison and dagger to Rosamond. Rosamond chooses the dagger and stabs herself. In the Field tragedy, which has some fine poetry, there is a departure from the old story. Rose is made not the daughter of the Cliffords, but a simple country maiden:

> She whom our first Plantagenet too well
> Loved, and for whom he built the marble maze
> Was no rich, crimson beauty of old line,
> As fabled in proud histories and lays;
> No Clifford, as 'tis boasted, but, in fine,
> A girl o' the country, delicately made
> Of blushes and simplicity and pure
> Free ardour, of her sweetness unafraid;
> For Rosa Mundi, of this truth be sure,
> Was Nature's Rose, not man's. . . .

But all these romances which the poets have used may be discarded as merely legendary. What seems to be absolutely historical is that within two years after Henry came to the throne of England, Rosamond broke the liaison with him and retired to the nunnery at Godstow, founded in the reign of King Stephen, "a little nunnery among the rich meadows of Evenlod."

In this little nunnery the discarded mistress of the King lived twenty years trying to atone for her sins by a life of the most austere penance. During those years, while she thought only of her penance, all was not pleasant with the King who had deceived her. Eleanor, who developed a bitterness against him, aroused her sons to rebellion against him, and after the rebellion of 1174 Henry was so incensed with his sons and his Queen that he openly avowed his connection with Rosamond, which had been a closed book for many years, by acknowledging her sons as legitimate. Eleanor was at that time practically a prisoner, disgraced, confined to her own palace for sixteen years. Becket had been murdered. Henry had gone to do penance at the martyr's grave. At last peace came after all the unnatural rebellion and then Henry went as a pilgrim to the shrine of the martyr to thank him for his victory. And during all the years Rosamond, heedless of what was going on in the great world, went on with her penance and her prayers. In the midst of all the troubles of the kingdom she died at Godstow. She was nearly forty years of age. "She died," says Miss Strickland, "practising the severest penances, in the high odor of sanctity, and may be considered the Magdalen of the middle ages. Tradition says she declared on her deathbed that when a certain tree she named in the convent garden was turned to stone, they would know the time she was received into glory. She died deeply venerated by the simple-hearted nuns of Godstow." Rosamond's father, lord Clifford, was still living at the time of her death. Many endowments of land had been made to the nunnery of Godstow by him and his family, and Henry, too, as well as many other friends, singled it out for their charity. It was not strange then that the tomb of Rosamond for many reasons became a noted place. The poor penitent must have turned in her grave as she saw all the honors paid to the tomb of a sinner. "According to the peculiar customs of the time," says Miss Strickland, "the grave was not closed, but a sort of temporary tabernacle, called in chronicle a hearse (of which the modern hatchment is a relic) was erected over the coffin; this was raised before the high altar, covered with a pall of fair white silk; tapers burnt around it, and banners with emblazonment waved over it. Thus lying in state, it awaited the time for the erection of a monument. Twenty years after, the stern moralist, St. Hugh, bishop of Lincoln, in a course of visitation of convents, came to Godstow and demanded, 'Who lay there in such state under that rich hearse?' And when the simple nuns replied, 'It was the corpse of their penitent sister, Rosamond Clifford,' the reformer, perhaps remembering she was the mother of his superior, the archbishop, declared, 'that the hearse of a harlot was not a fit spectacle for a choir of virgins to contemplate, nor was the front of God's altar a proper station for it.' He then gave orders for the expulsion of the coffin into the churchyard. The sisters of Godstow were forced to obey at the time; but after the death of St. Hugh they gathered the bones of Rosamond into a perfumed bag of leather, which they enclosed in a leaden case, and, with all the pertinacity of woman's affection, deposited them in their original place of interment, pretending that the transformation of the tree had taken place according to Rosamond's prophecy. Southey records a visit to the ruins of Godstow. The principal remnant serves for a cow-house. A nut tree grows out of the penitent's grave, which bears every year a profusion of nuts without kernels. King John thought proper to raise a tomb to the memory of Rosamond; it was embossed with fair brass having an inscription about its edges in Latin: Hic jacet, etc."

When the nunnery was dissolved the tomb of Rosamond was opened. When it was opened, says an old writer, "a very sweet smell came out of it." The Rose of the World had kept its sweetness bedewed with the penitential tears of twenty years.

Chapter 6

SAINT MARGARET OF CORTONA

THE great thirteenth century! To name it is to be thrilled at the manifestation of the power and glory of God through His saints who lived in that blessed period. It has its own long litany of saints—St. Elizabeth of Hungary, St. Gertrude, St. Francis of Assisi, St. Louis of France, St. Dominic, St. Bonaventure, St. Anthony of Padua, St. Thomas Aquinas—to name but a few of them—each of whom would have done honor enough to any age. And not the least in the list is she who is the only Penitent Saint among them—St. Margaret of Cortona. She has been called the "New Magdalene," so similar is her history to that of the great penitent of the Gospel—the same depths of degradation, the same heights of sanctity.

Laviano is a little hamlet in Tuscany, in Central Italy, twelve miles from Cortona. There Margaret Bartolomeo was born in the year 1247. It never was much of a place, even in Margaret's time; it is less now with its four or five houses and the little church of St. Vitus and St. Modestus. But there on the hill amid the pine trees, insignificant Laviano is yet of interest inasmuch as it still cherishes as a shrine the humble home where a great saint was born. And humble enough surely it was and is—a cottage, or shack rather, with the down-stairs room used as a shed. But the memory of Margaret hovers about the place. One can in fancy see her toddling as a child up the outside stairs that lead to the living room of the cottage where her picture now hangs.

Tancred Bartolomeo, the father, was a poor peasant. He had his little plot of ground as his share of the world and was happy enough in his humble circumstances. The first years of his married life were, indeed, full of happiness. He had married a peasant girl as poor as himself, a woman of great piety, well instructed in her religion. Two children were born to them, Margaret and a son, Bartolomeo, of whom we know very little. We get hints here and there of the simple piety of that home. Margaret tells us that when she was very small she used to kneel with her mother before the crucifix and repeat after her this prayer: "Lord Jesus, I pray to you for the salvation of all those whom you wish to be prayed for." The crucifix appealed to her childish heart as she was told the story of the Passion of Christ, and she loved to hold it and cover it with kisses. And how far, indeed, she was to wander from that little crucifix!

Things might have turned out differently if the good, pious mother had been spared to continue her work of sanctifying the soul of her child, but when Margaret was seven the mother died. She never forgot that mother, even through her years of sin. The memory of the lessons she had received from her was not the least of the influences which brought her back home after she had wandered far.

The trouble began with the second marriage of Tancred Bartolomeo. Two years after the death of his wife he married again. It is the traditional story of the harsh stepmother. There was very likely fault on both sides. The hatred was mutual. Margaret refused to obey the strange woman, and the stepmother in turn used that disobedience as an excuse for continued persecution of the motherless child. So this cat and dog life continued till the girl was in her seventeenth year. The home life was so distasteful that Margaret wanted to get away from it and marry, but the father would not hear of that. She was of great help in the home and on the little farm, and moreover he was too poor to provide her with a suitable dowry. So he kept her at home, trying as well as he could to do the impossible thing of keeping peace between the two women.

But the lack of affection at home made Margaret seek it outside. She did not have to seek far. She did not have to seek admirers; they thronged about her. She is described in those days as a true beauty. A fine figure, regular features, beautiful black hair, a fresh and brilliant complexion, with a carriage that made her seem more like the daughter of a nobleman than a poor peasant, and added to all this a quick intelligence and vivacity that showed her warm heart, she was the avowed belle of Laviano. She was beautiful, and she knew it. The adulation of all filled her with vanity. She decked herself out far beyond her station and then set out to break hearts. She was a confirmed flirt, with an eye to purchase with her beauty the comforts which were denied her in her father's house.

One day there came into the life of the peasant maiden the youth who ruined her. He was the son of Guglielmo di Pecora, lord of Valiano, and a knight of Rhodes. The family lived at Monte Pulciano, but had come to live for a while at their country seat in the Villa Palazzi. Young di Pecora had heard—as who had not?—of the village beauty. One day as he rode through Laviano he saw her and he was immediately smitten with her charm. Flirt as she was Margaret did not disdain the attention of the nobleman. She had ambitions, and fancied herself the lady of the castle. She demurred at first about becoming his mistress; the religious training she had received, the memory of her mother, perhaps, warned her against such a course. But the gay young blade, wiser in the ways of the world than his victim, soon found a way to win her. He represented to her the fine position he could give her, told her of the beautiful clothes she would wear, the jewels with which she could adorn herself. Even then he could not move her. And at last, seeing that she could be won in no other way, he promised that if she would elope with him he would marry her as soon as arrangements could be made. Thus with the hope of marrying the son of a lord Margaret left her home. There was to be an end to the drudgery at home, the fighting with her stepmother, the humdrum existence in the deserted village of Laviano.

The story is told that the two lovers, fearing the wrath of the father who was wise enough in the ways of the world to know that rich young noblemen ordinarily mean no good to peasant girls even when they promise to marry them, attempted to flee by crossing the marshes of Chiana in a boat. The boat struck a rock and both were nearly drowned, a warning to the girl to leave this way that was leading to destruction. But she had gone too far now to turn back. The fine promises again rang in her ears. Life would be different on the morrow when she would be adorned in the clothes of a fine lady. So the next morning the youth and his captive arrived at the palace. What a change in the life of the poor girl! Yesterday a worker in the fields, a drudge; today a lady with servants at her beck and call. We can easily imagine her sentiments as she came into a fairyland grander than anything of which she had ever dreamed. Her conscience perhaps troubled her with the knowledge that it was a life of sin; but had he not promised to make her his wife? A few days more and she could go back and look the villagers in the face, go to her disgraced father, and tell him that she was an honored wife and lift him up from his poverty. Oh, the fine dreams she dreamed! But they were dreams only. Di Pecora had fulfilled some of his promises. He had given her wealth, jewels, fine clothes, but he denied her the one thing greater than all these, a good name. Time and again she urged him to marry her, but as often he refused. He would marry her soon; there was no hurry. Then her baby was born, and now she felt that she knew he would marry her at last and save the name of their child from disgrace. But again he put off the day. No doubt it was the obstacle of blood that prevented him from doing justice to the girl who had submitted to him. Whatever the reason, nine years passed in this manner and Margaret was still the mistress, though she begged to be made the wife. Nine years of luxury and of a certain kind of happiness, but years of heartache as she realized that even while she was flattered by the nobles, while she rode through the streets of the town on her palfrey in her silken gown, her flowing hair wreathed with jewels as was the custom of the day, her name was a byword with all decent people. Better had she remained in poverty and married some poor peasant of Laviano. She was paying dearly for the fine feathers. "At Monte Pulciano," she said after her conversion, "I lost honor, dignity, peace; I lost everything except faith." For Margaret was not an abandoned woman. She was in many ways the victim of circumstances. We can well believe her when she tells us that she assented to her betrayer unwillingly. The old innocence was tugging at her heart. The contrast of what she was with the purity of her childhood made her afraid. She was conscious of her guilt, and often she would steal away from the social whirl of the palace to some quiet spot, there to pray and weep over her miserable condition. "Oh, how good it would be to pray here," she would say; "how well one could sing the praises of the Creator here, how well one would do penance here." Somehow in the midst of her evil life there was a feeling that she was going to be redeemed from it. "Never mind," she would say both to her flatterers and to those who were scandalized at her course, "you shall see, yes, you shall see a time when I shall be a saint; and you shall see pilgrims with their staff come to visit my tomb." They must have thought the lady crazy to prophesy sanctity of one in her condition. It is easy to fancy the laugh on one side and the looks of horror on the other that greeted such a statement. None of them—and who could blame them?—believed that there was much sanctity either in Di Pecora or his beautiful mistress. Some of the poor villagers might have believed it; indeed, they could have believed anything good of her for she had ever shown herself compassionate to them. Who shall say what part their fervent prayers played in the conversion of the good lady who had been so kind to them?

Thus the two lovers lived in sin for nine years. Margaret was now twenty-seven years of age, in her fullest beauty. From Monte Pulciano they had come to live for a time at the Villa Palazzi, the scene of her first fall. It was to be the scene, too, of her great conversion. It came about in this way:

Young Di Pecora had his enemies. What the special reason of their animosity was it is impossible to discover now; no doubt it was due to a dispute about land or to the dissatisfaction of some of his tenants. One day he left the palace to settle a matter of dispute about the boundaries of his country property. He never came back. His enemies came upon him secretly and murdered him; then seeking to conceal the crime dragged the corpse from the road and covered it with stones and brush under some oak trees. Evening came and the nobleman did not return. Margaret was troubled. It was the first time such an unexplained absence had occurred. A thousand different thoughts flashed through her mind as she waited in vain for his coming. Had he ceased to love her? Had he transferred his affections to another? Was she now to be abandoned with her young son and sent back in shame to her home for the neighbors to point the finger of scorn at her? There is no doubt that she was deeply attached to her paramour even in spite of his refusal to give her an honest name; so it was a dreary night as she stood through the long hours at the palace window waiting for the familiar sound of his footsteps. Morning broke and still he did not come. All day long she watched and wondered. Another dreary, sleepless night and still he did not come. The wonder became alarm, and she summoned the servants and sent them forth to seek tidings of their master while she waited hoping against hope that nothing had harmed the man she loved. At last a glad cry broke from her lips as she looked for the thousandth time from her window. She saw the master's greyhound running toward the castle. All her fears fell from her. Her loved one was coming home, for thus the dog had always preceded him. Down the castle stairs she ran to meet him, perhaps to playfully reproach him for causing her so much worry. But no master came. The faithful dog whined piteously and then fell at her feet apparently lifeless. When he revived he whined still more trying to convey a message to his mistress. Then he took hold of her gown and tried to pull her with him. She knew then that something had happened and she followed the greyhound out of the palace down the road. He stopped at the oak trees and began to dig and soon exposed part of the body of his master. Feverishly Margaret went to his assistance and with her hands tore away the stones and brushwood. It was he, her beloved. The terrible sight horrified her and she fell in a dead faint. When she recovered, there alone with the poor corpse and the faithful animal, her grief surged upon her. It was an anguish unbearable. He was dead. And she had loved him. She cursed his murderers. He was dead, had gone from her without making her an honest woman, without giving his name to their child. She was doomed to poverty again. Perhaps there was for a moment a bitter resentment against him who had so betrayed her. But immediately all resentment disappeared as she looked again at the body that was once so beautiful now becoming fast a thing of corruption. Her heart burst in pity for him. Fear for his eternal salvation came into her soul. Did he have a chance to repent of his evil deeds? Was his soul perhaps now in hell? If so, she had been the cause. Her miserable beauty had fascinated him. She had led him to destruction. A few years of sinful happiness and now all was at an end. Life and pleasure were, indeed, short. And

as with him so would it be with her. There as she
sat gazing at the repulsive sight of a rotting corpse she
wept bitterly as she thought of the wretched state of
his soul at that moment. Her own soul trembled with
fear. If she died at that moment she too would be
judged not only for her own sins but for her enslave-
ment of him. She too would be sent to hell for all
eternity. In that moment the horror of her sins crushed
her to the earth. She beat her breast and wept. Oh, if
God only would give her a chance to show Him that
she was sorry! If He would only permit her to live to
do penance for herself and for him who had been so
suddenly summoned before the Judgment seat! In that
one moment from Margaret the sinner, was born
Margaret the saint. She struggled to her feet, weak
in body but strong in soul. Slowly she dragged herself
back to the palace with the awful burden of sorrow.
How could she break the news to her little son, how
tell him that the father he worshiped would never
come home again? How could she face life again?

The anguishing days passed. The young Di Pecora
was laid to rest with his fathers, and Margaret was
left to live her life. Her decision was soon made.
No one knows what it cost her to follow the directions
of her conscience, but there was no turning back once
she had decided on her course of action. She put aside
all her finery for which she had paid so dearly, and
donned a peasant's dress of black, not for her mourning
only but as a sign to the world and to her own soul
that she was already to do penance for her sins. She

gathered together the jewels and money which her lover had given her and turned them over to his parents. She could keep no mementos of that life of sin. We can fancy that the parents of young Di Pecora sought to persuade her to change her mind, to live with them still, if not for her own sake at least for the sake of the boy. But she would not. She was no longer the grand lady; she was a poor sinner. To those who would call her Milady as was the custom she would say, "Ah, call me only sinner; it is the only name my scandalous life deserves." To the servants who loved her and who tried to console her she would say, "Think of me no longer as your mistress, but pray for me that God may forgive me my sins." And then one day, in spite of the entreaties of those who loved her, she went forth from the palace forever, leading her little son by the hand. She was going home, back to the father she had disgraced, back to the stepmother who had hated her.

The story of Margaret of Cortona is a story of courage. At no time in her long years of penance was greater courage required of her than here at the outset. She knew that she would not be welcomed at home. The thought of the cold reception she would get threatened to weaken her resolution. Why bring upon herself and her beloved son such humiliation? She was still very beautiful; she could still fascinate men as she had fascinated Di Pecora; she knew so many gallants who would follow her to the ends of the earth if she gave them the least encouragement. Why leave her life of ease, of flattery, of pleasure, to come back, an outcast to those who would despise her? The temptation was alluring, but it was no more than a temptation. In her heart was the fear of sudden death; if she did go back to a life of sin she might die at once and then Hell would be hers forever. It was that fear of damnation that kept her straight and urged her feet along the rocky road to Laviano.

It was as she had expected. Tancred Bartolomeo had been disgraced by his wayward daughter. He had been obliged to hang his head in shame. With the passing years he had lived it down to a great extent, so long as she would keep away from Laviano. But now she was back again, disgraced, and with an illegitimate child. His first greeting to the sorrowing woman was an outburst of indignation. But his anger wore away at sight of her distress. Her tears softened his hard heart. The memory of her childhood, of her sainted mother, brought back to him all the affection of the old days. And he ended by folding her in his arms and mingling his tears with hers. But the stepmother had to be reckoned with, too. There were no tender memories with her. She had never liked the girl; it was very unlikely that in the present trying circumstances she would develop any affection for her. She was adamant; there was not room enough in the same house for them both. For a while, however, she relented, moved by the pleading of her husband and touched somewhat by the tears of the abandoned woman. But it was only a momentary softening. She allowed Margaret and the boy to enter the old home.

It was like a glimpse of Heaven to Margaret, dearer to her than the palace she had just left. But the blue sky of hope became clouded once more. She was treated like a slave. She was made to understand that she was a menial. That was sweet penance to the reclaimed sinner, but it could not last. The hatred of the step-mother toward her revived. She gradually poisoned the mind of her husband, and at length Margaret and the boy were driven out into the world. Today there may still be seen near the cottage in Laviano the shoots of a fig tree. Tradition has it that it is the remnant of the tree under which Margaret and her little son sat and wept the day they were driven from home. It was another place of trial, for the old temptations crowded upon her; temptations to go back to her life of sin, to walk the easy paths rather than the stony way that stretched before her. Violent were the tempta-tions, but she fought them and conquered them; and then, as if to assure her that God was with her, she seemed to hear a voice directing her to go to Cortona and put herself under the direction of the Franciscans. St. Francis of Assisi himself had preached at Cortona in 1221, establishing the Third Order, and had built a convent there. It was to the good monks who were modeling their lives after the great founder that she was now directed.

It was a long journey, twelve miles, for the weak woman and the little lad who had been accustomed to every luxury, a veritable Way of the Cross. It was necessary for her to pass the spot where she had found the dead body of her murdered lover. What emotion was hers as she knelt at what had been his temporary grave, the place of his judgment. There were prayers for his poor soul, prayers for herself and child, prayers of thanksgiving that God had spared her and had given her the wish to do penance. In memory of that event there is now a beautiful little chapel on the spot, containing a picture of Margaret and her son kneeling there. It is called the Chapel of Repentance.

The two outcasts resumed their journey toward Cortona and as they entered the city they chanced to meet the Countess Marinaria and Countess Raneria Moscari, mother-in-law and daughter-in-law, two excellent women who were to play an important part in the life of Margaret. It was not chance but the grace of God that brought about the meeting. At first they did not recognize the woman whom once they had known, very likely, as a grand lady; she was but a forlorn traveler who appealed to their kind hearts. Their kindness brought from her the whole story. Their compassion for her increased as they listened, for they were pious women, and in order to help the penitent in her good dispositions they promised to use their influence with the Franciscans to whom the voice had directed her. And, meanwhile, they pressed her to take refuge in their home, where she insisted on being not their guest but their humble servant. They at once assumed the care of educating the boy. They introduced Margaret to

Father Rinaldo, then the head of the Franciscan monastery, who placed her under the direction of a zealous, holy priest, Father Bevegnati, who subsequently wrote the life of the saint.

From that moment Margaret entered upon a life of austerity which she never relaxed. She was done with the old life, attractive as it had been. She sought to crush all memory of it; she even forbade the boy ever to mention the name of his father or speak of the days of Monte Pulciano. She did not wish to say a word to condemn the man who was dead; she, not he, had been the cause of the evil life. So at any rate she believed. Hers must be all the blame. She was the great sinner; she must become the great penitent. So she took as her model St. Mary Magdalen. No penance was severe enough. She fasted almost absolutely, sustaining herself on a bit of bread and water; she wore a hair shirt, scourged herself and sought continual mortifications. Her confessor tried to make her be more lenient with herself. "Father," said she, "peace between my soul and this miserable body is no longer possible. Let me treat it as one treats an irreconcilable adversary, and do not listen to its recriminations. It did not complain when it was living in luxury. O my body, wilt thou not help me to serve thy Creator? Why art thou not so eager to render Him homage as thou wert to violate His law? No dissimulation, no murmuring; thou hast conquered me, I shall conquer thee." The good priest had no argument against such sincerity.

In spite of the severe mortifications the face of the

woman retained its wonderful beauty, a material love-
liness to which the spiritual was now added. She
became the enemy of that material beauty. Her face
had ruined her; she would ruin it. She scratched it,
beat it, bruised it with stones, deformed it with coals,
stained her features, cut off her hair, and she would
even have deformed her nose and lips had she not been
restrained from that by the good countesses and again
by her confessor. In her zeal for penance she could
not understand such restraint. They should understand
that she was a sinner. She wanted all to call her the
poor sinner, the great sinner. She wanted to show God
by these external signs as well as in her soul that she
was sorry for the past. She begged Father Bevegnati
to allow her at once to put on the habit of the Third
Order to show that she was a penitent, but he wisely
deferred the investiture in order that he might have
time to prove the lasting sincerity of the ardent penitent. It was a precaution hardly necessary, for he
knew that here was an extraordinary case. She made
her general confession to him with heartbreaking sobs,
as fervently as if it were in the presence of the Eternal
Judge. The words of the *Miserere* were now her continual chant, and the crucifix in which she saw the
veritable work of her sins became the perpetual subject of her meditations. Day after day she came back
to the church to confess again and again, to excite herself to newer and greater sorrow for her sins.

But this quiet method of penance was not enough for
Margaret. She wanted to do public penance. She had

scandalized the people of Monte Pulciano by her wicked deeds; she desired to make an act of reparation. Thus she begged Father Bevegnati to allow her to go back there in rags, with shaven head and veiled face and a rope about her neck with some one to lead her and cry out, "Here comes Margaret the sinner. Behold her, that infamous sinner, who by her vanity, pride and scandals has ruined so many souls in this city."

Again the confessor thought such a course indiscreet and Margaret was not allowed this opportunity of humiliating herself and being considered a mad woman in the eyes of those over whom she had once queened it. But her zeal for penance could not be curbed. She felt that she was too well off in the fine home of the Countesses and she begged them to let her go to live in some poor hovel which was more suited to one of her character. Feeling the blessing of her presence, they would not part with her, but to satisfy her they fixed up a little place near their home and insisted upon providing her and the boy with the necessary food. Even that was too luxurious for Margaret. She gave her bed to the little fellow and slept on the floor or on a straw mat with a stone for her pillow. A far cry surely from the magnificence of the palace! She ate little of the food provided for her. She gave it to the poor, and then to humble herself all the more went from door to door to beg her bread, stopping the people on the street to tell them what a miserable sinner she was and begging them to pray for her. She even humbled herself in the house of God, taking her place beneath the pulpit where she could not be seen. The story of this marvelous penitent soon spread throughout the town. All admired such heroism. All wanted to have a share in her prayers. For this they sought every means of being kind to her, giving her clothes which she immediately gave to the sick and the poor.

Margaret was not an idler. Fearing that her begging might be taking the bit out of the mouths of some needier than herself she decided to work. She wove flax and wool as she had done in her girlhood days in Laviano. With that she also served as a midwife, accepting no pay for her services but the most miserable food. Her services were in great demand—no one but Margaret must hold the new baby at the baptismal font. She could not understand such kindness to her. Did not these people know what a low woman she was? Every moment she could steal from her duties she spent in a corner weeping and praying.

The story got about the city that certain people in whose house Margaret had been working had seen her lifted bodily in an ecstasy, and now more than ever she became an object not of scorn but of reverence. But such a misunderstanding of her must not be permitted to continue! They must understand that she was a public sinner. So one Sunday she determined, with the approval of her confessor, to do public penance in the village of Laviano. It was a thrilling scene, and no doubt the villagers talked about it for many a day. All the people were at Mass in the little church and among them no doubt was Bartomoleo and his shrewish wife. Suddenly a woman entered. She was barefoot, her hair was cut close, and a rope was about her neck. She advanced and prostrated herself before the altar. During the Mass she remained there, no one recognizing her. When the Mass was ended she arose and turning to her old neighbors told them who she was, that she was the vile Margaret Bartolomeo who had once brought lasting shame upon her native place. There was not a dry eye in the church when she finished this public act of contrition. One woman in particular, a noble lady by the name of Manentessa who had often advised the girl against her evil ways, was particularly touched as Margaret threw herself at her feet and begged her pardon for having laughed at her warnings. She folded the penitent to her bosom and took her to her own home. So impressed was she by the account Margaret gave of the Third Order that she promised that she, too, would soon enroll herself in it. History says nothing about the sentiments of Margaret's father or stepmother on that occasion. No doubt the stepmother especially took this public shaming of the family name as an added reason for her antipathy to the girl, of the fall of whom into evil ways her harshness had been no little cause.

Margaret had now been living this penitential life three years—surely a long enough trial one would think. When she returned to Cortona, attracted by the presence there of the Franciscan order, she begged again to be allowed to don the habit of the Third Order. But still her confessor put her off. She must be tried still more. She was young and beautiful, she had given terrible scandal; she was not yet worthy. "Ah," said she, "why do you tell me that? Have I not faithfully done whatever you prescribed these last three years? And as for the dangers which you dread from my still unfaded beauty, here I am ready to execute what I long since would have done but for your prohibition. Let me cut off this nose, mangle these lips, and I will be more disfigured than you wish, and secure of all you ask." Finally her perseverance won. In the year 1276, when she was in her thirtieth year, she ran to the convent as if impelled by some superior power and cried out: "Hesitate no longer to clothe me with the habit of the Third Order, you whom the Lord has charged with the direction of my soul. I have so loved my God, so great is my confidence in His mercy since He has forgiven me and He Himself has so bound me to His love, that I no longer dread any creature or any temptation. I have fled from the world, I have lived in the company of pious persons, I have changed my life. Is it not enough? Why still defer it? What are you afraid of?"

Margaret had been tried enough; her confessor could hold out no longer. She was at once invested with the desired habit, the gray tunic, the cord and veil, while her tears of sorrow and gratitude flowed abundantly. As a proof of her gratitude to God she made on that occasion three resolutions: to live solely on alms in the future, to increase her mortifications, and to live in a more solitary and more humble place. The boy was still with her, and in order that she might devote herself more wholly to God the Countesses arranged to send him to Arezzo for his education. It was not that Margaret was a heartless mother that she was willing to be separated from her beloved child. She had learned the real philosophy of life, that it is eternity that counts. She knew that this arrangement was better for herself, better for the boy, who finally became a religious and died a very holy death. But that is to anticipate. During the few days he remained with her before leaving for school she forbade him to speak of anything but God. She was already forming him to sanctity.

Free to devote herself entirely to the work of sanctifying her soul, Margaret became as a Tertiary even more zealous than before. She fasted longer, she scourged herself more vehemently, she put on sharper haircloth, she slept less; in a word she employed every moment of the day and night in penitential austerity. She rarely spoke; her life was hidden with Christ. The report of her austerities, her sanctity, spread everywhere. To her door came the sick and the poor, the afflicted in soul or body, and even the devout, to ask her advice. The place was so frequented that she feared the many interviews might wean her somewhat from her penances, so through the aid of her benefactresses a poor abandoned hut was obtained for her near the church of the Franciscans. Thus she was able to spend a great deal of her time in church. At an early hour she was there and during the recitation of the

Divine office by the monks she would remain kneeling before the crucifix sorrowing for her sins. That old crucifix is still treasured today in the new church in honor of St. Margaret. Treasure it is, for one day as she knelt before it a voice from the Cross spoke to her: "What wishest thou, my poor sinner?" asked the Lord; and Margaret answered, "Lord Jesus, I seek only You, I wish only for You."

Prostrated in confusion, she wondered that the great God should speak to her. There was always with her that wonder, the wonder that God had forgiven such a sinner and taken her back to Himself. "Lord," she said one day, "how does it happen that You have cast Your eyes on me who am only dust and ashes, mire and darkness? Why, Lord, grant so many favors to such a contemptible creature?" "Because," said the Lord, "I have destined thee to be the net of sinners. I wish that thou shouldst be a light to those who are seated in the darkness of vice; I wish that the example of thy conversion should preach hopefulness to those who are despairing, and that it should be to repentant sinners what the morning dew is to plants parched by the sun's heat; I wish that ages to come may be convinced that I am always ready to open the arms of My mercy to the prodigal son who returns to Me in the sincerity of his heart."

But the fight was by no means ended. It was to be lifelong. Memories of the nine years of sin came back again and again to tempt her. Visions of the old pleasures, the old sins when she was a great lady loved by the handsome young nobleman, rose up to haunt her. In her ears sounded the old love songs that had serenaded her. Violent temptations they were, but she drove them away by more earnest prayer and by scourging herself more relentlessly. But with this perpetual remembrance of her sins there came also the temptation to despair. Who was she that could hope to be able to atone for all that she had done? But Margaret had too much confidence in God to fall into despair. God had been good to her. Then the pendulum of temptation swung to the other extreme. The tempter sought to fill her with spiritual pride. But once more she conquered his wiles. To humble herself she stood on the roof of her poor hut and cried out so that all the city might hear: "All ye people of Cortona, arise, arise, and with stones in your hands drive this wicked, scandalous woman out of your city."

The many and varied temptations made her redouble her austerities. There was no doubt about her penance. Yet in spite of that the day came when even she whose later life had been one of open sacrifice came under a cloud of suspicion. Some one hinted that she was not all that she pretended, that her supposed great penance was a sham. Gradually the suspicion spread through the city. Public resentment grew against her. Her old life was recalled. How could such a sinner repent, was asked. She must be a hypocrite, she must be demented, or worse than that she must be possessed of the devil. So from being reverenced as the special object of God's mercy, she was now despised as one who had brought shame on the city by her very presence. So great, indeed, was the public condemnation that even the Franciscans began to wonder if they had been deceived in being so kind to the penitent. They even gave her to understand that they would be better pleased if she did not come to their church so often, and for fear that she was the subject of diabolical delusion they ordered Father Bevegnati to discontinue his conferences with her and to visit her hut only when she was dangerously ill. It was the time of her dereliction when even the priests of her beloved order seemed to fail her. But she made no complaint; who was she, indeed, to make complaint? Her only complaint could be that she had once offended God; her only fear that she might offend Him again; her only prayer that God would send her immeasurable suffering to keep her from sin. And God did send her suffering. Every part of her body was in constant pain. There was hardly an ill to which the flesh is heir that she did not endure—convulsions, fevers, splitting headaches; yet she begged for more.

It would be a mistake to think of Margaret merely as one immersed in her own penances. The great work of every man is his own salvation. There is nothing selfish about that. "What doth it profit a man if he gain the whole world and suffer the loss of his own soul?" But her case is like that of all the great penitents. The more they afflicted themselves, the more they did penance for their sins, the more helpful they became to others. St. John Camillus was never done doing penance for his wicked youth, but with those penitential practices there went a tender charity for the sick and poor. And so, too, with Margaret. The conviction of the awfulness of sin made her long to reclaim other sinners. She prayed continually for them. They were her friends. They came to her from everywhere, even from France and Spain, to ask her advice and to get courage from her example to break the chains that enslaved them. Such spiritual popularity only increased the animosity of the public, the holy public that sneered at the presumption of a poor woman, a woman that had been a sinner, daring to advise others. History repeats itself. But the many souls converted through her good advice and example and prayers could estimate her at her true value in spite of the knowing public.

And Margaret's was not only a spiritual help to her neighbors. Even in her days of sin she had been kind to the poor—perhaps that had won the grace of conversion for her. And now in these days when she knew the value of charity that kindness increased. She gave everything she could lay her hands on to the poor —the clothes off her back, the very bit of bread she was about to put in her mouth. She tended the sick, delighting to care for the most loathsome diseases. This apostolate of hers among the sick was the beginning of the establishment of the hospital of Our Lady of Mercy in Cortona.

Margaret's soul was ever wrapt in prayer. The name of Jesus was always on her lips, her refuge always in the crucifix. Yet she was considered a hypocrite! And thus it went on for twenty-three long years, a life of suffering, of penance, of prayer, sometimes of ecstasy and visions, a life of service of the sick and poor, a life of help to poor sinners. And one day the news spread through the city that Margaret was about to die. Our Lord had appeared to her and told her that He was going to take her Home. At once whatever resentment there had been against the woman disappeared. Crowds came from all parts to visit her in her poor little hut, all grieving that she was going to depart from them, all penitent that they had ever misjudged such an object of God's special love. They saw her in all her beauty, for in spite of the terrible penances and ills she had borne her wonderful beauty returned at the end and she seemed more like a young girl than a middle-aged woman who had spent a quarter of a century afflicting herself and seeking to make herself repulsive. There was nothing now to take away the peace of soul of the penitent. She had fought the good fight, and she had won. So at daybreak on the twenty-second of February, 1298, in the fiftieth year of her age, she passed to God. Margaret was buried in the oratory which through her efforts had been erected in honor of St. Basil. To her tomb there everybody came, the sick in body and the sick in soul, and many miracles were wrought through her intercession. Her body was never corrupted by the grave. It is still preserved for veneration in the new church built in Cortona in her honor, and thither year after year on her feast come thousands from every part of the country to pay their tribute of love to the great penitent. The prophecy which she unwittingly made in the days of her sin in the palace of the Di Pecoras that crowds would come to her tomb as to a shrine has been fulfilled. There in her gray habit she lies waiting through all the years the glorious day of resurrection.

Chapter 7

BLESSED ANGELA OF FOLIGNO

In the little Latin edition of the *Visions and Instructions of Blessed Angela of Foligno,* published at Cologne in 1851, and edited by Father Lainmertz, parish priest of Kessenich, there is a frontispiece representing the penitent woman. It is the picture of an old woman, bowed down, not so much by the weight of years as by sorrow—sorrow for her sins. In her arms she bears all the instruments of the Passion, the Cross, the lance, the reed and sponge, the nails; in one emaciated hand is a scourging whip, in the other a bundle of scourging rods. A very different picture is the fresco in the church of Santa Anna, Foligno, from the brush of Pierantonio Mezzastris, which portrays the penitent as she was at the time of her conversion, a young woman of remarkable beauty. Look on this picture and on that. Between them lies the long, hard way of the Cross by which the Umbrian Magdalen came to her eternal peace.

Angela of Foligno is deserving of study not only on account of her theological genius, which made Maximilian Sandaeus, the Jesuit, call her "the mistress of theologians," but also for her example of austere penance, the chief manifestation of which was in her whole-souled love of poverty, after the example of him who was almost her contemporary, St. Francis of Assisi. The poverty-loving Francis, the poverty-loving Angela need to be heard today when so many in the world are goaded even to anarchy by too much worry over the material morrow. Was there ever a time when such examples were not needed? Back in 1851 when the little Latin edition appeared the editor thought Angela's message a timely one. "We think it very fitting," he wrote, "that in these times especially when all are crying that poverty and the other ills of human life are the greatest of evils, and think that every effort should be made to remove them from the world, a certain voice from far distant times should be heard which vindicates to poverty the pristine honor given to poverty by Christ the Lord, and shows to the human race the delights which are hidden in that same poverty."

At any rate the need of such examples has not lessened in our time.

It was Angela's good fortune that when she came to do penance she had the wonderful example of Francis within calling distance, for she was born within thirty years of his death. It was not so long before her time the young gallant had been heard "serenading the Umbrian moon." The music of that serenade had gone on the wind, indeed, when the rich young man had given up all to sing the praises of his Lady Poverty, and now in this other Umbrian soul the spirit of Francis was working strains of music. The influence of St.

Francis of Assisi upon his contemporaries cannot be exaggerated. Thousands had left the world to follow him the full way; others, innumerable, whom duty bade remain in the world, sought their sanctity through the milder penitence of the Third Order. We would hardly have had Angela without Francis, so faithfully does she model her life according to that new spirit which he brought to the world of his day. It is for that reason she is called "a simple Franciscan soul." Therein lies her claim to greatness. She was no great campaigner on the battlefield of the world; the be-all and the end-all of her heroism was—and in fine it is so in the lives of all the saints—within the confines of her own heart. Angela conquered herself as Francis conquered himself. There is the epitome of sanctity.

Beneath the Umbrian moon, then, Angela was born at Foligno, three miles from Assisi, in the year 1248. It was at Foligno that St. Francis sold the horse and the load of cloth he had taken from his father's house to do charity to the poor. From a material point of view her lot was a happy one. She belonged to a rich family which evidently had turned a deaf ear to the invitation of the saint of Assisi to sell all and give to the poor. To such a family Francis must have seemed peculiar, to say the least.

It was a worldly family, if one may judge by the life led by Angela. There was plainly a desire to marry her off. She must have a rich marriage, and nothing beyond that was worth considering. Anyway when Angela was still very young she married a man of her own social rank and wealth—a loveless marriage, we are tempted to believe, seeing that she was not very long faithful to her vows. It would be easy to write romance into the life of the young wife, but there are not many facts to go on. By some of her biographers she is called the "Countess of Civitella." The few facts we have justify us, however, in describing the young Umbrian beauty as a frivolous girl whose one thought in life was to have a good time regardless of the consequences. She was the social butterfly, full of vanity, very charming and conscious of her charm, yet withal of very little brains. The type can be picked out today very readily. The beautiful Angela was an easy prey to flatterers. The vanity soon ended in sin. In spite of the fact that she was a wife and mother she allowed herself to be led into the crime of adultery, not once but innumerable times. Lower and lower she fell until she became positively shameless. One lover succeeded another; one after another all were thrown aside as soon as they had succumbed to her wiles.

How long Angela continued in this wicked course of life we do not know. Nor do we know just what circumstances led to the break with the old life. It is immaterial. The one thing sure is that a great grace came into the soul of the sinful woman. Angela was sated with sin, disgusted with herself, and desired to come back to God. How she walked that journey we do not have to imagine. Angela herself tells us simply in that *Book of Revelations* which Father Arnold of the Friars Minor wrote at her dictation. It is one of the most human documents ever written, ringing as true as that similar soul-study—the *Confessions* of St. Augustine.

"I," says Angela, "in going towards the way of penance traveled eighteen steps before I knew the imperfection of my life." Her true conversion to God may thus be seen in her description of these "steps," the narrative of which may be thus abridged.

In the first step she began to consider her sins and obtained a knowledge of them. It was a frightful vision to her. She was filled with the fear of being damned to hell and she wept bitterly. But in spite of that fear she was not, as she tells us in the description of the second step, fully converted. She blushed so for her sins that she could not fully confess them, and hence often communicated unconfessed, receiving the Body of the Lord with sins on her soul. There was no peace in her soul; day and night her conscience troubled her, and at last she prayed to St. Francis to find her a suitable confessor who would know her sins and to whom she could confess properly. That night, as she tells the story, an old man appeared to her—none other than St. Francis himself—and said to her, "Sister, if you had asked me sooner, I would have done sooner what you have asked."

The next morning on her way to the Church of the Franciscans Angela found preaching in the Church of St. Felician "a friar who was a true Chaplain of Christ." As soon as the sermon was over she made a general confession to him and received absolution. But still she felt no love, but only bitterness, shame and sorrow. In the third step she began to do satisfaction for her sins. She felt sorrow, but no consolation. In the next step she thought of the Divine mercy which had drawn her out of hell. Her soul began to be enlightened; she grieved more bitterly for her sins and applied herself to greater penance. It must be understood that she remained for some time in these various states of soul. It was but a gradual ascent to perfection.

In the fifth step Angela condemned herself unsparingly, knowing how worthy of Hell she was, and all the while her sorrow for sin increased. In the sixth she came to have a more profound knowledge of her sins, and realized that in offending the Creator she had offended all creatures made for her, and she asked the Blessed Virgin and all the saints to intercede for her that God might have mercy on her soul. "Seventhly," she says, "was given to me the special grace of gazing on the Cross, on which with the eyes of the heart and of the body I beheld Jesus Christ dead for us; but this vision and contemplation were, as yet, insipid to me, though I conceived a great grief by means of them."

In the eighth step Angela came to a greater knowledge of how Christ died for her sins, and she offered herself wholly to Him, promising Him to keep perpetual chastity and not to offend Him with any of her members. The ninth step is best described in her own words: "Afterwards was given me, in the ninth place," she says, "a desire to seek the Way of the Cross, that

I might stand at its foot and find the refuge to which all sinners fly. And I was illuminated and instructed, and the Way of the Cross was made known to me in the following manner. For it was revealed to me that, if I wished to go to the Cross, I should strip myself so as to travel thither more lightly and more freely; in other words, that I should forgive all who had offended me, and that I should strip myself of all earthly things, of all men and women, friends and relations, and of my possessions and of my very self, and give my heart to Christ Who had conferred on me such great benefits as I have mentioned, and thus walk over a road of thorns, a road, that is, of tribulation. And so I began to give up good clothes and dresses and delicate food, and also headdresses. But as yet this was a cause of shame and suffering to me, because I did not feel much the love of God, and I was living with my husband, so that it was bitter to me when I heard or sustained any injury; I suffered, however, as patiently as I could. Now it happened at that time by the will of God that my mother died, who was a great impediment to me in the way of the Lord, and my husband also died, and all my sons in a short space of time. And because I had commenced the aforesaid Road of the Cross and had begged God to deliver me from them, I received a great consolation from their death, although I suffered somewhat with them in their death, yet I thought that henceforward, as God had granted me this grace, my heart would be forever in His Heart and Will, and the Will and Heart of God in my heart."

In the tenth step Angela desired to know what to do to please God. Waking and sleeping she seemed to see Christ on the Cross, who bade her look at His wounds. He showed her what He had borne for her, showed her all her sins and that by those sins she had wounded Him. She knew now a greater sorrow for her sins, and wept so bitterly that the tears burned her flesh, so much so that she had to apply cold water to alleviate the pain. In the eleventh step she began to do greater penance. She desired to abandon all the world, to become poor. But with that desire there came the counter temptations. Her weak nature suggested to her that she was yet so young and that there would be danger as well as shame for her if she had to beg her bread. Then, too, she might die of hunger, of cold, of nakedness, and moreover all her friends would dissuade her from such a course. But Angela, still young, still rich, still beautiful, won the victory over herself, and caring little if all these calamities came to her as a result of her sacrifices she made up her mind to embrace Holy Poverty. In the twelfth step she asked a sign by which she would always have the memory of the Passion of Christ; and in the thirteenth she tells of a dream she had in which she saw the Heart of Christ Who said to her, "In this Heart there is no falsehood, but all there is true." This happened, she naïvely tells us, because she had made fun of a certain preacher. The frivolous Angela was not yet fully conquered.

In the fourteenth step she came to a greater knowledge of herself. One day Christ appeared to her and bade her put her lips to the wound in His side. She did so, and it was given her to understand that in that blood He would wash her. "And at this point," she says, "I began to receive great consolation, although the consideration of the Passion caused me sadness, and I asked the Lord that He would make me to shed and pour out all my blood for His love's sake as He had done for me, and I desired for the sake of His love, that all my limbs should be afflicted and should suffer a vile and more bitter death than His Passion, and I took thought and desired to find someone to kill me, so long as I should suffer for His faith or for His love, and I thought that I would beg Him to grant me this grace, namely, that as Christ was crucified on a tree He should crucify me on a river bank or in some very vile way. And, because I was not worthy to die as the holy martyrs had died, I desired to die a viler and more bitter death, and I could not think of a death vile enough for my desire, which should be altogether unlike the death of the saints, for of their death I deemed myself altogether unworthy."

In the fifteenth step Angela besought the Blessed Virgin and St. John to obtain for her that she might feel such sorrow at least as they had felt at Christ's Passion. All the while Angela had to fight against severe temptations. "But this time," she says, "was given me a desire of expropriating myself with my whole will, and although I was much assaulted by the devil, and frequently tempted not to do so, and was prevented having communication with the friars minor and with all from whom it was fitting for me to take counsel, on no account, whatever good or evil things might have happened to me, could I have abstained from devoting all my goods to the poor, and, even if I should not have been able to do this, from at least stripping myself completely of them all." Still, her soul remained bitter on account of her sins, and she did not know whether what she was doing was pleasing to God, but with bitter groaning she cried to Him, saying, "Lord, even if I am damned, I will nevertheless do penance and will strip myself of everything and serve Thee."

After this bitterness, however, a change came over Angela's soul in the sixteenth step. One day while in church she recited the *Our Father,* and the prayer was expounded in her heart word by word. God placed Himself so in her heart that she could not express her feelings of the Divine goodness and her own unworthiness. "O sinners," she says, "in what heaviness my soul advances to penance." In the seventeenth step she tells how the Blessed Virgin acquired for her a more living faith by which her former faith seemed dead in comparison, and her former tears small in comparison with her new tears. In many ways her soul received consolation, yet there was also a mixture of bitterness because she did not have certitude as to her state of soul. In the eighteenth, and last, step, she began to have such delight in prayer that she wanted to pray always, and not even spare time to eat or sleep. Nothing wearied her, so ardent was her devotion. But she was not entirely wrapt up in herself. With this struggle of soul went a great love for the poor. She sold her farm, the best piece of land she possessed, and gave the proceeds to the poor. Some of her neighbors thought she was possessed, but, heedless of what they thought she continued the devotions that so enraptured her. So great was her devotion that whenever she looked at a picture of the Passion she burned with a fever, and finally her friends used to hide such pictures so that she would not see them. It is not surprising to learn that at this time she was given many consolations and visions.

In reading of the visions of Angela one is struck by the common sense of the woman. There was little chance of her being deceived. Her sense of sin kept her humble. And always through the spirited life of this convert the one thing that stands forth is that realization of what an evil sin is. She tells us that lest the greatness and number of her visions and revelations might make her proud, she was afflicted with many temptations in body and soul. She can scarcely describe the afflictions and passions endured. Every one of her members suffered horribly. She was never free from pain and fatigue. She was continually weak, so full of suffering that she had to lie down continually. She could hardly move, hardly eat. She even felt herself afflicted by demons. She could have torn herself apart with the suffering. Her old sins came back to haunt her, and with them new temptations.

Even vices she had never committed assailed her. In a word her sufferings of soul were horrible.

"Likewise," she says, "there fought in my soul a certain humility and a certain pride of the greatest loathsomeness. Humility—because I see that I have fallen from all good, and see myself beyond all virtue and beyond all grace, and see in myself such a multitude of sins and defects that I am not able to think that God wishes to have mercy on me. And I see myself the house of the devil, and a worker for and truster in devils, and see myself their daughter, and see myself beyond all rectitude and beyond all truth, and worthy of the lowest and last depths of Hell." At such times she wanted to go through the street crying out that she was a hypocrite. "Hear ye, that I am a hypocrite and a child of pride, a deceiver and an abomination to God." One recalls the like desire of that other great penitent, St. Margaret of Cortona.

Angela would have been willing to suffer martyrdom in exchange for these torments of soul. They lasted two years, however. They purified her soul and they were succeeded by great consolations. She received from God no less than ten visions, or consolations, and meanwhile she prayed unceasingly thinking only of God.

It was at this time that Angela promised to follow the rule of St. Francis, and begged the saint to obtain for her that she would be faithful to that rule. Under the direction of Father Arnold she took the habit of

the Third Order. We have not many details of her
external life. At first she lived with a religious companion near the church of the friars minor. She had
not only given her goods to the poor, but she gave
them her personal service. She would gather the sick
in her humble home, care for them, heal their sores,
and go through the streets begging for the means to
sustain them. It was not easy work, and Angela sometimes had to resort to heroic measures to overcome her
squeamishness in dressing the sores of lepers.

The fame of Angela's holiness soon gathered about
her many other Tertiaries, both men and women. Later
on she established at Foligno a community of sisters
who to the rule of the Third Order added the three
vows of religion. The community was not enclosed,
in order that the members might be able to devote
themselves to charitable works. Angela's whole life
after her conversion might be summed up in the statement that she dressed ulcers and meditated on the
Passion of Christ. And this for many years.

It is edifying to read what Father Arnold says of her
in his preface to the revelation he wrote at her dictation. He confesses that his written word is unable
to convey the wonder of her revelations, for when he
would read what he had written, even Angela was dissatisfied with the words as not expressing all that she
had felt. "After her conversion," he writes, "she did
penance as great as her body could bear, as I myself
know." "She was," he continued, "most fervent in
prayer, and most discreet in confession. Whence one

time when this faithful servant of Christ confessed to me as she was accustomed, with such a perfect knowledge of her sins, and with so great contrition with tears from the beginning of her confession to the end, and with such humility that I wept in my heart, believing most surely that if the whole world was deceived, God would not permit that this woman of such rectitude and truth could be deceived. And when on the following night she was sick apparently unto death she came with great pain the following morning to the Church of the Friars, and then I said Mass and communicated her; and I know that she never communicated without God giving her some great grace and as it were a new grace continually. So great was the efficacy of the visions and illuminations and consolations which she received in her soul that very often they were evident in her body. Thus sometimes while standing with me, her soul was lifted up, and she was unable to understand anything of what I was reading to her. She was changed in face and in body from the joy of the Divine allocutions, and from the devotion and delight of consolations, so much that sometimes her eyes were as brilliant as candles, and her face as a rose. And sometimes she was made full and bright and angelical and admirable in her whole countenance beyond human condition; and she forgot to eat and drink as if her spirit did not exist in her corporal body. Her companion, a most devoted virgin, related that one day when they were walking along the street her whole countenance became so bright, and joyful and ruddy,

her eyes so big and resplendent, she did not seem to
be the same person."

Yet these great consolations from God never let
Angela forget that she had been a grievous sinner.
She never minced words in enumerating her many
iniquities. What was there in the world for her then
but penitence and pain? She had sinned; she must
atone. Hers was not a half-hearted penance. She
must give herself entirely to the Master she had once
offended. So through the long years—Angela was
sixty-one when she died—she went her simple way,
tending the sick, doing penance, teaching her sisters
in religion the wonders of the life that is hidden with
Christ in God. Hers was a story of love.

One day, toward the end of her life, she said to her
companion, "Let us go to the hospital, and perhaps
we will find Christ there among the poor, the suffering
and afflicted." The two women brought all that they
had to give away, some head coverings, and gave them
to the hospital servant telling her to sell them and
buy something for the poor in the hospital to eat. Then
they washed the feet of the patients and even tended
a leper. But it is in her so-called last will that the
soul of Angela shines forth. When she was about to
die she gave a last admonition to her religious children
of the community she had established at Foligno. "My
little ones," she said, "what I say to you I say only
for the love of God, and because I promised you I
would carry to the grave nothing that would be of
service to you. In all that I am going to say, however,

there is nothing of mine, but all is of God. For it pleased the Divine goodness to give me a care and solicitude for all His sons and daughters who are in this world, on this and the other side of the sea. I guarded them as well as I could, I grieved over them, and suffered much for them as you may well believe. O my God, now I give them back to Thee, and I ask Thee through Thy ineffable charity to guard them from every evil, and keep them in all good, in a love for poverty, humiliation and suffering, and in the transforming of their life, and in the imitation of Thy life and perfection, which by word and deed and example it pleased Thee to show us.

"O my most beloved children, I exhort you in this last exhortation that you strive to be little and truly humble and meek, not only externally in deed, but deep in your heart, that you may be true scholars and true disciples of Him who said—'Learn of Me, for I am meek and humble of heart.' Care not for power, honors and preferments. O my little children, strive to be little, that Christ may exalt you in the perfection of merits and His grace. Be so humble that continually you may think yourselves as nothing. Accursed are those self-sufficiencies which kill the soul, as powers, honor and preferment. Flee them, since there is great danger and deception in them; though there may be smaller deception in them than in spiritual pride, namely, in knowing how to speak of God, to understand the Scriptures, to make fine discourses, to have the heart occupied with spiritual things. For very

often these fall into error, and are with greater diffi-
culty corrected than they who have pride in temporal
things. Therefore regard yourselves as nothing. Oh,
how unknown is this spirit of nothingness! Truly the
soul can have no better wisdom or learning than to see
its own nothingness and stand in its own prison.

"O my little children, strive to have charity, without which there is no salvation, no merit. Behold, God
says: 'All Mine is thine.' Oh, who are you to merit
this, that all God's goods should be yours? Indeed,
there is nothing that can merit this but charity. O my
little children, and fathers and brothers, study to love
one another, and have this mutual charity and love,
for by this the soul merits to inherit the Divine goods,
and I exhort you, that you not only wish to have this
charity even for one another, but for everybody. For
I tell you that my soul has received more from God
when I wept and grieved over the sins of others than
over my own. And the world jests about this, what
I say, that a man could weep for the sins of his neighbor as for his own, or even more than for his own,
because it seems to be contrary to nature. But charity
which does this is not of this world. O my little children, strive to have this charity, and judge nobody.
And if you see a man sin mortally, I do not tell you
that you should not be displeased at his sin, and that
you should not grieve and abhor that sin, but I tell
you that you should not judge the sinners, nor despise
them because you know not the judgments of God; for
in the eyes of men many seem to be damned who are

in the eyes of God saved; and many in the eyes of men seem to be saved who before God are accursed and damned. And would that I knew how to tell you that there are some whom you have despised, of whom I have firm hope that God will lead them back to His own right hand. I leave you no other testament than this, that I recommend to you mutual love and profound humility. And I leave you my entire inheritance, which is that of Christ Jesus, namely, poverty, sorrow, and humility, namely, the life of Christ. Those who will have this inheritance—the life of Christ—will be my children; for they are the children of God, and there is no doubt but that afterwards they will have the inheritance of eternal life."

Having spoken thus, says her biographer, she placed her hand on the heads of everyone and said: "Blessed be you by the Lord and by me, my little children, you and all the others who are not here, and as it was signified and demonstrated to me by the Lord, so I give this eternal blessing to you present and absent, and may Christ give that blessing to you with that hand of His which was nailed to the Cross."

So through many days Angela lay in her agony. Her only food was the Sacred Species. Already she had begun to taste the joys of Heaven and heard her Lord call her—"My very beloved child." "Do you wish to die and leave us?" one day her religious asked. "I have hidden so much from you," she replied, "but now I hide nothing, and I tell you now I must go."

"On the same day," writes her biographer, "all her

sufferings ceasing, with which for many days before every member within and without was horribly and in every way afflicted, she lay in such great quiet of body and happiness of soul that she seemed to taste already of the joy promised to her. Then we asked her if this joy was already given her, and she replied that she had begun to feel it. And in this calm of body and joy of soul lying most happy till after the Complin of Saturday, many of her brethren standing about her and reciting the office of that day, the octave of the Holy Innocents, at the last hour of the day, as if she was greatly sleeping, she passed to eternal rest. And her most holy soul, freed from the flesh, and absorbed in the abyss of Divine Infinity, received from Christ her Spouse the state of innocence and immortality to reign with Christ, whither may He also lead us by virtue of His Cross and through the merits of His Virgin Mother and through the intercession of this most holy mother of ours, Angela."

The remains of the holy penitent were laid in the Church of St. Francis at Foligno. How long ago it seems, and yet—another proof of the perpetual youth of her children to Mother Church—relics of this dear saint are still preserved at Rome, Naples, Cremona, Antwerp and other places. The saints never die, even from earth. After reading the story of her soul, the greatness of her sorrow for sin, the severity of her penances, we are not surprised to be told that numerous miracles were wrought at her tomb, and that from the very beginning Angela was the object of veneration.

The little Italian book of her Visions and Instructions, translated in 1510 from the Latin, was one of the earliest popular books of devotion printed in the vernacular in Italy. The popularity of her *Visions* is easy to understand. They are as one scholar has called them, "an extraordinary blend of naïve candor and passion."

"Mistress of theologians," Angela may be called; yet we prefer to think of her as the commonplace, frivolous, vain, sinful woman, of weak nature, who through sorrow for sin became a "simple Franciscan soul," and attained holiness. Angela is one of the greatest of the great penitents, who fill with hope the rest of us poor sinners.

Chapter 8

BLESSED CLARE OF RIMINI

SAY Rimini, and immediately you think not of the saint of Rimini but the sinner of Rimini. Francesca da Rimini by her terrible sin and her tragic ending has made forever unforgettable the place of her damnation.* Paolo and Francesca—the undying example that the wages of sin is death. "Francesca," sings Dante, "your sad fate even to tears my grief and pity moves." Dante was a young man twenty-five years of age when the beautiful Francesca went to her doom in 1285. The story hardly needs retelling—how the son of the great Malatesta, Giovanni the Lame, notorious for his ugliness, had as general served so well Giovanni da Polenta of Ravenna that he was rewarded with the hand of Polenta's daughter, the beautiful Francesca. As soon as Francesca, however, beheld Giovanni's brother, Paolo the Handsome, she fell in love with him and he with her. That love was their destruction. Says Francesca in Dante's immortal poem:

> One day
> For our delight we read of Lancelot,
> How his love thralled. Alone we were, and no
> Suspicion near us, ofttimes by that reading
> Our eyes were drawn together, and the hue

---

* Of course, no one can state as a certitude that any individual has been damned—that is, that he went to Hell. The author is only setting forth what would seem to be indicated by the external evidence. —*Publisher*, 2006.

145

Fled from our altered cheek. But at one point
Alone we fell. When of that smile we read,
The wishèd smile, rapturously kissed
By one so deep in love, then he, who ne'er
From me shall separate, at once my lips
All trembling kissed. The book and writer both
Were love's purveyors. In its leaves that day
We read no more.

The wronged husband, discovering them, murdered them both on the spot, and Dante represents them as forever doomed to go through Hell joined each to the other, forever powerless to escape from their sin.

Those were days of endless conspiracy and crime in Rimini, where the Malatesta tribe tyrannized over all. Dante, who had been converted from a sinful life, does not mince matters about the corruptions of his times. It is well to bear all this in mind as background for the life of the sinful woman who, happier than Francesca, did not die in her sin but by the grace of God came to be a great penitent and a great saint. Clare of Rimini and Francesca of Rimini—the same in sin, but how different in their ending. Clare the Blessed; Francesca the Cursed! The contrast, as well as the sameness of their lives, is all the more striking when we realize that they were almost contemporaries. Clare was a little girl of three—she was born in 1285—when Paolo and Francesca were murdered in their sin. As she grew up she must have listened many times to the tale of the horrible tragedy that had happened in her own social set. It was only yesterday. No doubt she

often bemoaned the fate of the beautiful young lovers,
as her contemporary Dante bemoaned it. It came very
close to home, for Clare's family also boasted of noble
blood, nobler than that of the cruel Malatesta that had
enslaved Rimini.

The family of the Agolanti, to which she belonged,
was rich as well as noble. It was a combination that
prevailed to her undoing. She was very young when
she was married, and life, in spite of the unsettled
condition of the times, lay beautiful before her. But
the shadows soon fell. It was a time when no one
was safe. Internal strife was continual. We do not
get all the details, but she was married only a short
time when misfortune came and deprived her of her
parents and her young husband. No doubt it is a
hidden chapter in the history of the Malatesta con-
spiracies. But the young widow in spite of the tragedies that had fallen to her lot was far from crushed.
Perhaps she rejoiced in the freedom that had come to
her by the deaths of those who had restrained her.
At any rate, we soon find her enjoying life to the full
in the town which knew how to be gay and how to sin
in the midst of fighting and conspiracy. War is ever
a friend of lust. The gay young widow soon passed
from heedless frivolity to downright immorality. The
fate of Francesca gave her little fear.

She married a second time, evidently without love,
for she continued her life of sin as before. She was
a thorough product of the license of the times, living
for the world and its pleasures with very little thought

of God. Evidently the husband was a complaisant sort of individual, with none of the Malatesta desire to avenge broken marriage vows.

Clare continued her wicked life up to the time she was thirty-four years of age. And then like a bolt from the blue the grace of God struck her down. The grace of God for her; the sword for Francesca.

In spite of her life of sin, Clare clung to the external observance of religion. She was very likely more a weakling than a confirmed criminal. One day she went to Mass in a Franciscan church. It was a mere matter of form. There was no devotion in her soul. She was only the grand lady of the world fulfilling a social obligation, just as Pompadour might assist at Mass in the royal chapel of Louis XV. A bit of hypocrisy, and nothing more. She had no thought of prayer. Prayer was not for great ladies who lived a life of public sin. And so while the Mass proceeded she let her thoughts wander at will, thinking of her lovers, thinking of her gowns, of her social successes, and eager for the tiresome service to be ended. But in the midst of her imaginings suddenly she seemed to hear a voice, as if it were the voice of a child, saying to her, "Clare, try to say one *Pater* and *Ave** to the glory of God, with attention, and do not think of anything else." It was the great moment of grace, like the "Take and Read" that came to St. Augustine, another sinner, and to her credit she opened her heart to that grace. She obeyed the mysterious command and said the prayers with all the attention and fervor she could command, and then

---

* *Pater Noster* and *Ave Maria*—that is, *Our Father* and *Hail Mary.* —*Publisher*, 2006.

carried along by the grace she began to think of the terrible sins with which her soul was sullied. It was but a moment, but in that moment the sinner died and the saint was born.

The processes of conversion are hard to follow. They are not always long and methodical. Sometimes they are instantaneous, like the miraculous cure of the blind man—"I was blind, now I see." Hence some psychologists would sneer at the statement in the life of Clare of Rimini that, very shortly after this happening of the mysterious voice, while she was in this same church on another occasion, the Blessed Virgin, surrounded by angels, appeared to her. How ridiculous! they would say. The Blessed Virgin appearing to this sinful woman, notorious for her bad reputation! It was the same charge made against even a Greater One—"This man receiveth sinners and eateth with them." The Friend of publicans and sinners! It is so easy for man to set limits to the mercy of God. There is for us no more consoling title given to Our Lady than "Refuge of Sinners." Did she so show her love to the poor, miserable Clare as to come to her in person? It is not incredible. Clare assures us of the fact, and her sudden transformation from a lover of the world and its sinful pleasures into an ardent penitent who henceforth regarded with disgust all the things she had once held dear, is proof enough that she was granted the extraordinary favor which she so humbly describes. It is the only way to account for her sudden, complete and lasting conversion.

Immediately after this vision had been vouchsafed her, she hastened home to tell her husband of the great change that had been made in her soul, and begged him to coöperate with her so that henceforth she might do for God what hitherto she had done for the world. No doubt the conversion of his wayward wife was pleasing news to him. Whether it was or not, he does not seem to have protested against the spirit of unworldliness which she insisted on introducing into her household. At once she laid aside the fine garments to which she had always given so much attention, and put on the humble dress of the Third Order of St. Francis, all the while lamenting her past sins as a true penitent. For a grand lady of the world to put aside such vanities was little short of heroic. But it was only the beginning. While her husband lived, her desires to do penance were necessarily curtailed, but when he died, a short time after her miraculous conversion, she set no limits to her penance. She became the penitent in earnest. To punish her flesh that had so grievously sinned, she wore a hair shirt and a coat of mail, went barefoot, slept on the bare ground, and took no food but bread and water.

But her penance consisted of more than bodily austerities. She continued to pray unceasingly, keeping her vigils during most of the night, bemoaning her sins and beseeching God to pardon her. As an added penance for Lent, she used to spend her prayerful nights at the city walls no matter how inclement the weather. A part of her life during those early days of fervor she lived in an abandoned tower near one of the churches.

No need to say that perseverance in such an extraordinary course of austerity was not easy. Clare had been too long an ally of Satan for him to give her up without a struggle. Oftentimes there returned to her the vision of the sinful delights she had once enjoyed. There was the temptation to escape from those self-inflicted horrors and go back to her old companions in vice. Human nature is always weak. But they were only temptations. They humiliated her while they strengthened her. In answer to the memories of the old allurements she increased her penances and prayed all the more fervently.

Clare, however, while concerned principally with the salvation of her own soul, did not stop there. She had found the peace of God for herself and she yearned to make others know how sweet it was. The saints are never selfish. They are always distinguished for their charity to their neighbors. Clare wanted to be of help to her neighbor. Happily the first call upon her charity came from one of her own brothers. Very likely he had been one of the victims of the Malatesta tyrants, just as his father before him. Whatever side he was on, however, in those times of never-ending dissension, he had been obliged to flee from Rimini and was now hiding in Urbino, where he had fallen desperately ill. Clare, with that special affection for him which all her penances had not destroyed but rather strengthened and indeed sanctified, hastened to his aid and nursed him back to health. We may be sure that she did not confine her care to his bodily ills, but took advantage of his condition to help him set his soul in order. As soon as he was better she returned to her beloved Rimini. It was not without a purpose. Rimini had witnessed her sin; Rimini must witness her expiation.

But it was surely an expiation of love, not merely the expiation by austerities that might frighten, but the expiation through deeds of charity, that won the affection of all the poor of Rimini. Clare now lived solely for others. Wherever there was suffering, there was she doing her utmost to alleviate it. She had considerable means of her own and all this she employed to aid the poor, for her own wants were insignificant. Food and clothes for the poor, medicine for the sick—daily she provided these; and when her own resources failed she would go begging from door to door so that the sufferers might not lack these comforts. She cared for the sick personally, trying to soothe their sufferings, and even dressing the most loathsome sores.

Where once she had been a scandal, now she was a continual source of edification. The nine days wonder of the conversion of the great lady soon passed. Likely there were many who prophesied that it was too good to last. But as the years went on and the sinner was transformed into the saint, Clare the charity-worker became an accepted fact in the life of the city. She had her enemies of course. It was good she had. They kept her humble. They lied about her and made her the victim of their petty persecutions. They resented the reproofs which she in her zeal sometimes addressed to them. Their pride was hurt, and they tried to undermine her influence by accusing her of heresy and even by declaring that she was possessed by the devil. But the calumny was pleasant music to the ears of the penitent. She believed that she was a greater criminal than even her worst enemies could ever imagine. She had condemned herself; their condemnation mattered little. Her only return for their hate and suspicion was to pray for them.

But not all the people of Rimini felt thus to her. Her unselfish charity had won the gratitude of many, and at least the respect of the best people of the town. And Clare availed herself of this high regard of her friends to do the work of God among them. In many a home she was an angel of peace. Clare could speak with authority of the evils of sin. Many a time she went to women who were leading the same kind of wicked life she herself had once led and preached so effectively to them that she won them back to virtue and penance. There was one noted case of a young widow of great family whom she converted and who ever after associated herself with the charitable work of Clare.

The old biographer of this holy penitent tells us one very striking example of her charity. The Poor Clares of a neighboring town had been compelled, owing to the breaking out of one of the perpetual wars of the times, to abandon their monastery and seek refuge in Rimini. They were in desperate straits, and at once Clare went begging for them from door to door. One day when they were without firewood, she went out into the country and returned carrying upon her shoulders through the streets of Rimini, where once she had ridden in glory, the trunk of an old tree. Who knows what a Way of the Cross that journey was to her who could boast of generations of noble blood? That incident alone would indicate how much she had mastered herself.

Clare from the time of her conversion had donned the garb of the Third Order and had professed the Franciscan rule. She was eager to bring others to that rule, and at last succeeded in forming several pious women into a community which she placed under the rule of St. Clare. While she professed that rule herself, she would not bind herself to the enclosed life, feeling that it was in the designs of God that she should still carry on in the world her apostleship of charity. One work led to another. Aided by some wealthy friends, she bought some houses and established a monastery for these spiritual children of hers, which foundation she called Our Lady of the Angels, perhaps in memory of that wonderful vision at the instant of her conversion when she beheld Our Lady surrounded by angels.

So year followed year, and every year furthered the sanctification of the penitent. It was a long period of penance—thirty years—yet all too short for her to prove her sorrow to the God she had once so grievously offended. God had long ago forgiven her. She was

now a soul upon whom he poured all His delights.
He gave her the gift of prophecy, she worked miracles,
and she talked with Him in her prayers as St. Teresa
talked with Him.   At one time toward the end of her
life she remained in an ecstasy of contemplation for
three months.   Our Lord Himself, with St. John the
Baptist and the Apostles, appeared to her.   He showed
her the wound in His side, and bade her beg from
Him all the graces she desired.   Clare simply asked
Him to grant the conversion of sinners and to give
herself the grace of compassion for His sufferings.   In
connection with the Passion of Our Lord to which
Clare had such devotion it is interesting to note that
nearly two centuries later the House of Rimini pro-
duced another saintly woman who wrote beautifully
of the sufferings of Our Lord.   This was Battista
Varani, whose mother was a daughter of Sigismund
Malatesta, Prince of Rimini.   In her the spirit of Clare
found a new expression.

The conversion of sinners was the thing that
appealed most to the piety of Clare.   She had known
the misery of sin herself; hence she knew the misery
in which all sinners were, and she could conceive no
greater love for them than to see them delivered, as
she had been delivered, from the bondage of death.
The folly of sin, the folly of doing what one must be
sorry for, that was the lesson which Clare tried to
convey by her ceaseless tears.

So she crucified herself for thirty long years, and at
last to this broken-hearted penitent, this woman sixty-

four years of age, came the blessed relief of death. She died February 10, 1346, and was buried in the chapel of the monastery which she had founded, and where her sanctity was attested to by many miracles. Later her remains were removed to the cathedral of Rimini.

The scandal of Rimini is now its glory; Clare of Rimini has atoned for the sin of Francesca of Rimini.

Chapter 9

SAINT HYACINTHA OF MARISCOTTI

COUNTLESS are the saintly sons and daughters of St. Francis of Assisi. "For six hundred years," says Cardinal Manning, "his children have multiplied above all others. In all lands, of all languages, in every state of life, men and women, poor and rich, lettered and unlearned, soldier and civilian, layman and priest, princes and kings, bishops and pontiffs, in whatsoever condition of life they might be, the Franciscan type is in all the same."

Not the least among them is St. Hyacintha of Mariscotti, Virgin of the Third Order Regular, she who in the midst of her severe penitential life firmly believed in all her humility that she was the greatest sinner that ever lived. That is the true psychology of the saints. St. Teresa, who never lost her baptismal innocence, confessed herself the greatest sinner ever, and, what is more, really believed that she was. Somehow the saints are not as tolerant of themselves as are the rest of us in regard to our poor, sinful selves. How far and how grieviously Hyacintha sinned we cannot tell. Perhaps she really had been the great sinner she confessed herself to be. No need, however, to know the details. It is enough to know that the day came when she put behind her forever her frivolous, if not criminal, life, and atoned for it with such bodily austerity, such fervent love and such heartfelt sorrow that from being at the very verge of Hell she about-faced and triumphantly entered Heaven. The sinner became a great saint.

Had she never sinned, her story would bear telling as the example of a heroic soul that set aside family and social position and all those things so dear to the human heart, in order to serve God alone. For in a worldly sense she did sacrifice much.

As to family name and noble blood no child ever had a fairer inheritance than Clarice of Mariscotti, the name with which she was baptized. Her father was Marc-Antonio of Mariscotti, a member of one of the most distinguished families of Italy, tracing back to the days of Charlemagne when a Scotchman, Marius Scotus, settled there. We find the family marrying into the noblest families of Italy, the Orsini, the Conti, the Farnese and others. Clarice's mother was Octavia Orsini, all in all, perhaps, the most distinguished family that ever existed in any country. The name Orsini was for many centuries one to conjure with. To be an Orsini was to have the world before you.

Even from her infancy Clarice gave signs of that fine mentality which later distinguished her, a mentality that so often reminds us of the talent of Teresa of Avila. She was a charming little girl, and, much to the delight of her parents, manifested a piety that was extraordinary in one so young. They quite believed

that she was a child of special election, a belief that
was strengthened by what they considered a miracle
that saved her when at the age of seven she nearly fell
into a well.

But the hopes grew dimmer as the years went on.
Much to the chagrin of the pious parents, the girl as
she grew up cared for nothing but pleasure and dress
and vanity.   Again she reminds us of the girlhood of
St. Teresa, who confesses how near she came to losing
her soul by her vanity.

In order to correct this worldly tendency of Clarice,
the doting father and mother, worried out of their
lives, sent her to be educated by the Franciscan nuns
at Viterbo, where her elder sister was a religious.   But
it was an effort apparently wasted.   Clarice cared little
whether her sister were a nun or not.   She ridiculed
her admonitions.   She was only her sister after all,
nun or no nun, and girls do not take their sisters too
seriously.   It was so, too, with the advice of the other
nuns.   They wasted their breath on her.   She was
going to have a good time no matter what they said.
She came home from the convent school more worldly
than when she had entered.   She firmly believed that
the time spent there had been worse than wasted and
she was bitterly resentful toward those who had sent
her there.   This resentment was intensified by the fact
that her younger sister, Hortense, was going to be
married to a marquis.   It galled her pride to think
that she had been passed over.   It was her right to
be married first, and here was that child Hortense

snubbing her by being the first to get a husband. Perhaps the prospective suitors were afraid of the haughty, heedless Clarice. That did not help matters anyway. Piqued at what she considered an injustice, she began to make life even more unbearable to all at home. She ruined the peace of the house. Finally her father, heartily sick of her tantrums, suggested to her that she ought to be a nun. The Count must have been desperate when he suggested such a solution of his difficulties, for he must have known what a sorry kind of nun this headstrong, vain, quick-tempered, worldly daughter of his would make. But anything to get her out of the house where she was making things so intolerable. In her chagrin, as if replying to a dare, the heedless girl took him at his word. If he wanted her to be a nun, well, she would be a nun. She might as well be that as anything else. And heedless as usual, with little thought of the matter, she entered the convent, where her sister already was, at Viterbo. She took the name of Sister Hyacintha.

How the good nuns ever consented to take among them one who had as a student made their lives so miserable is a mystery. Many a time, indeed, they would have been glad to get rid of Sister Hyacintha. Nun she was in name only. It was the same haughty, frivolous, worldly Clarice with a religious habit and a new name. Nothing more. She was still of the world and would be of the world to the end. She had made up her mind to that. She was a nun against her will. She made no secret of her dispositions. At any rate she was no hypocrite. So when one day her father came to see her, hoping perhaps to find her in better disposition, she astounded him by saying to him, "I am a nun but I mean to live according to my rank." The father was speechless. She was still the same Clarice, convent or no convent. One could hardly call it a convent as far as she was concerned. Having plenty of wealth at her disposal and knowing how influential her family was, this follower of the poor St. Francis, hardly seeing the ridiculousness of her action, insisted that her room be furnished with every luxury. She demanded and obtained every comfort and convenience that she had been accustomed to enjoy in her palatial home. She was bound to enjoy life as much as she could. A fig for the rule! Religious exercises were a tiresome interference to get rid of with as little effort as possible. No wonder the other nuns were scandalized at this parody of the religious life. Surely they cannot be blamed if it never entered their minds that this lax nun was in God's good time to out-distance them and become a great saint.

Sister Hyacintha continued this manner of life for ten years. How with such coldness and laxity she continued so long in what must have been a veritable prison, in spite of all the bodily comforts she enjoyed, is beyond us. All we can say is that there must have been a lot of good in the girl, for all that. And we are not surprised at being told by her biographer that she had in spite of everything a lively faith and a great respect for the mysteries of religion. One can readily see in her the strong will which when sanctified, as it was later on, would be just as stubborn in the pursuit of sanctity as it had been to seek its own comfort.

The grace of God was in readiness all the while to recast the clay into a vessel of election. The conversion chanced this way. One day when she was confined to her bed with a slight illness, she sent for the spiritual director, Father Anthony Bianchetti, a Franciscan, to come and hear her confession. He was a fine priest and a wise spiritual guide, just the right man for such a circumstance as this. No doubt he had heard before of the strange case of this quasi-nun who turned her convent cell into milady's boudoir. Now he would give her the lesson she so badly needed. Scarcely had he entered the room and beheld the luxury that surrounded the so-called religious when he turned on his heel and started to leave the room. He refused to hear her confession, and told her that Heaven was not made for the vain and the proud. It was the psychological moment, or rather the moment of grace. Sister Hyacintha, humiliated by such a reproach, was no longer the haughty woman of the world. With the words of the priest had come a grace that made her fear. "Is there no hope for me?" she cried out to him. "Have I shut myself up in a cloister only to lose my soul? Must I give up all hope of salvation?"

We know what the good priest's answer would be. Of course there was hope for her, but there was one necessary condition, and that was that she change her life and atone for the bad example she had given to her sisters in religion for the past ten years.

With Sister Hyacintha there was no more trifling with grace. She was crushed by the sudden realization of the scandal she had given as well as of the way in which she had trifled with God. She burst into tears, broken-hearted sobs. It was indeed the parting of the ways. The saint was born in that instant. As soon as her confessor was gone she proceeded at once to put into execution her desire to repair the scandal of her life. Dressed in the meanest habit she could find, she repaired to the refectory where the sisters then were, threw herself upon her knees and began to scourge herself, the while in tears she asked pardon of all for the scandal she had given them. Needless to say the community was amazed at this sudden conversion, as well as delighted.

Nevertheless, for a while it seemed too good to be true. Habits of years are not cast aside easily. It was not a pleasant road—this way to sanctity. And poor Sister Hyacintha had many a temptation to go back to the lax life from which she had been rescued. She was indeed slipping back, when as a new grace from God she fell into a serious illness, a warning to her to have no more trifling with her soul. Her conversion this time was complete and lasting. There was no more looking back to the flesh pots of Egypt.

Her first move was to get rid of all the luxury with which she had surrounded herself and to wed herself in truth to the Poverty to which she had been vowed.

The boudoir was dismantled and the cell appeared from beneath its fine furnishings. A few vine branches with a stone for pillow served as her bed. The finery of her habits was cast aside and she dressed in rags with a hair shirt beneath them. The days of dainty fare were over. Now when she did eat—for she fasted almost continually—bitter herbs were the only food she would take. To these mortifications were added the daily scourgings, against which her pampered body must have rebelled. In a word, the new convert set no limit to the penances she imposed upon herself. It was, however, a mistaken ardor, and later on she admitted the folly of this undirected self-torture. Nothing sated her desire for suffering. At times she would go into the convent garden in the bitter cold of winter and put her feet into icy water, then again take a heavy cross upon her shoulders and make the Way of the Cross in that fashion, disciplining herself at every station. She wore a crown of thorns, drank absinthe on Friday in memory of the vinegar and gall, tortured her flesh with nettles, hot wax, fire and snow. The day came, however, when she realized that no matter how necessary these sufferings might be, they were not everything. More important still was the interior mortification, the perfection of the soul. We find her writing to a friend who had asked her advice about bodily mortification: "Mortification is not really that which sanctifies; for that we must have interior virtue. Ah, my daughter, of what use to me have been so many years of fasting on bread and water?

What benefit have I derived from so many scourgings till the blood flowed? What has all this done for me? Nothing, absolutely nothing. I have afflicted myself, but I am not mortified." Written with the common sense of St. Teresa! It is like a passage from one of Teresa's letters. But at the same time it has all the humility, the self-depreciation of St. Teresa, for in spite of her denials Hyacintha was internally mortified and had acquired a great deal through those sufferings, the very mention of which makes us quail. It is always so easy for us to say that certain saints were unwise in their self-inflicted tortures; it helps us to salve our own conscience.

But, great as were these bodily mortifications on the part of Hyacintha, her mortification of soul was greater still. She regarded herself as the greatest sinner that ever lived, and hence unworthy to dwell in a convent among so many holy souls. In her own mind she was the least of all the nuns, and she begged to be allowed to do the most menial of all the tasks, such as washing the dishes and sweeping the floor, and even rejoiced in being permitted to perform what in her days as a great lady she had considered as repulsive tasks. What a change in her! A short time before she would have resented the very insinuation that she should humble herself to such menial work. But it was a long time since Clarice had told her father that she intended to live according to her rank, nun or no nun. It was because she really believed herself a great sinner that she humbled herself, always keeping her eyes on the ground. When asked why she did this, she replied, "I fear Hell, which my sins deserve so much." When she heard of some notorious criminal she would say, "Alas, what is that in comparison with my former transgressions! I am much more guilty in God's sight than all these great sinners."

Some, indeed, took her at her word and were willing to believe that she was as great a criminal as she confessed. As a result they despised her and insulted her, all of which was the sweetest music to her ears.

But with all these sufferings of body and soul, she ever kept her common sense in spirituality. Again she reminds us of the common sense of St. Teresa. Thus to one sister who is disturbed because she cannot take more time from her sleep to give to prayer, she replies: "Be sure, sister, that if you do not sleep as much as is necessary, you will fail to do good, for not less than seven hours sleep is required according to the practice of the strictest Orders. The power of sleeping little is a special gift of God, and the gift is not granted to everyone. God knows well what he is doing. Our difficulties and our resignation are more pleasing to Him than vigils and forced prayers. Sleep, then, seven hours in holy peace in the hearts of Jesus and Mary. If God wills, you will become a saint without sleeping less. Besides all the saints in Paradise did not practice long vigils." To another sister she wrote, "Do not think that God is a tyrant. . . . Drive away sadness, I implore and pray you." But with all her broad-mindedness she was never lax as far as the spirit of the Order was concerned. Thus she wrote to the superior of a convent who desired a modification of the rule in regard to the use of food: "Oh, how terrible an account must be given on the Day of Judgment of the abuses tolerated in monasteries. I pray and entreat you by the sufferings of our Heavenly Spouse to care nothing for what may be said. How many poor suffer hunger, and nuns desire superfluities!"

Great saint that she was, Hyacintha was first of all a woman of prayer. Prayer was her very existence. She had mastered the science completely. She might advise others against shortening their sleep, but she herself spent most of the night in prayer. God had raised her to a high degree of contemplation. But more than all these spiritual delights she cherished the Cross. "The greatest perfection," she writes, "consists in the Cross and suffering. I do not know how to speak of consolations, but I consider the way of the Cross the safest." Again it is as St. Teresa she cries out, "The Cross! the Cross! To suffer! To suffer! and to persevere bravely without consolation. This is the true sign of the spirit of God." Where now is the haughty descendant of the Orsini who had insisted that her cell be furnished like a boudoir? All the past weakness and worldliness are gone, consumed in the fire of Divine Love.

There was never a saint yet that was not filled with charity to his neighbor. It is but a corollary of the love of God. There was no one kinder than Sister Hyacintha, no one more tolerant of the faults of others.

Within the convent and without she was the soul of neighborliness. The young girl students regarded her as a mother. If Sister Hyacintha had a sense of humor, and I am sure she had, she must have smiled many a time while correcting the students as she thought of her own student days when she was the despair of the nuns. Perhaps she understood them better than she was understood in her school days. She could allow for a lot now, feeling that no one had ever sinned as she had. This humility of hers explains her success in converting sinners. She knew how to meet them more than halfway.

There is one little incident in her life which shows her extraordinary love for the poor. She was always alleviating distress, going without necessary food herself in order to give it to others. It was the pious custom of the Mariscotti family to have a number of Masses said at the death of any member. Hyacintha begged her brother to give her now the money that would be spent at her death in order that she might use it for the poor. She was willing, she said, to bear the pains of Purgatory without this relief so long as she might have more to give to the unfortunate.

Indeed, one would be obliged to dilate on every virtue to describe thoroughly this holy penitent, for there was none that she did not practice in a heroic degree. Holy penitent, I say, for in spite of the miracles she wrought, in spite of her ecstasies, in spite of her wonderful charity, I rather like to think of her as the poor sinner who by the way of penance came from the very mouth of Hell to the gates of Heaven.

She died January 30, 1640, at the age of fifty-five. It was a pope of the Orsini family, Benedict XIII, who beatified her. Popes and princes have given glory to the blood of the Orsini, but none such glory as gave Octavia Orsini's daughter, the humble penitent, Clarice.

Chapter 10

CATALINA DE CARDONA, "THE SINNER"

THERE never was a finer judge of character, spiritual or secular, in the world or out of it, than St. Teresa of Avila. Praise from her is praise indeed. So that when you find her with her great common sense, her sense of humor and her realization of the weakness of human nature, growing enthusiastic over anybody, you may be sure that the object of her admiration is quite out of the ordinary. And surely she is enthusiastic to a great degree over the remarkable penitent, Catalina de Cardona, who is recognized as one of the glories of her age. To call Catalina a penitent is something of a misnomer, just as it was a misnomer for her to call herself "The Sinner." It was just that same humility that made Teresa consider herself the greatest sinner that ever lived when we know that she never sullied her baptismal innocence. Saints regard the slightest imperfections with a horror that makes the rest of us tremble. They regard themselves as sinners, hence their lives of heroic penance; hence, too, their delight, as in the case of St. Teresa, in meditating on the lives of those who once had been great sinners and who had been converted even unto sanctity. There is a very striking passage in the life of Mary Queen

of Scots, the guilt or innocence of whose life seems
fated never to be settled until the day of judgment,
although her death had all the characteristics of martyrdom for the faith.   During the night before her execution she searched in the *Lives of the Saints,* which her
ladies were accustomed to read to her, for the story of
some great sinner whom God had pardoned.   She
stopped at the story of the penitent thief which Jean
Kennedy was reading to her, and declared that it was
the most reassuring example of human confidence and
Divine mercy.   "He was a great sinner," she said, "but
not so great as I.   I implore Our Lord in memory of
His Passion to remember and have mercy upon me as
He had upon him in the hour of death."

And St. Teresa, who had never been a great sinner,
found as her favorite among all the saints none other
than Mary Magdalen.   "I had a very great devotion,"
she writes, "to the glorious Magdalen, and very frequently used to think of her conversion, especially when
I went to Communion.   I used to recommend myself
to that glorious saint, that she might obtain me pardon."   And again: "On the feast of the Magdalen,
when thinking of the great love I am bound to have
for Our Lord, according to the words He spoke to me
in reference to this saint, and having great desires to
imitate her, Our Lord was very gracious to me and
said I was to be henceforth strong."   Sinner that she
believed herself to be, she yearned to give herself to a
life of the most austere penance.   "I began with a
renewed love of the most Sacred Humanity; my prayer

began to be solid, like a house the foundations of which are strong; and I was inclined to practice greater penance, having been negligent in this matter hitherto because of my great infirmities. The holy man who heard my confession told me that certain penances would not hurt me, and that God perhaps sent me so much sickness because I did no penance; His Majesty would therefore impose it Himself. He ordered me to practice certain acts of mortification not very pleasant for me. I did so because I felt that Our Lord was enjoining it all, and giving him grace to command me in such a way as to make me obedient unto him."

St. Teresa now treated her body with extreme severity, disciplining herself even to blood, yet with a common sense that saved her from any foolish extremes. Being such a great penitent herself, she knew therefore how to estimate such a character as Catalina de Cardona. It is in the *Book of the Foundations* that Teresa tells the story of the woman whom she so longs to imitate. She first came in contact with Catalina's cave of penance on the occasion of a journey to Villanueva for the purpose of establishing there a Carmelite convent to contain some nine women who were then living in community at that place. Four of these women, daughters of pious and noble parents, had been attracted, as so many others, partly by curiosity and partly by veneration, around Catalina de Cardona. They had wished to serve God under the guidance of the holy anchoress, but as she would not consent to this, their brother, who was a priest, advised them to lead the

life of Beatas in the world, while Catalina, although
unwilling to undertake their direction, prophesied that
one day they would found a convent of Carmelite nuns.
About this time another woman, a widow with four
daughters who was animated with the same holy
designs, invited them to join her household, and
together with still another woman they accepted the
invitation and formed a sort of community, waiting for
God to direct them further in the way of the religious
life. The people of Villanueva with the parish priest
at the head of the procession led them to the hermitage
of St. Anne, close to the house where the widow lived.
This was in 1574. All the townspeople had the greatest admiration for these holy women and were eager to
see them nuns, and in 1576 they sent a delegation to
Teresa, who was then at Toledo, to ask her to found a
Carmelite convent for them. But Teresa was not enthusiastic over the matter. They persisted again and again,
but for common-sense reasons of her own and out of
her great experience she still refused. But one day
when she was at Communion, God said to her, "Where
was the treasury that supplied the means for the foundations already made?" He told her then to accept the
house without any misgiving as it would be greatly to
His honor and the progress of souls. She left Malagon,
February 13, 1580, and on the way stopped at the
monastery of Our Lady of Succor, which was situated
three miles from Villanueva. Among those who were
accompanying Teresa was the prior of this monastery,
and the friars came forth to meet him and to conduct

him into the monastery church. Teresa and her companions followed them, the first thought in her mind being for the great Catalina de Cardona, who had been the instrument of God in the foundation of the monastery. She writes: "Certainly I went in with so much inward joy that I would have looked on a much longer journey as profitably made, though I was very sorry for the death of the saint by whom Our Lord founded the house; I did not deserve to see her, though I desired it greatly." She continues then: "I think it will not be a waste of time to say something in this place of her life, and how it came to pass that Our Lord would have the monastery founded which, as I learn, has been of so much advantage to many souls in the country round about. I do so, that you, my sisters, beholding the penance done by this saint, may see how far we are behind her, and make efforts to serve Our Lord with renewed courage; for there is no reason why we should do less than she did, seeing that we are not sprung from so refined and noble a race, for, though this be of no consequence, I speak of it because she once lived in great comfort according to her rank, for she was a child of the ducal house of Cardona and was known as Donna Catalina de Cardona. When she had written to me a certain number of times she signed herself simply, 'The Sinner.' "

This extraordinary penitent who sought to hide her noble name under the title of "The Sinner" was the daughter of Don Ramon de Cardona, who was descended from the royal house of Aragon. When she was but eight years old she was left an orphan by the death of her father, her mother having died some time previously, and she was taken into the home of the Princess of Salerno, a near relative of her mother. She had a vision of her father suffering in Purgatory and he assured her that she could release him from his pains by her penances. At once, out of the great love she bore her father, she began to mortify herself and to discipline herself until she had the assurance that he had been delivered from suffering.

The Princess soon after this brought her to Spain, just about the time that Teresa, who was four years older than Catalina, was laying the foundations of the reform of Carmel. Catalina, still filled with the penitential idea, retired to the desert and began a life of heroic austerity. She was called away from her secluded life of penance by the death of the Princess, and for a time was put in charge of the household of Ruy Gomez, having under her care the Prince Don Carlos and his brother Don Juan of Austria. But even in this noble household she lived as well as she could the life of the desert, still practicing her austerities, touching no meat at all and even fasting strictly four days a week. It was an heroic life, indeed, for her companions then were all great men and ladies of rank. But one can have a hermitage even in a palace, and Catalina, because she was surrounded by so much of the glory of the world, took greater care of her soul and redoubled her penance. It was the same old story of the hair shirt beneath the robe of velvet. But the worldly surroundings palled on her and she yearned to go into solitude, where unobserved she could do the penances she wanted to do. Her confessors, however, would not consent to this. "But," as St. Teresa observes, "as the world is now so very discreet, and the great work of God wrought in His saints, men and women, who serve Him in the deserts, is almost forgotten, I am not surprised that they thought her desire foolish." Nevertheless God was watching over the soul of this woman whose heart was so full of zeal for pain. He sent her in time to a holy confessor who was himself doing heroic penance, and he told her not to hold back but to obey the evident will of God. The great St. Peter of Alcantara also encouraged her to follow the life she ached for, and immediately she put her designs into execution. Ruy Gomez together with his wife set out on a visit to an estate which he had just bought, and Catalina accompanied them. She bided her time, and at the first opportunity she dressed herself as a man in order not to attract attention, and then set out for the life of real penance. She consulted a holy hermit whom she had known at Madrid and who had come to see Ruy Gomez on some business, and he approved of her resolution. Thereupon Catalina, in her man's clothes, together with the hermit and another priest, set out before dawn and made their way to La Roda. They found a little cave, so small that it hardly could hold her, and there the two priests left her to her prayers and her penances. It all reads like a page from the age of the Fathers of the Desert rather than from the age of Shakespeare. The poor hermits left with her to sustain her three loaves of bread, all that stood between her and starvation. "But," remarks Teresa, "what love must she have had! for she did not think of any means of finding food, nor of the danger that might ensue, nor of the evil speaking that would result from her disappearance. Oh, how deeply must that soul have drunk of the wine of God!"

St. Teresa relates that she had heard many details of the great austerity of the life of Catalina, how she treated her body with the most fearful penances during many years and how she received from God the most extraordinary graces. Yet with all these graces she was a soul of the utmost simplicity. When she went to visit the nuns at the convent of St. Joseph in Toledo she told them about the great favors God had shown her, but all so simply that no one ever suspected her of any vainglory. At that time of her visit she had been in her little cave eight years, living for days at a time on roots and herbs. When the three loaves of bread which the hermits had left with her had been eaten she had nothing at all until, three years later, a poor shepherd chanced upon the cave and discovered her gathering roots and herbs for her daily meal. He gave her a small supply of bread and meal, of cakes baked over the embers, and she partook of this luxurious banquet once in three days. So accustomed did she become to this rude mode of living that later on when she went about collecting funds to build a monastery she would occasionally be compelled to eat a sardine, but, wasted as she was, she felt that such a delicacy did her more harm than good. Daily she would discipline herself with a heavy chain, sometimes for the length of two hours, so that her garments, of the coarsest sackcloth, were always clotted with blood. To these penances were added the attacks of evil spirits, who, she says, came to her in the guise of mastiffs and serpents, and assailed her. But much as she suffered from them she did not fear them, for she knew that the power of God was with her. She loved her cave where God gave her so many graces, and even after she succeeded in founding the monastery she still lived and slept in her hermitage, leaving it only for the Divine Office. Before her own monastery was established she used to go to hear Mass at a monastery a quarter of a mile distant from her cave, but even then so keen was her desire for doing penance that she would sometimes make the journey on her knees. Her dress was made of kersey and she wore with it a tunic of the coarsest cloth so fashioned that people thought she was a man.

It did not take long for the fame of the holy woman to spread. People began to visit her in her cave, so great was their devotion to her whom they really considered a saint. They considered it an honor to converse with her, but the continued encroachment upon her devotions wearied her, and she said they were killing her. There were times when the whole plain near her cave was filled with the carriages of the great ones of the world, and so great was the crowd at times that, soon after the friars were established in the monastery built through her efforts, she had to be raised on high in order to give her blessing to the people. She had been living in the cave eight years when one night as she was praying she saw the walls crumbling, as the earth had been loosened by the moisture. The dirt fell upon her, and in the morning she was found half buried. It was then that the instruments of her penance which she had so carefully concealed were discovered. The people cleared the cave and made it larger and protected it against the wet. But soon after she fell very seriously ill, so ill that she thought she was going to die.

But the time of her reward had not yet come. God had other work for her to do. This work was the founding of the Carmelite monastery which brought so much glory to the place and so much joy to the poor penitent. In her zeal for the glory of God and the salvation of souls, she began to wish that a monastery of friars should be established in the vicinity of her cave. One day when she was praying before the crucifix Our Lord showed her a white mantle, and she was given to understand that it belonged to the Carmelites, of whom she had never heard. Making inquiries, she found out that there was such a community of friars at Pastrana, where it had been founded by Ruy Gomez after much persuasion on the part of Father Mariano. Ruy Gomez, Prince of Eboli, was the first Duke of Pastrana and was treasurer of Spain and the Indies. One meets his name often in the correspondence of St. Teresa, and especially the name of his wife, the

Princess Eboli, a pious woman, the mother of ten children. The Prince died in 1573. Catalina saw him in a vision and he told her that he had been saved by his alms but that he was suffering great woe. In aid of his soul she disciplined herself to blood, and had Masses said for him, and in a second vision he told her what relief he had received.

Catalina, as soon as she heard of the Carmelites at Pastrana, had herself conducted thither, and there, May 3, 1571, the Prince of Eboli and the Duke, who was the successor of St. Francis Borgia, and many others went out to meet her. In that monastery of Pastrana she took the habit of Our Lady, but since she had no intention of becoming a nun, she donned the habit of a lay brother, for the reason that she thought the life of the Carmelite nuns too soft for her and feared that if she entered the community her superiors would stop her great austerities.

Immediately she set about the work of collecting for the new monastery which she wished to have built near her cave, and for that reason went at first to Madrid. So great was the sensation she caused, for the fame of her virtue had long been known there, that she found it impossible to escape the crowds, who went so far as to cut off pieces of her habit and mantle as souvenirs. From Madrid she went to Toledo where she stayed with the Carmelites. The sisters afterwards declared that there was a fragrance as of relics about her, a fragrance that remained even about her habit, which they kept as a relic, giving her another habit in exchange. They never ceased to have the greatest veneration for her. At the court and elsewhere she collected the means to found the new monastery, and was loaded with gifts of vestments and altar vessels. When a certain ecclesiastic said to her that woolen vestments and leaden chalices were good enough for poor friars, she replied, "You, a worm of the earth, have a service of silver, and want the King of Kings to be satisfied with lead!"

In a very short time she was so successful in collecting funds that the monastery was built, the church being erected on the very spot where she had her beloved cave, and another cave or hermitage was made for her close by, with a solid tomb inside it. There she lived for the rest of her life.

But even in spite of the great veneration for her and her known austerities there were some who questioned her sanctity, and it was determined to make an official investigation of her manner of life. It is not strange, since it was not many years before that a pretended mystic had deceived even the wisest. Clare of Cordova, who was in religion Magdalen of the Cross, had by her pretended miracles, her visions and revelations aroused the admiration of all Spain. She was a member of the Franciscan order and after many years in the convent at Cordova, where she had edified and astounded the community by her austerities, she was made abbess. Her fame spread everywhere, so much so that even kings and popes consulted her, as she was supposed to be a prophet. She even went into ecstasies, and at times in those ecstasies was lifted two or three feet from the ground. But at last, after having deceived the whole world, she was touched by the grace of God, and threw herself at the feet of the Franciscan visitor and declared that her whole life for the past thirty years had been a lie. She was condemned by the Inquisition to read an avowal of her misdeeds in the cathedral of Seville, and was then exiled to a distant convent where she spent the rest of her life in the hardest penance. This had happened in 1546. So that lest the faithful might be deceived by another such penitent, it was determined to investigate the case of Catalina de Cardona. Father Salazar of the Jesuits was sent by the Inquisition to visit the woman in her cave. He was so amazed by what he saw and heard that his report silenced all clamors forever.

Catalina lived five years and a half after the foundation of the monastery which was so dear to her heart. She foretold the time of her death. She died May 11, 1577, and was buried with the greatest solemnity, multitudes crowding about the body which they had good reason to believe had belonged to a saint. So ended the life which St. Teresa says "seems supernatural, and indeed so does her former life, considering how severe it was." Teresa continues: "She is now lying in a chapel of Our Lady, to whom she was so extremely devout, but only for a time, till a larger church than the one they have at present shall be built, as only fitting to contain her blessed body." From that time on the monastery, owing to the fact that it held her body, became a place of great devotion, and even the whole neighborhood, on account of the desert and the cave, was regarded as a place especially holy.

St. Teresa evidently meditated much on the life of the saintly penitent. In her third "Relation" she says: "Once when thinking of the great penances practiced by Donna Catalina de Cardona and how I might have done more, considering the desires which Our Lord had given me at times, if it had not been for my obedience to my confessors, I asked myself whether it would not be as well if I disobeyed them for the future in this matter. Our Lord said to me: 'No, my daughter; thou art on the sound and safe road. Seest thou all her penances? I think more of thy obedience.' "

And Teresa ends her story of Catalina de Cardona thus :"During my stay there I was greatly comforted, though to my exceeding great shame, and the shame lasts, because I saw that she who there had borne so sharp a penance was a woman like myself, and more tenderly nurtured, for she was of a nobler race, and not so great a sinner as I am; on this subject there is no comparison possible between us, for I received much greater graces from Our Lord in many ways, and that I am not this moment in Hell for my great sins is a very great one. To follow in her steps, if I can, is my only comfort; but that is not much, for all my life has been wasted in desires; as for works I have none. May God of His compassion succor me in Whom I have always put my trust, for the sake of His Most Holy Son and the Virgin Our Lady, whose habit by the goodness of Our Lord I wear. One day after Communion in that hallowed church I became profoundly recollected and fell into a trance in which my senses were withheld. In that trance I saw the holy woman as a glorious body by an intellectual vision. There were angels with her; she told me not to grow faint, but strive to go on with these foundations. I understood thereby, though she did not say so expressly, that she helped me before God. She also told me something else, but there is no reason why I should repeat it here. I was very much comforted and had a desire to labor; and I hope, in the goodness of Our Lord, that, with such good help as her prayers are, I may be able to serve Him in some measure. You see now, my sisters, that her troubles are over already, and that the bliss she is in has no end. Let us strive now for the love of Our Lord to follow this our sister; hating ourselves as she hated herself, we shall finish our journey, for everything passes rapidly away and comes to an end."

It is the tribute of one great penitent to another. And surely Catalina de Cardona must have been a wonderful soul when the story of her penitential pains and tears could minister so to the humility of a St. Teresa.

Chapter 11

BEATRICE CENCI

IT is hard oftentimes to get at historical truth. The sources of history are not always the documents consigned to files to grow musty with the passing of the years. The people who have lived the events recorded insist on handing down their own version of the affair. Friend clashes with enemy, and the partisans of both clash through the ages. Hence so often the two lines of tradition, the black and the white, one contradicting the other, so well exemplified in the story of Mary Queen of Scots. And in spite of all your documents, in spite of all your rehabilitations, people will continue to believe just what they want to believe and nothing more. If a thing is not true, well, it is *ben trovato*. It serves the purpose, like many a fictitious coat of arms. Sometimes the true, impartial scholar will come along and establish the truth in mooted questions. But, in spite of that, the tradition disproved goes on just as if the scholar had never existed. And especially if the false tradition helps to prove a certain thesis. Still it is maintained that indulgences were and still are sold; still, that the Jesuit teaches that the end justifies the means. For it is chiefly in the domain of religion that these false traditions defy all historical research.

It must be maintained at all costs that the Catholic Church is wrong, that popes are crafty and cruel, rapacious and hypocritical, tyrants and foes to liberty; that all was horribly dark and evil till the shining light of the glorious Reformation; and every tradition that serves to perpetuate that assumption must be kept going no matter what the unbiased historian may say. And in no case has this ever been as plainly demonstrated as in the legend that has grown up about Beatrice Cenci.

A long time ago Shelley wrote his famous tragedy of *The Cenci*. A poor enough thing it appears to us today and very far from the great poetry which his contemporaries considered it. It is filled with mouthings and rantings. Shelley told the story in his own way, and prefaced the play with the "facts" on which he based his plot. No doubt he was honest enough, even though too willing to accept the anti-papal and anti-Catholic version of the notorious crime. But whether Shelley was honest or dishonest, his tragedy was meat and drink to the Protestant voraciousness of the time. Nothing good could come out of Rome. Here was another proof of it in the case of Beatrice Cenci, this poor, sweet girl done to death by the cruelty of a Pope who put aside all claims of justice and mercy in order to enrich himself with the wealth of a crushed family. Beatrice Cenci thus in due time became the rallying cry of all who hated the popes and wanted to rob them of their temporal power. In 1872 a committee was appointed to take means to place in the Capitol an inscription, "destined to recall the name and the misfortune of Beatrice Cenci, and at the same time the villainous iniquity of the priests." And even as late as 1906 a Roman association decided to invite the free-thinkers of the world to erect a marble monument in honor of the martyr Beatrice Cenci. But the newspaper that published the report of the meeting insisted that "in this affair of Beatrice Cenci the matter should be done prudently, and before starting a subscription historical truth should be examined thoroughly." So it was that Corrado Ricci, historian and art critic, while starting out merely with the idea of investigating the facts of the so-called portrait of Beatrice Cenci, painted by Guido Reni—which picture by the way he has demonstrated is not a portrait of Beatrice at all—finally came to devote himself for five years to a minute study of the case, going to the sources which had been so long neglected. And as the result of that honest study Beatrice Cenci stands forth very different from the picture the Pope's enemies have painted. She is no longer the "Roman Virgin" who, to avenge herself for the incestuous attack which her father made upon her virtue, brutally put him to death. But this "Roman Virgin" so piteously portrayed by Shelley and other romancers is shown forth as one who carried on an adulterous connection and gave birth to an illegitimate son; a proud, high-strung girl who in her resentment at the cruel manner in which she was treated by her father, who was in reality the vilest, most brutal person that could be imagined, finally soiled her hands with his blood and was doomed to pay the penalty by the loss of her head. Another historical lie has been scotched, but it will take more than Ricci's monumental work to make the enemies of the Church drop such a dainty morsel as the virgin-martyr Beatrice. And yet, great criminal that Beatrice Cenci was, one cannot read her true story without a surge of pity for the unfortunate girl who was carried away by her hate to do an unnatural deed, parricidal murder, and then through penitential tears sought to make her peace with God.

Beatrice Cenci was born at Rome, February 6, 1577. The Cenci were a noble family of many generations past. For centuries before the time of Beatrice, as well as since then, the family could boast of its scholars, its lawyers, its senators, its prelates and its cardinals. But at the time of our story it was fallen on evil times and had very little dignity to boast of. On the contrary, in spite of its great wealth, it had gone as low as it could go in the person of Beatrice's father, Francesco Cenci. When the father of Francesco died, the boy, then thirteen years of age, found himself the head of the Cenci, the possessor of an enormous fortune and vast domains. But he was the last one on earth to be given the responsibility of managing such an estate and of representing the noble Cenci. There was something of the perverted being, the degenerate, about him, even from his youth. He was convicted time and again of the most indecent, the most horrible deeds even as a boy; and the child was father to the man. Even though he was married at an early age in the effort of his mother and his guardians to reform him, he never till the day of his awful death lived a decent life. The court records of the time are full of his escapades. Now we find him banished for his immorality, now hiding himself in flight from the hand of the law, now haled before the tribunal of justice to be heavily fined, only to return to his vices and his cruelties as soon as he was freed.

At the age of fourteen he married Ersilia Santacroce, also fourteen, and to them were born twelve children. But the young wife finally succumbed to his cruelty, cruelty that was nothing short of tyrannical. She died April 16, 1584. The somber, forbidding palace of the Cenci resounded not with laughter and happiness but with the bitter cries of those who quailed before the brutality of the master of the house, who today would be examined for his sanity.

Francesco, however, was soon convinced that he could not ride roughshod over everybody. He had something of the coward in him, as is always characteristic of the tyrant and the bully. When Sixtus the Fifth came to the Chair of Peter, a pontiff who was always just and stern—and he needed to be in those days of lawless brigandage—he struck fear into the hearts of the lawbreakers, whether they were rich or poor, nobles or plebeians. Francesco, seeing that his great wealth and noble name would not avail to save him from the hand of the law, became more careful of his life outside the palace walls, but he vented all his wickedness, his unnatural cruelty, upon the members of his own family. He hated his children, and they in turn hated him. They had inherited his strange, hot blood of anger and lust, and the older they grew the more they resembled him. They grew up violent and wicked, most of them, and as soon as possible they left the palace, which had none of the attractions of a home, and went to squander their lives where they chose, demanding however that their father pay their debts. a thing that was always the source of violent misunderstandings.

After the stern Sixtus died, Francesco, too long kept in captivity, broke forth again into an orgy of impiety and degraded vice. Yet, crafty as he was, he thought it advisable, in order to save his face before the world, to make certain gifts to charity, and in that way he obtained before many people in the world the reputation of being an excellent father. All the blame was thrown upon the children. He was regarded as a saint abroad, a devil at home.

Among these children, brought up in such unloving surroundings, breathing nothing but hate and hearing nothing but bickerings, was the wonderfully beautiful Beatrice. When at the age of sixteen she left the convent school where she had been educated, she had all the qualifications of a noble Roman lady. Even the vulgar Francesco must have had a certain momentary pride in his beautiful daughter. She was intelligent, her judgment was sure, and for that reason, and also perhaps because he saw that she had a violent, energetic temperament similar to his own, he made her his favorite and gave her the management of the palace even in preference to this oldest daughter, Antonina, and his second wife, the poor, miserable weakling of a Lucretia, who was very soon to be engaged in plotting his murder. This Lucretia Petroni, whom he took as his second wife in 1593, was also of a distinguished Roman family. Left a widow with nine children, and with very little to support them, she had accepted Francesco Cenci, not out of any love for him, for she knew his horrible character, but merely as a financial investment. He had promised to pay for the upbringing of her children, and in an evil day she had married him. She had little intelligence and no will of her own, and so was hardly the one to cope with the cruel and crafty lord of the palace. She soon paid dearly for the wealthy match with the loss of her liberty. Francesco became viler and rottener than ever, an addict to such unmentionable vices that it is the best charity to him to maintain that his mind was affected. Evil as he himself was, he fancied that everybody else was just as evil. He became obsessed with the idea that some of his victims were trying to poison him. For that reason he was constantly changing his servants, changing his place of residence, hiding himself from the light as if there were a curse upon him. He accused his own son Giacomo of attempting to poison him and summoned him to court to answer the accusation. But Giacomo, though capable of committing such a crime, was found not guilty. Francesco of course hated his sons more than ever after that, and when some time

afterwards another son, Rocco, was killed in an ugly
street brawl, Francesco declared that it was a judgment of God in his favor. The sons would not tolerate
such cruelty; they fought hate with hate. But poor
Beatrice, turned from the quiet of the convent school
into this home that was more like a Hell, had to bear
all the miseries which her father could not inflict upon
anyone else. All in all it was a hating, fighting family
that seems from start to finish to have been possessed
by the devil. If any man ever deserved a miserable
death it was this noble, Francesco Cenci. And this
should be borne in mind in considering the hate-engen-
dered crime that finally brought the fair head of
Beatrice to the block. No one can condone the terrible
deed, but the crimes of the murdered father, his cruelty
to his own flesh and blood, can help to explain the
answering hate that could be sated only with the blood
of the hated thing.

As the days went on, fate too went on driving to the
tragedy. Francesco seemed to take a perverse delight
in persecuting his children and in proving by his tyranny
that he was the master of the house. His heart became
harder every moment. He seemed bent on the ruination of his own line. The two oldest sons, Giacomo
and Cristoforo, noting with alarm his wild spending
and the heavy fines exacted for his crimes, attempted
to have him legally restrained from wasting the family
fortune. They were considering, too, their sister
Beatrice, who, they argued, should be now given in marriage and with a dowry as big as that which Antonina

had received on her marriage. These legal proceedings were not calculated to soften the heart of Francesco, who could not bear that anyone could presume to dispute his will.

Francesco, in his bitterness at the action of these sons who had fled from his wrath, decided to leave Rome His daughters Lavinia and Antonina were married; the two younger sons, Paolo and Bernardo, were at school; and besides that he himself was unwell, suffering from a fever. There was nothing now to keep him at Rome where he felt the animosity of his neighbors and the disgrace of the vile crime of which he had been convicted, so one day in April, taking with him his wife, the unfortunate Lucretia, and his daughter Beatrice and two servants, he set out for the castle of Petrella, giving the women to understand that they were merely going on a pleasure trip; otherwise they would not have left Rome.

The castle of Petrella was the property of Marzio Colonna, and it was from this nobleman that Cenci had obtained permission to live there. Francesco must have chuckled to himself at the thought of the surprise the women would get when they saw the castle, which was in aspect, as it was to be in reality for them, a prison. Their hearts, indeed, sank when on the following day they found themselves in the gloomy fortress to which they had been actually lured. To Beatrice especially, just beginning to live, it must have seemed like the entrance to her tomb. She who longed to get away from the vile being who called himself her father, who yearned to be married the same as her sisters, now saw all her hopes deferred, perhaps gone forever. Her father had squandered fortunes to gratify his passions and to buy indemnity from the law, but he was too miserly to provide her with the necessary dowry.

The castle of Petrella was soon to be the scene of one of the most infamous crimes in all history, and the very first person Beatrice met as she entered under the shadow of its walls was the one man destined to serve as the instrument of her hate. This was Olimpio Calvetti, the governor or castellan of the castle, a position which he held due to the kindness of Colonna, who had taken an interest in him. He was then forty-five years of age, a tall, handsome fellow with black hair, black eyes, black beard and moustaches, and so well preserved in spite of the hard life he had led that he looked much younger than he really was. Originally a tailor by trade, he had served as a soldier and had fought at the famous battle of Lepanto. His life as a soldier had made him insolent and sanguinary, and he had even killed his man, not a strange thing in those days. After his release from prison on this occasion, Colonna, with whom he had served in the army, made him the keeper of Petrella, and thus got him away from Rome, the scene of his troubles. But the change of scene did not change his heart. Soon after that he killed another man and was condemned to death; but Colonna again had him freed and brought him back to Petrella, where he married a girl named Plautilla and by whom he had two children, a daughter Vittoria, now four years of age, whom he idolized, and a son Prospero. Olimpio was contented and happy enough with his wife and children till the Cencis, and especially the beautiful Beatrice, crossed his path. The devils that had been driven out of his soul returned with legions and destroyed him. Olimpio lost his soul* as well as his head through his unholy love for Beatrice.

Francesco Cenci remained at Petrella about a month, and then, perhaps because he found the life there too boring for one of his propensities, made a journey to Rome. As soon as he had left the castle the poor, persecuted, pining women got in touch with friends at Rome and begged them to help them escape from their living grave. Francesco somehow got wind of their appeals and when he returned to the castle he determined that the women should have no further communication with their friends, so he actually turned the castle into a prison, fastening the doors and the windows day and night, and arranging the apartments of Lucretia and Beatrice in such a way that they could have no association with anyone else in or about the castle. He threatened Beatrice with violence if she made any effort to get away or if she made any complaint about him, and then, confiding the keys to the eldest of the servants, he set off for Rome again, summoned thither by business with his creditors. No doubt he flattered himself that this time he could go in peace, seeing that he had made things so secure at home.

The petty persecution and the imprisonment affected the two women differently. Lucretia wept at the indig-

---

* See the footnote on p. 145. —*Publisher*, 2006.

nity, but she soon resigned herself to her fate. She was the kind that would silently bear a lot of abuse for the sake of a home. But not so with Beatrice. She was young, full of life; she was deprived of all the pleasures which a girl in her station had a right to look for. The stillness of the castle increased, and with it her hate for her father. She did not regard him as her father, but as a tyrant, a jailer, her avowed enemy. Petrella was indeed a jail. Not even the servants could stand it. They left, others came, and these too left after a short experience. But the daughter of the house did not have the liberty enjoyed by the servants.

The girl dwelt upon her unhappy lot so long and so bitterly that at last she determined she would stand it no longer. She would escape and go back to Rome to the protection of her friends. To this end she sought to enlist in her aid Marzio Catalano. He was a coppersmith by trade, but was in reality a jack-of-all-trades. He was a happy-go-lucky creature. He could sing and dance and play several instruments, and was something of a wandering minstrel, playing on the streets for the people to dance and even bringing his music to the castle of Petrella, in the hope of picking up a little money for the support of his wife and family. His coming to the castle seemed providential to the suffering Beatrice. She confided in him. She urged him to help her escape, promising that she would richly reward him for his efforts, and even threatening that if he did not help her she would settle the matter by killing herself. But he refused to take part in such an affair. He dreaded the anger of the Cenci and the Colonna, but he was willing to go as far as to carry letters to her brothers in Rome. Beatrice grasped at this poor straw. She wrote a pitiful letter to her brothers urging them to rescue her and her stepmother from their living death. But again this plan was fated to fail. She was betrayed. Francesco in Rome got wind of the letter, and, boiling with wrath, hurried back to Petrella to have his vengeance. He beat and whipped Beatrice unmercifully, and then threw her into a room where he kept her a close prisoner for three days. Three days more for the girl to nourish her hate. "I will make the lord Francesco repent for the blows he has given me," she said to Lucretia. And she meant it. She was biding her time. The new servants left, and none could be found willing to take their place. Francesco cared little about the lack of servants, for he had these two women, his wife and daughter, to be his slaves. It would humiliate them all the more. Slavery it was, degrading slavery. He was brutal, filthy in his personal habits, living more like an animal than a man, and even though the priests from the church in the village came to say Mass for him every morning in the castle chapel, it was more a matter of routine and outward show than anything else, since Francesco had very little true religion in his whole makeup.

Meanwhile Beatrice thought of but one thing—to have her father dead. It became an obsession with her. She was the power of vengeance in the whole miserable business. Hers was the dominant will that persuaded the others even against their better nature to stain their hands with blood. And first of all her victims was Olimpio. The gallant swashbuckler pitied the wretched girl, and pitying her he soon grew to love her, or to develop an infamous passion for her.

Beatrice, whether she lured him on in order to gain domination over him and thus compel him to do the murder for her sake, or whether she developed a criminal passion for the handsome soldier, soon made him forget his wife and his idolized children. She showed, that, much as she despised and hated her father, she was his true daughter. The moral law had little appeal to her and she was soon in an adulterous union with Olimpio, and with such abandon on the part of both that Plautilla, naturally jealous of her attractive husband, and many others in the valley were soon aware of it. Beatrice was far from being the "Roman Virgin" which the enemies of the Pope have continued to call her. There is little choice, in a word, between her and Francesco, though he has received all the odium and she all the sympathy.

About this time another one of Francesco's sons, Cristoforo, twenty-six years old, was killed in an ugly brawl over a woman, and Francesco brought the younger sons, Bernardo and Paolo, to be under his eye at Petrella. But almost immediately they escaped the prison, while the father vainly pursued them. His discomfiture did not make him feel more kindly toward Beatrice, who thought she saw a way out of the diffi-

culty. It was a time when the country districts were
infested with bandits, though Sixtus the Fifth had done
much to put down their lawlessness, and Beatrice and
her fellow conspirators conceived the idea of arranging
matters so that Francesco would fall a prey to these
marauders; but it was too uncertain a plot and was at
once given up as hopeless. Whether Francesco suspected the liaison of his daughter with Olimpio, or
whether he feared that the soldier might be induced
to aid her to escape, he ordered him to leave the castle
and never come back. Olimpio obeyed, as he could do
nothing else, but his passion for the girl was too strong
and too flattering to his vanity, and so he continued to
visit her clandestinely by means of ladders which he
contrived. Their meetings night after night were not
merely love trysts. Beatrice knew that Olimpio was a
slave to her charms, and she decided to use him as the
instrument of her vengeance. She drove him on to the
murder. She promised to make him wealthy, to make
him a great personage, to aid in educating his little
daughter Vittoria. It was a rosy future she painted
for him and his family, and all he would have to do
was to kill a tyrant that deserved death. Lust and
romance and ambition took possession of Olimpio's
soul. That is one of the horrible charges to be made
against Beatrice Cenci, that she hopelessly ruined the
man she professed to love.

Olimpio went to Rome and had an interview with the
three brothers of Beatrice. Giacomo, the oldest, hated
his father, as we have seen, but he told Olimpio to

go slowly as "the lord Francesco had seven devils like a cat." He, too, promised Olimpio a great reward if Francesco was put out of the way, but he suggested poison as the safest and easiest method. But when Olimpio returned to Beatrice with the suggestion about the poison she declared it impossible, since her father was so suspicious of everybody that he would never take a drink from her without first making her prove it harmless by drinking of it herself in his presence. No, there was only one way to get rid of him; he must be murdered in cold blood, and Olimpio must be the one to do it. She had even studied out the plan to be followed. They would murder him in his bed and then throw the body over the balustrade into the ravine below the courtyard, so fixing things that the impression would be given that he had fallen accidentally. Olimpio agreed. He even wanted to do the murder alone, but Beatrice insisted that Catalano should take part in it, so that being implicated in the crime he would be compelled to keep his mouth shut and not betray them. Catalano, however, was not keen about being mixed up in the affair, even though Olimpio made him promises of all sorts of rewards. His better nature, for he was not essentially evil, made him hesitate, and he tried to dissuade Beatrice, telling her what an enormous sin it was for her to kill her father. But she coldly and insolently replied, "Of that I will render an account to God." And the poor music-maker agreed to help in the murder.

On the night of Sunday, September 6, 1598, Olimpio

and Catalano entered the castle by means of the ladders, while Francesco was asleep. Beatrice met them. She was calm. She told them that she would give her father some opium in his drink, and that while he was under the power of the drug they could despatch him. Lucretia, she said, was a party to the plot. She hid them in the castle for the night, and was so lost to decency that she entertained her lover, Olimpio. But the opium did not have the desired effect, and again it was necessary to put off the hour of the crime. Fate was trying its hardest to save the miserable Francesco.

Olimpio's jealous wife, worried over his long absence from home, came to the castle seeking him. Indignant at her spying, he followed her home and beat her, but that night he returned to the castle again, slave that he was to the charms of Beatrice. Meanwhile Lucretia and Catalano had discussed the matter and had agreed to have nothing to do with the murder. Beatrice, however, scorned such weakness. Nothing would change her mind. Once more everything was set for the crime, and then Lucretia remembered that it was the feast of Our Lady's Nativity. Already the church bells were ushering in the festal day, and again she made time by persuading the others that it was unseemly to do such a crime on such a feast! Olimpio and Catalano, perhaps disgusted with such wavering, perhaps glad at being prevented, left the castle and even took the ladders with them, for they had decided to have nothing to do with the crime, much to the displeasure of Beatrice, who loaded them with abuse for their cowardice.

But scarcely was Olimpio home and in bed than he began to think of the girl he loved. No more dallying. He would prove his love for her by doing as she wished. At four o'clock in the morning he arose and dressed, then hurried to the house of Catalano and aroused him. The poor Catalano did not want to go but he was weak in the hands of the masterly Olimpio, and at last he suffered himself to be persuaded. They hurried to the castle, entered it in the usual way by means of the ladders, and awakened Beatrice, who was surprised to see them back. Little time was lost in talk. The deed was to be done and done quickly before another change of heart. The two men entered the room where Francesco was sleeping, while the women, Lucretia and Beatrice, remained in the ante-chamber. Olimpio threw himself upon the sleeping man and hit him again and again with a hammer, while Catalano with a rolling pin beat the victim's legs and prevented him from rising. The murder was over in a few minutes, and Olimpio and Catalano came from the chamber of horrors, saying to the waiting women simply, "It's done."

Feverishly then all four worked to remove the traces of the actual crime. A hole was made in the floor of the terrace to make it appear that it had given way as Francesco was walking there, and then they took the corpse from the bed, now saturated with blood, and pushed it down the hole. The men then hurried from the castle to their homes, while the women busied themselves in trying to remove all traces of the blood, a thing in which they failed miserably. But as soon as the cleaning was done, as they believed satisfactorily, they proceeded to give the alarm, and very soon the castle was filled with the people from the village, among them the three priests of the village church, all listening intently to the details of the accidental death of Francesco Cenci.

At first the story told by the women was accepted without question, but those who observed all the details a little more closely had their own suspicions. But for a while these whispered suspicions did not start any action. Francesco was hurried away to be buried, almost with indecent haste, Olimpio taking it upon himself to be the master of ceremonies. He could not get Francesco buried quickly enough, a circumstance that later worked against him. The brothers in Rome were sent for, and they came to bring Lucretia and Beatrice away from the scene of horror. It was remarked that they did not even visit the tomb of their father, and that also was set down against them for the day of reckoning. Back in Rome, all went to live in the Cenci palace, all breathing a sigh of relief that Francesco was buried deep, and without any suspicion as to the manner of his death. They were all safe, safe now from the tyranny of Francesco, safe from the prying eyes of justice. And Olimpio, the servant, now raised to the level of the nobles whose lives he held in his hand, acted as if he were the head of the Cenci family.

But they were not as safe as they imagined. There were so many suspicious circumstances about the case that rumors began to spread in the country and later in Rome, and so persistent were they that an investigation of the crime was begun on November 5. No need to go into the details of the investigation. The one thing that we note is that Beatrice made a very bad impression on the authorities. She was bold and even insolent, showing plainly her resentment at being questioned at all about the death of her father. But this insolence, this attitude of injured innocence, did not help her case. The investigation dragged along to February 3, when Catalano, put to the torture, confessed his part in the crime and reconstructed the scene of the murder. It was a sorry day for Beatrice when she had insisted that he should be implicated in order to make him keep his mouth shut. But in spite of this damning confession Beatrice would admit nothing and was as arrogant and insolent to the court as Francesco had ever been. No doubt she felt confident that nothing could convict her. If only Olimpio would get away before they tortured him into a confession of guilt! Olimpio, seeing the danger, did flee, but Giacomo, knowing that none of them would ever be safe as long as Olimpio lived, hired assassins who hunted him out and put him to death. Another sigh of relief for the Cenci; dead men tell no tales. But in spite of the disappearance of Olimpio the investigation went on inexorably. Giacomo and Lucretia were put to the torture and at last they confessed their part in the crime, though attributing all the blame to Beatrice. But even in the face of these confessions, even confronted with the unfortunate pair, who accused her, she maintained her innocence. Put to the torture herself, she cast all the blame upon Lucretia and Olimpio. Her boldness all through the trial made many of her contemporaries believe that she was the personification of outraged innocence. The report of the torture she suffered was so exaggerated that the people regarded her as a heroine who was being hounded by the law for a crime she never committed. But the record of the trial when read in cold blood shows that she was convicted by all the rules of justice. Even her lawyer, Farinaccio, knew that it was a hopeless case, and knowing that, he sought to defend the girl by a tour de force, by maintaining that Francesco had violated her, and that to avenge her honor she had killed him. It was a popular appeal made to the prejudices of the crowd, but the horrible accusation against the dead man did not have a shred of real evidence. Beatrice did have a child, but the father of that child was Olimpio Calvetti. She was not then the "Roman Virgin" violated by her father, not the pure little girl over whom Shelley weeps, but an unfortunate woman who had cast away her virtue in the most horrible circumstances.

But the law had all the evidence before it, and according to that evidence, Giacomo and Lucretia, Bernardo and Beatrice, were found guilty. Poor Catalano had died in prison. The sentence was pronounced. Giacomo was to be beaten with a hammer in the same manner that his father had been killed, then torn with pincers, beheaded and then quartered. Beatrice and Lucretia were sentenced to be beheaded. Bernardo was saved from the sentence of death, although he was not aware of the clemency that had been extended to him until he was brought to the scaffold. The two brothers were attended in prison by members of the Confraternity of Mercy. They declared that they wished to die as good Christians. They heard Mass and received Holy Communion with great devotion. Giacomo went to his doom with a truly contrite heart. He was resigned to his fate.

But Beatrice, when the time came for her to prepare for death was the most resigned of all. The grace of God had touched her heart and she realized the horror of the crime she had committed. Yet with that realization there was the greatest confidence in the goodness of God. The journal of the Confraternity of Mercy recorded: "Beatrice when exhorted to put herself in the hands of the Lord, and confessed by our chaplain, said that she was happy to die as a true Christian, and abandoned herself entirely to His holy will, and asked pardon of God for all her sins." She asked to be buried in the chapel of San Pietro in the place chosen by the religious, and then sent a message to the Holy Father begging him, "that for the love of God he would do her the favor that her will would be carried out." In that will she left practically all that she owned to charity. One item is very touching: "I leave to Reverend Mother Superior, Sister Ippolita, nun in the Monastery of Monte Citorio, formerly my teacher, three hundred

scudi in money that she may pray God for my soul."
How the heart of the poor girl must have wept as she
thought of the happy innocent days under Sister Ippolita.

At the dawn of the day set for the execution Mass
was celebrated, and Lucretia and Beatrice received Holy
Communion with great devotion, and after that spent
the time in prayer and in helping each other to meet
their fate with exhortations to courage and fervor. The
decree of punishment was carried out with stern justice
in spite of all the appeals for clemency, and all went
to their death—Giacomo and Lucretia and Beatrice—
seeking to atone by their sorrow for the crime into which
they had been betrayed by their own hate.

Beatrice did not flinch even on the march to the
scaffold. So unmoved was she, so straight and unbend-
ing, so calm, that her very attitude of strength made
the weeping multitude of onlookers believe that here
was a virgin martyr going to a glorious doom. The
crowd pitied her, and with that pity came indignation
against all the authorities and especially against the
Pope, Clement VIII, for assenting to her execution.
But severe as the punishment was, the Pope could
hardly have done anything else. A man with the spirit
of St. Philip Neri, who had been his confessor for
thirty years, he was a good, upright, holy priest. Personally he would have been moved to compassion, but
the crime of parricide was so horrible that he felt that
justice demanded the punishment decreed.

With a light step Beatrice Cenci mounted the scaffold and calmly placed her beautiful head upon the block. In a second it was all over.

For several hours the corpses of the criminals were exposed, and thousands passed by in procession, giving their tributes of flowers and tears to the once beautiful Beatrice.

So passed the poor criminal, Beatrice Cenci, criminal in more ways than one, little guessing that other generations would use her tomb as the rallying ground to fight the faith in which she was glad to die. Spite of her crimes, one cannot but have pity for the hounded, tyrannized girl who fought hate with hate and gave her soul to vengeance. Criminal she was, but somehow the remembrance I like to keep of her is that of the lowly penitent in the prison cell, happy to die as a true Christian and begging God to pardon her sins. Great sinner, she was at the last a great penitent.

Chapter 12

THE PRINCESS PALATINE

"I DO not believe," said Cardinal de Retz, speaking of the Princess Palatine, "that Queen Elizabeth of England had more capacity for ruling a state. I have seen her in the midst of factions, I have seen her in the Cabinet, and I have found her everywhere sincere in conduct." Mazarin himself said of her and Madame de Longueville and the Duchess of Chevreuse that they were "capable of governing and overturning three kingdoms."

But it is not on account of her statecraft, her talent for political intrigue, that I choose to tell her story, but for the reason that she, at one time one of the most notorious women in France, became by the grace of God one of the most humble of penitents, to such a degree that at her death she merited having Bossuet preach what to my mind is his greatest funeral oration, even superior to that which he pronounced over La Vallière.

The Princess Palatine has been called a "genuine heroine of romance." Romance, true; but more than all a heroine of one of the finest spiritual romances ever written.

Anne de Gonzague de Cleves, Princess Palatine, was

born in 1616. She was the fifth of the six children, the second of three daughters, of Charles de Gonzague, Duke of Nevers, of Rethel, of Mantua and Montferrat, and his wife, Catherine of Lorraine. Hers was an inheritance of noble blood from generations past, although noble blood and noble lineage did not always insure happiness. Charles de Gonzague was a strange character. Though a very fine Catholic, even devout, his ideas were chimerical. He founded an order of chivalry and even built an Armada against the infidels, which was, by the way, destroyed by fire in a day. He was always a disturber in French politics.

While Anne was still very young, no more than two years of age, her mother died, in 1618, and the father arranged for the care of his children as best he could under the protection of Catherine de Gonzague, Duchess de Longueville, the mother-in-law of the famous Madame de Longueville. Marie, the oldest girl, remained under the care of the Duchess; Benedicte, the youngest, was sent to the convent at Avenay, where, according to the strange abuse of the time she was made abbess at an age when, says Bossuet, "her cross was but a play-toy in her hands"; and Anne was sent to the convent of Faremontier. There in this retreat of holiness under its holy abbess, Françoise de la Chastre, she remained twelve years. "No plant," says Bossuet, "was cultivated with greater care." These were the happiest years of the girl's existence, for she loved the religious life, and in spite of her subsequent wanderings and sins it left an indelible impression on her.

At the end of her stay at Faremontier she went to Avenay to live with her sister Benedicte, the abbess, who in spite of the strange way in which she had been appointed to the position was, indeed, a model of every virtue. Anne loved her sister Benedicte better than anything else in the world. And Avenay made such an impression on her that she thought very seriously of becoming a religious. This would have pleased her father anyway, for he had destined his two younger girls for the cloister—he had "immolated" Benedicte, says Bossuet, in order to make easier the worldly advance of the family in the person of Marie. Marie was a great beauty and evidently of great ambition. The Duke of Orleans, the brother of Louis XIII, had wanted to marry her, but the Queen, Marie de Medici, who was Marie's godmother, had other plans for her son, and in order to prevent the marriage she contrived to have the girl sent as a kind of prisoner to the castle of Vincennes. It was a successful ruse on the part of the Queen, for the Duke soon forgot the girl he had pretended to love. Marie was full of the world. Like her father she believed that her younger sisters should take a back seat and let her dominate the stage. Later on she was greatly loved by the famous Cinq-Mars who was beheaded for treason. In spite of all her plans to get a great husband, it seemed as if she were destined to be disappointed, when to the surprise of all she succeeded in getting a throne by marrying the King of Poland. When the King, Wladislas, was looking for a wife, the pictures of Marie and her sister Anne were sent to him. He liked Anne's picture best, but he ended by choosing neither one of the sisters. He married another noble lady. When this first wife died, however, he came back to Marie and married her. The wedding is described in all the memoirs of the time as a magnificent affair. After the death of Wladislas Marie married his brother and successor to the throne, Jean Casimir, in 1648. It may be said in passing that she made an excellent queen and was truly one of the illustrious women of the century.

All this, however, is anticipating. In 1637 the father of the girls died, and Anne and Benedicte were recalled to court from their convent home to settle up his affairs. Benedicte was considered as the one best fitted to reconcile the various interests of the family. Anne was then twenty-one and remarkably beautiful. She soon forgot the convent and her desire to be a nun, especially when she met Henry de Guise. Henry had been named to the archbishopric of Reims, at the age of fifteen—another abuse of the times—but of course had never taken orders. He first fell in love with Benedicte but dropped her as soon as he set eyes on Anne. He was something of a scatterbrain, but adventurous and a brave soldier. After the death of his father he succeeded as Duke de Guise and gave up his archbishopric, which he had held only in name. He conquered Naples and then went to Germany. On his return to France he found that his first love, Benedicte, had died. Anne was more beautiful than ever. He persuaded her to marry him and went through some kind of ceremony with her. Then he was off to Flanders to the service of the German emperor. Anne, really believing that she was his wife, disguised herself by dressing as a man and followed him. She called herself Madame de Guise and referred to the Duke as "my husband." But she soon realized that she had been duped. While she was at Besançon and he at Brussels, she learned that he had married the Countess de Bossut. But the Duke soon abandoned the Countess, too. Anne, however, refused to be crushed. As if nothing had happened, she returned to Paris and resumed her old name of Princess de Gonzague.

In 1645, the same year that her sister Marie married the King of Poland, Anne married Prince Edward, son of Frederick V, Elector of the Palatinate and King of Bavaria, who at the famous battle of Prague, in 1620, had lost the throne of Bohemia, and of Elizabeth Stuart, daughter of King James I of England. They were a strange family, all of them adventurers and some of them pirates. Edward was a Protestant, if he was anything at all, but Anne succeeded in converting him as well as his sister Louise to the Catholic faith. Anne married secretly and without the consent of the court and was therefore in disgrace, but the Queen of England patched up matters for her and she took her place at court with her very ugly and very jealous husband. She was a great success. As Bossuet says, "The court never saw anything more engaging, and without speaking of her penetration, of the infinite fertility of her expedients, all ceded to the charm of her association." Anne soon became one of the most ardent and most intriguing politicians at court. She was noted for her loyalty to her friends, and was adept in conciliating opposing interests. The name of the Princess Palatine, which name she acquired by her marriage, is found very often in the memoirs of the time in regard to the important part which she played in the Fronde, or civil war, where she exercised the great influence which de Retz attributes to her. She and Madame de Longueville were ever close friends and coworkers.

Some time after the end of the Fronde, on March 18, 1663, Anne's husband died. She was then forty-seven years of age, the mother of four children, a son who had died in infancy and three daughters, one of whom married, in 1663, Henri Jules de Bourbon, son of the Great Condé with whom Anne had been associated in the civil war, and another, Benedicte, the Duke of Brunswick. The Queen of Poland adopted the daughter Anne and was arranging to have her succeed to the throne of Poland, but she died in 1667, before the affair was settled. A woman of forty-seven, the mother of married daughters, the Princess Palatine was old enough to know better, but soon she began to astonish the court by her evil life and by her loose religious opinions which she did not hesitate to express. She had many lovers and went all over the world, leaving, as one writer says, scraps of her virtue everywhere.

This wicked life continued for ten years. Her name

was a byword, and yet in spite of that she enjoyed great popularity. She had many good qualities—she was generous, liberal, grateful, faithful to her promises, and just; or as Bossuet puts it, "faithful to man, not to God." All the poets of the day wrote in honor and praise of her. She was called learned and literary, but nevertheless she was far from happy. Religion, that religion which she so loved in the convent days that she yearned to be a nun, was now a thing of the past. She confesses that she so lost the faith that she could hardly restrain her laughter when she heard anyone speak of the mysteries of religion. Religion as well as morality were a joke to her.

At times, however, the old faith stirred within her. Once she retired to the country to regulate her conscience and business affairs, and spent in charitable work more than a million francs. But she did not persevere in her good endeavors. Faith was gone absolutely. Called back by business to the court, she put aside all thought of her conscience. It was while she was in this unbelieving state that an extraordinary circumstance converted her. She relates it in the confession which she wrote at the request of Abbot de Rancé, the noted penitent of La Trappe.

One night she had a dream. It seemed to her that she was walking alone in the forest. She met a blind man in a little hut. She approached him and asked if he were blind from birth or if his blindness were due to some accident. He told her that he had been born blind. "You do not know then," said she, "the light which is so beautiful and pleasant, and the sun which has so much brilliancy and beauty?"

"I have never rejoiced in that beautiful object," said he, "and I can form no idea of it. I cannot but believe that it is of a ravishing beauty."

Then, changing his voice and visage, he said with a tone of authority, "My example should teach you that there are things very excellent and very admirable which escape our sight and which are not less true and desirable though we cannot understand or imagine them." Even in her dream she applied these words to herself, and so much was she impressed with them that when she awoke she knew that she was changed in soul. Her faith, that faith which she had said was impossible, had returned. She arose with haste, her heart filled with joy, and went to Mass. The Real Presence had been the hardest mystery for her to believe, but now she seemed to feel it. From that day forth her faith never wavered.

The hard task now was to prepare for her confession. It took her three months to get ready for the ordeal. So much did it prey upon her mind that when the day of the confession arrived she fell into a syncope, during which she says that she suffered the torments of Hell. Her confessor came, but she was unable to go to confession and was obliged to defer it till the next day. She could think of nothing but death and damnation. All hope had fled. And then God seemed to instruct her once more in a dream. In that dream she saw a chicken seized by a dog. She rescued the chicken and in spite of the efforts of the dog she clung to it and would not give it back. She applied the simple dream to herself, to her soul which God had rescued from the jaws of Hell. Immediately she felt a new peace and confidence in God. He would not let her be destroyed now that He had reclaimed her from sin. With that new confidence, with her faith and hope now alive once more as in the old convent days, she changed her life entirely. "No dress but simplicity, no ornament but modesty," says Bossuet of her. When she came back to her grand world, her conversion created a great deal of talk. Many, perhaps, thought it but a passing whim, but they soon realized how sincere the new penitent was. She told them all that she had renounced the vanities of earth forever. And she went so far as to renounce all the diversions of the court, even the most innocent. To her now all that was a waste of time. There was no room in her life for anything but the service of God and atonement for her sinful life. She began at once the rigid penance which was to continue for twelve years to the end of her days. She became essentially a woman of prayer. In her home one exercise of piety succeeded another. The hours of prayer were never changed for anybody and all the members of the household were obliged to participate. She read the Scriptures and pious books continually and kept an absolute silence as much as she could. She worked continually, making garments for the poor and linens for the altar. She was the soul of charity. She gave great alms and even went with-

out comforts herself in order that she might have more
to give to the needy.   Her pet charities were the care
of old women and the providing of dowries for marriageable girls.   Always her penances were most rigor-
ous, and in addition to these she was never free from
pain.   She suffered torments, especially in her last illness, when the pain was excruciating.   But she never
complained.   She felt that no suffering was great
enough to atone for her wickedness, and she sanctified
the pain by bearing it patiently.   And the soul suffered as well as the body.   She was afraid of sin, afraid
of relapsing, for she knew herself well enough to distrust herself.   Yet with all the distrust of her own
powers, she never lost her confidence in the mercy of
God.   "I am going to see how God will treat me,"
she said toward the end, "but I hope in His mercy."
The mercy of God—that was all that counted now.
"There is no more Princess Palatine," she said; "those
great names with which we deafened ourselves exist
no more."   And again: "I am going from these things,
I am carried by an inevitable force; all flees, all dimin-
ishes, all disappears from my eyes."

And at last the poor penitent, worn out by ill health,
worn out by her penances, died at the Palace of the
Luxembourg, July 6, 1684, at the age of sixty-eight.   By
her wish her heart was sent to be interred at Faremontier where she had spent so many happy days and
where she had wished at one time to be a religious,
and her body was buried in the chapel of Val de Grace,
by the side of her beloved sister Benedicte.

The funeral services were held at the Carmelites, and Bossuet preached the sermon, August 9, 1688, in the presence of many great ones of the court. It was the Great Condé who asked Bossuet to do this final honor to her.

So passed the niece of an emperor, the sister of a queen, the wife of a king's son, and the mother of two great princesses. "I wish," said Bossuet, "that all souls far from God, that all those who persuade themselves that one cannot conquer himself nor sustain his constancy amid combats and sorrows, that all those, in fine, who despair of their conversion or their perseverance, were present in this assembly. This discourse would make them understand that a soul faithful to grace, in spite of the most invincible obstacles, elevates itself to the most eminent perfection."

Bossuet was not the one to mince matters. Everybody knew that this woman had been a great sinner, and, instead of covering up that fact, he used it in order to draw a great spiritual lesson. "Let us," he said, "enter more profoundly into the ways of Divine Providence, and let us not fear to make our Princess appear in the different states in which she has been. Let those be afraid to discover the faults of holy souls who do not know how powerful is the arm of God to make these faults serve not only to His glory but also to the perfection of the elect. For us, my brethren, who know how the denials of St. Peter served him, how the persecutions which St. Paul made the Church suffer, served him, how to St. Augustine his errors and to all penitent saints their sins, let us not fear to put the Princess Palatine in the rank and to follow her even into the unbelief into which she fell at last. It is from that we will see her come forth full of glory and virtue, and we will with her bless the hand that rescued her, happy if the care which God took of her will make us fear the justice which abandons us to ourselves and desire the mercy which snatches us from it."

Chapter 13

MADAME DE LONGUEVILLE

THE contemporaries of Madame de Longueville referred to her proudly as "the most illustrious penitent in years." And even allowing a great deal for the fulsome praise of her Jansenistic admirers, who were grateful to her for the manner in which she had befriended them, there is no reason to rob her of the glory she acquired, not by her rank or by her meddling in affairs of state, but by her tears, her penances, and more than all by the crushing of her innate colossal pride. In her youth she was once very near to sanctity. Then came days when she almost lost her soul. Then the grace of conversion which made her an "illustrious penitent" in the eyes of the world. and at least a humble penitent in the eyes of God.

It has been said of the women of the seventeenth century that they were not less illustrious than the men. Anyway, however that might be, one had a right to expect great things from the daughter of Charlotte Marguerite de Montmorency. Charlotte, the daughter of the great constable, was the most beautiful woman of her time. Born in 1593, she was fifteen when she came to the court of Henry IV, who immediately fell in love with her. She had already been promised in marriage but the King broke off the engagement and in 1609 insisted that she wed his nephew, Henri de Bourbon, the Prince de Condé, hoping that thus she would more readily fall a victim to himself. But the Prince, sensing the danger and seeing the covetousness in the eyes of his royal uncle, fled with his bride to Brussels. Henry, indignant, moved heaven and earth to have the elopers sent back to his court, so madly was he infatuated with Charlotte, but before he could succeed in this new lust of his he was assassinated in 1610. The Prince, who had courage enough to defy a king in order to save his honor, returned to France immediately and took sides against the Queen Marie de Medici. It was a triumphal return, but because it was feared that he would claim the throne, he was arrested and thrown into prison, first in the Bastille and then at Vincennes, in which latter place he remained in captivity three years. He had been born a Protestant but had become a Catholic, and was, indeed, ardent in his new faith. He asked to have his wife share his prison with him, and it is surely a tribute to her loyalty and to her strength of character that, though she had little true love for him, she consented to his request and uncomplainingly shared his imprisonment till the end. It was while she was in prison that her daughter was born, Anne Genevieve de Bourbon, the future Madame de Longueville. Two months later the prisoners were released and took their place in the world once more. Two other children were born, the Duke d'Enghien, the Great Condé, in 1621, and the Prince de Conti, in 1629.

If Charlotte de Montmorency was beautiful enough to turn the head of a king, her daughter Anne was more beautiful still. It was considered compliment enough to say to the girl that she was as beautiful as her mother. In all the memoirs of the times that is one point that is never disputed. Even the women praised her beauty, and that is no faint praise. She had all the characteristics of true beauty—she was tall, of a fine figure, with blue eyes, golden hair that ended in innumerable curls, and a complexion that had the tint of pearls. And she knew how to carry her beauty. "She was," said one of her Jansenistic friends, "the most perfect actress in the world." Cousin describes her charm as "aristocratic nonchalance." She was a regal beauty, and more than that a regal lady. "This princess," said Rochefoucauld, who dropped her after she had sacrificed all for him, "had all the advantages of spirit and beauty to such a degree and with so much agreement that it seemed as if nature had taken pleasure in forming a work perfect and complete." Some one describes her as having the "bon air." "In her," says de Retz, "a particular charm made her one of the most lovable persons in France." "It was impossible to see her without loving her and desiring to please her," says Madame de Motteville; and finally the Grand Mademoiselle, who did not like her, admits that she was as "beautiful as an angel."

All these tributes of course were paid to her in her womanhood. But even as a young girl her beauty was remarkable. And yet with all that she was so unspoiled in her girlhood that she even wanted to be a Carmelite nun.

The religious life played a very important part in the France of that time. There had come a new religious spirit. New institutions of piety had sprung up. Richelieu, St. Vincent de Paul, Berulle, had done much for the revival of a spirit of faith. The Sorbonne, the new seminaries, reform in many directions, had contributed much to religion. And not the least of the forces that helped the Church were the Carmelites, established in France in 1602, and the Sisters of Charity, in 1640. St. Teresa had died in 1582, so that it was scarcely twenty years later that her spirit came to France. It was two princesses de Longueville who had been instrumental in bringing the Carmelites to France, and later on Charlotte de Montmorency was a generous patroness of Carmel, which was called "a little Heaven on earth." Naturally, then, the place was very dear to her. She had an apartment there where she retired very often for the purpose of making a retreat. Loving the Carmelite convent so much, she communicated her ardor to her daughter Anne. She brought her to the convent and had her go through the spiritual exercises with her. The young girl was very much impressed with the solemnity of the place. She became genuinely attached to it, and made many friends among the nuns, many of whom, by the way, had been great ladies in the world and bore the noblest names of France. Some of them were like Mademoiselle d'Epernon, who, says Mademoiselle Montpensier, "preferred the crown of thorns to that of Poland." Anne formed a lasting friendship with these holy women, a friendship that endured even during the days when she wandered far away from God. We may well believe that their prayers saved her at the end. But in those days she was very near to God and very near to the nuns. She was exceptionally pious, and would live at the convent for days at a time, following the rule and conversing only of holy things. Her mother gave many gifts and jewels and money, and Anne, too, found her greatest happiness in enriching the convent. Even the young Duke d'Enghien was not outdone by the ladies in generosity.

When Anne was about thirteen, her mother's brother, Henri de Montmorency, convicted of conspiracy against the throne, had been put to death by order of Richelieu. He had a happy end. "Father," he said to his confessor, "I pray you to put me at this moment in the shortest and surest path to Heaven that you can, having nothing more to hope or wish for but God." "I thank you, gentlemen," he said to the commissioners, "and I beg you to tell all of them of your body from me that I hold this decree of the King's justice for a decree of God's mercy." At least, in those days, everybody was eager to die well. Even Richelieu had said to his confessor, "Treat me as the commonest of Christians." When Henry de Talleyrand, Count of Chalais, very much of a freeliver, was condemned to death for plotting against Richelieu, he sent one of his friends to assure his mother of his repentance. "Tell him," she replied, "that I am very glad to have the consolation he gives me of his dying in God; if I did not think that the sight of me would be too much for him, I would go to him and not leave him until his head was severed from his body; but being unable to be of any help to him in that way, I am going to pray God for him." And she returned into the church of the nuns of St. Claire.

The Princess de Condé was crushed by the tragedy of her brother Montmorency, and Anne was so overcome that she wanted to leave the world at once. Her confessor, Father Le Jeune, S. J., a man of great piety, feeling that she had a true vocation, young as she was, advised her to become a Carmelite. But her father, as soon as he learned of her intention, put his foot down. It may be that he felt she was not sure of herself. Anyway he wanted her to know the world better before she decided to leave it. She must come out into the gay society of Paris. There was a great ball to be given at the time and he insisted that she make her debut at it. Anne did not want to go. She was full of the thought of the Carmelites. She went to them with her troubles, and asked their advice about her going to the ball. After much deliberation they decided that she should go since her parents wished it, but that under her fine raiment she should wear a hair shirt. They warned her to be on her guard. Anne put on her hair shirt and went to the ball, but with pride and self-confidence. Her beauty created a sensation. She was the belle of the ball, and what is more, she liked it. She was flattered on all sides and she liked that too.

She came from her first ball a different girl. She was still pious, she still loved the Carmelites, but she loved the world a little better. Gone was her vocation; gone, too, was the hair shirt.

That first winter out was one round of pleasure. The young girl delighted in the social whirl and especially in the social diversions at the summer place of the family at Chantilly, where youth and laughter had their fling. She soon became one of the most brilliant ornaments of the Hotel Rambouillet, the most noted of all the salons, where distinction of every kind was so well recognized for many years (1620-1648). It was there, it may be said, she received her true education. She was not a learned woman, she was intellectually lazy. While her brother, the Duke, was finely educated at the Jesuits, she, according to the custom of the day, received just such a smattering of education as her mother could give her. But she made the most of it. It was said that she conversed divinely; her sweet voice made up for much of the shallowness of her intellectual training.

But with all the gaiety there was still a deep spirit of religion animating the girl. Her friends were not all gay butterflies. Among them we note Mademoiselle de Vigean, one of the most beautiful girls in France, who later became a Carmelite as Sister Martha of Jesus. Anne's brother, the Duke, had against his will been persuaded for affairs of state to marry a niece of Richelieu, Mademoiselle de Brezé. All the while he was head over heels in love with Mademoiselle de Vigean. But she, knowing how hopeless the case was and disdaining to be the mistress of the Duke, fled from the danger and became a Carmelite, and a truly wonderful nun. Hers was not a singular case. In those days there were many striking examples of women who held their virtue dear. Catherine de Soubise, Duchesse de Deux Ponts, had replied to the dishonorable overtures of Henry IV, "Sire, I am too poor to become your wife, and too well born to become your mistress." So too Louise de la Fayette. At seventeen she was maid of honor to Anne of Austria. She attracted the attention of Louis XIII, but she was a girl of unimpeachable virtue. Richelieu showed his enmity to her, and she was so terrified that she fled to the convent of the Visitation, and despite the entreaties of the king she refused to return to the court. She founded later on the Convent of Chaillot, and as Mother Angelique died there in 1665. The story is also told of Madame de Soyon, how when the Duke of Orleans, for whose Duchess she was one of the ladies of honor, became infatuated with her she suddenly disappeared from court and shut herself up with the Carmelites, whence no persuasion or threats could remove her.

The great curse to Anne de Bourbon, as to so many French women who figure none too pleasantly in the memoirs of those days, was to be married to a man she did not love. At the age of nineteen she had been promised to the Prince de Joinville, son of the Duke de Guise, but he died in Italy. She was twenty-three when she married the Duke de Longueville, a widower, aged forty-seven, with a daughter as old as his second wife. It was the greatest family in France after the princes of the blood, but at that the marriage was something of a condescension on the part of the De Bourbons. But Anne felt that it was her duty to marry the man as long as her father had made the match. And she was apparently gay and happy enough. Her husband was a grand seigneur and a brave man. His morals, however, were nothing to brag about, for before and after his marriage with Anne he had carried on a liaison with the notorious Duchess de Montbazon, who of course hated the new wife with a hatred that was reciprocated. But Anne determined to make the best of it. She was a dutiful wife and in a few years she bore him four children.

In spite of the fact that she was something of a coquette and craved admiration, no breath of scandal touched her for a long time. Nevertheless hers was a precarious position. Beautiful, flattered, with a husband unfaithful to her, she at last began to fall in with the all too prevalent manners of the times. Knowing her charms, she began to play with fire and to try her success with coquetry.

She was twenty-nine or thirty when her husband was sent to Münster on a political mission; in the spring she followed him there, but in spite of the honors paid to her she was not very happy. While she was there her father died and she returned to France, glad to do so. It was an unfortunate return, for at this time she met the Prince de Marcillac, afterwards the Duke de Rochefoucauld, the man, vain, mean, cowardly, a slave to ambition, who was the cause of her moral destruction. Yet in all she might have remained a thoroughly good wife were it not for her overweaning ambition for her brother, now Prince de Condé. One of the bravest soldiers that ever lived, his great victory at Rocroy had made him so popular that Mazarin feared him. Anne was eager to enslave everybody to the cause of her darling brother. And with that ambition for him to shine, she also had an innate ambition to be something of a manager, a political force, herself. It has been said by some that her liaison with Rochefoucauld was more a matter of ambition than of love; others say that she really loved him and thought only of his glory. However that may be, it is sure that he did not really love her but only used her to advance himself. He was six years older than Anne, a fine soldier, a polished gentleman and of handsome appearance. He wanted to be avenged on the Queen and Mazarin. To do this he had need of Condé. His aim was to reach him through the sister whom Condé dearly loved. Win her, you won him, and so Rochefoucauld determined to get her, and succeeded. He was angry because he had not obtained from Mazarin the governorship of Havre or the command of the cavalry. He persuaded Anne to turn against Mazarin on the plea that that Cardinal had not given her dear brother all that he had merited. It was thus for love of her brother and for love of Rochefoucauld that she became embroiled in the Fronde or civil war.

She soon broke with her brother, but clung to her lover.

After the siege of Paris and the Peace of 1649, she demanded certain court privileges for him, privileges upon which he had set his heart, showing that she thought only of him and his interests. He had duped her. She was as putty in his hands. She had sacrificed all for him, duty, peace of mind, reputation. She had lost her soul to help him in his ambitions, and as soon as those ambitions were satisfied he, the selfish place-seeker, thought no more of her. She was too blind, however, to see that, and when later Mazarin revoked the privileges which he had granted, and war was on once more, she again took sides with Rochefoucauld, won over her husband to his cause, and finally succeeded in making her own brother a traitor to his country—and all for the sake of this sinful affection. When her brothers were thrown into prison she fled to Normandy, but even then was so under the power of her love that she went so far as to treat with the Spaniards.

The proud beauty who had once wanted to be a Carmelite had fallen low. How low is evidenced by the fact that when she returned to France she was unfaithful even to Rochefoucauld and entered into a liaison with the Duke de Nemours. The new love was of short duration, for Nemours was killed in a duel after he had abandoned Anne for another woman. But the Nemours affair played into the hands of Rochefoucauld. The latter had never really loved the woman who had sacrificed all for him, and now he was glad to break with her and get rid of her, since she could serve his ambition no longer. The noted author of the *Maxims* does not show up well in this affair. He was an ingrate; more, he was a cad, and when he wrote his *Memoirs* he tore to shreds the reputation of Madame de Longueville.

She was now a disillusioned woman, abandoned by all her friends. Her youth was gone; her beauty was going. When she was at a convent in Bordeaux, at the time she was waiting for the Peace, she wrote to her dear Carmelites: "I desire nothing so ardently at present as to see this war ended, to go and live with you for the rest of my days. . . . If I have had attachments to the world, of such a nature as you can imagine, they are broken and even crushed. This news will not be displeasing to you. I trust that in order to give me a feeling for God, which I have not yet, and without which I would nevertheless do what I have told you, you will do me the favor to write to me often and confirm me in the horror that I have for the world. Tell me what books you advise me to read."

Before this she had written other letters to them, once when she had lost a little daughter, and again when her mother died. When the Princess, the once beautiful Charlotte de Montmorency, was dying her thoughts were about the daughter whom she had trained so well, but who had brought disgrace on her name. She said to Madame de Briènne, "My dear friend, send word to that poor, miserable woman about the state you see me in, and tell her to learn how to die." In the letter that Anne wrote to the Carmelites asking for the account of her mother's death, she says: "It is in afflicting myself that I should solace myself. This account will have that sad effect, and that is why I ask it of you, for you know well that it is not rest that ought to follow such a grief as mine, but torment secret and everlasting; for this also I prepare myself, and to bear it in the sight of God and of those crimes of mine which have made His hand heavy upon me. He will perhaps find pleasing the humiliation of my heart and the chains of my profound miseries. . . . Adieu, my dear Mother, my tears are blinding me; and if it were the will of God that they should cause the end of my life, they would seem to me rather the instruments of my good than the effects of my wickedness."

All the while God was knocking at the door of the heart of the disillusioned woman. The thoughts of her pious, dead youth were haunting her. One day when she was speaking to the Abbé Tétu, one of her ladies handed her a book, which happened to be a pious one. The good Abbé complimented her on her choice of reading. "Alas," she said, "I asked for a book to take away my boredom, and look at what they gave me." "Madame," replied the Abbé, "these books sometimes take away boredom better than the others."

By order of the court she left Bourdeaux and proceeded to Moulins. From there she made a visit to the widow of her uncle, Henry de Montmorency, who had been executed. This excellent woman had on the death of her husband entered religion and was now superior of a convent. She talked with her niece and gave her books to read. She was an excellent religious and her example made a great impression on the sinner who was trying to find her way back to God. It was she who under God brought back the wayward woman. One day while Anne was reading one of the books which her aunt had given to her, the grace of God touched her troubled soul. "It was," she says, "as if a curtain were drawn from before the eyes of my soul; all the charms of truth gathered under one single object, presented themselves before me; faith, which had been so dead and buried under my passions, renewed itself; I found myself as a person who after a long sleep where she has dreamed that she was great, happy, honored and esteemed by all the world, suddenly awakes and finds herself loaded with chains, pierced with wounds, crushed with languor, and shut in a dark prison."

This was the decisive day of her conversion and she always kept it as an anniversary. Twenty-five years later she wrote to her confessor: "I count the years before men, but I do not count them before God, knowing that they are much more empty of good than the preceding years were of evil. I ask of you permission to wear two mornings between now and the second of August a cincture of iron to expiate both my present sins and those from which God drew me in those days."

Needless to say her aunt was delighted with the conversion and took it upon herself to guide her and encourage her in the way of penance. Anne remained ten months at Moulins and was then joined there by her husband, who brought her to Normandy. She was suffering in soul, paying the penalty of her sins. The *Memoirs* of Rochefoucauld appeared and humiliated her to the dust. But she would have no vengeance taken upon him. "I have so offended God," she wrote to her brother Condé, "that it is just He should punish me; and I see well that His chastisements are but designs of mercy on my soul." As yet she had no spiritual director and she wrote for advice on the matter to her aunt, also to the former Mademoiselle de Vigean and to Abbé, later Cardinal, de Camus. "God will lead you further than you think," he replied to her, "and demand of you things of which it is not yet time to speak to you. When we examine our conduct on the principles of the Gospel we find there frightful voids." The penitent woman thought and wrote of nothing but penance. Her husband thought that her conversion was but a passing whim but he soon discovered that she was very much in earnest. They had been separated for a long time but her conversion had established a new union between them.

It was then that she fell in with the nuns of Port Royal, who were later to be so mixed up with the evils of Jansenism. She made her general confession to Father Singlin, November 24, 1661, and she confesses to us that it was he who discovered to her her chief fault that had been the cause of her undoing—her colossal pride.

From the moment of her conversion Anne had given herself whole-heartedly to the practices of penances, but when her husband died, May, 1663, she threw herself even more eagerly into the work of punishing herself for her past. She built a little place for herself at Port Royal and divided her time between that place and the Carmelites. She was at Carmel when La Vallière entered, and it is said that none wept more bitterly than Madame de Longueville whose life had been as wicked as that of the King's mistress. She had plenty of troubles in those days. The bad conduct of her eldest son, the death of another son, the Count de St. Paul, who was killed in battle, a loss that crushed her—all these were troubles that she sought to sanctify as penances sent by God for her to endure. But added to these sorrows she wore herself out with instruments of penance. She always kept at hand some instrument of the kind. One day when she drew out her handkerchief her courtly friends were amazed to see an iron girdle fall out. But harder to bear than the instruments of torture was the humiliation to her pride. Her humility at the end was her true crown. She had plenty of enemies. Many had never forgiven her for the part she had played in the Fronde and for the destruction she had brought to many places in that civil war, although she had later sacrificed most of her fortune and even her jewels in order to make restitution. She heard of the insults that were heaped upon her name, but she said to God, "Strike again." One day when she was on her way to the Carmelites, she was insulted by an officer. Her friends were indignant and wanted to punish him immediately for the slur. "Stop," she cried to them, "let no one do him any harm. I deserve even greater insults."

There is no doubt that her penitential austerities hastened her end. She had always feared death and judgment, but she was calm when death came. She received the Sacraments with fervor and gave expression to her trust in Jesus Christ. She made her will, leaving much to Carmel and to Port Royal and to charity. She died at Carmel, that beloved Carmel which as a pious girl she had so desired to enter. She was there at last in peace after a stormy life. She died April 15, 1679, at the age of fifty-nine. The Bishop of Autun preached the funeral sermon. Her body was interred in the Carmelite convent and her heart was sent to the nuns of Port Royal. She had done much for Port Royal in the days of the Jansenistic controversy and had been instrumental in establishing the famous "Peace of the Church." A month after her death Port Royal was closed by order of the King.

Two days after her death, Monsieur de Pontchateau, a penitent himself, wrote: "Behold Madame de Longueville gone on the great voyage of Eternity whence there is no return. . . . I believe her happy and that God will show mercy to her. She greatly loved the Church and the poor, which are the two objects of our charity on earth, and I remember to have seen many of her letters in the beginning of her conversion which were full of sentiments very penitent and very humble. She had them, then, and the pains which she endured for the past year, served as penance."

We are told by one of her biographers that at the beginning of her conversion she slept on the bare ground, took the discipline and wore an iron girdle. "The body has sinned," she said, "let the body be punished." The day she died, her brother, the Prince de Condé, whom she had loved so well, came to visit her. The priest in order to increase her confidence in God's mercy recited the *Salve Regina*. When he came to the words, "And after this our exile," she struggled to rise in the bed and extended her hands toward Heaven. Then she struck her breast and joined her hands.

"I do not like exaggeration," wrote M. de Pont-chateau, "but it must be confessed that there was much of the extraordinary in the penance of Madame de Longueville, both as regards the body and the mind. . . . It is not that I wish to make out that she was a saint who has gone to enjoy God immediately upon leaving this world, but it is true that one will see few people of such quality embrace a life like hers, and abide firmly to the end in the great truths of religion, in a great contempt of herself, which was visible even in her attire and in a uniformity, as regards her essential duties, such as she has always displayed. She had her faults; who is without them? She saw them and mourned over them; that is all God requires of us."

There is a story that one day Madame de Longueville in the days of her sin met Father Le Jeune who had once advised her to enter Carmel. He had been absent for some twelve years on the foreign missions, during which time some of his fingers had been mutilated. She had told him that since she had seen him last she had abandoned herself to the depravity of her heart and that she doubted if she would ever be freed from the slavery of her sin. She asked him to say Mass for her and to tell her what God would inspire him to know about her. He answered her that she would one day be converted. Who knows how much the prayers of the poor, suffering missionary priest contributed to the reclamation of the sinful woman?

The epitaph on her grave in Carmel speaks of her conversion as "solid and entire." Another Magdalen had found her peace at the feet of the forgiving Lord.

Chapter 14

LOUISE DE LA VALLIÈRE

THE story of Louise de la Vallière is one of the world's great tragedies—a story of innocence, of lust, of royal ingratitude, of disillusionment, of penance, and —let us hope—of final sanctity. It is in many respects that of Goethe's Marguerite, but with a final touch of the grace of God such as Goethe could not imagine. Say "Mistress of the King," and you visualise the long line of abandoned women who made the Bourbon line a byword in history; but somehow I can think of La Vallière only as the golden-haired, blue-eyed girl, innocent of the world, powerless to cope with a corrupt court and a more corrupt king, and then as the austere penitent of the Carmelites, seeking to atone through thirty-six long years for her sins and for the scandal she had given.

It is not a pleasant story, much of it. Neither is the story of Mary Magdalen before her conversion; but through the weave of it all runs the golden thread of the mercy of God. Stones were cast at La Vallière as at Mary Magdalen, generally by those who were not without sin themselves, and just as the inspired writer did not hesitate to tell the story of the woman who had been a sinner, so, too, the Christian who knows

that "there but for the grace of God go I" can find
in the life of Louise de la Vallière the old lesson that
sin does not pay, and, too, that the mercy of God
endureth forever.

Louise Françoise la Baume de la Vallière was born
at Tours in the August of 1644. Her father was
Laurent de la Baume le Blanc, third Marquis de la
Vallière, the name being taken from the chateau of La
Vallière, a small property near Amboise of which he
was the governor. He was also distinguished for his
service in the army. Her mother, Françoise le Prevot,
was the daughter of a seigneur. Her uncle, her mother's
brother, was the bishop of Nantes, a prelate of eminent
piety, who resigned his see in 1677, and died in 1709 at
the age of ninety-three. It is well to remember this
background of piety and nobility in following the career
of Louise de la Vallière.

When she was about seven years of age her father
died, leaving to his family little more than a proud
name. The widow soon took as her second husband
the Marquis de St. Remi, an official in the household
of Gaston, Duke of Orleans, the brother of Louis XIII,
and consequently the family went to live at the court
of Blois or Orleans, where Louise passed the early
years of her girlhood with the younger princesses and
their famous step-sister, the Grande Mademoiselle de
Montpensier. St. Remi's daughter by a former marriage, a girl of fifteen, also lived there. Mademoiselle
de Montpensier says of Louise in those days that "she
was pretty." It was a monotonous little court, for the

Duke was at the time practically banished from the capital, but to Louise it was nothing short of Paradise. She was an unofficial maid of honor to Madame la Duchesse, who was very kind to her, and she had the pleasant companionship of the other young girls of the court. She was then a gay, care-free girl, happy with her flowers, her birds, her innocent sports. She was pious, modest, candid. Once when the young people at the court were conducting themselves unbecomingly, the Duke said, "As to Mademoiselle de la Vallière I am sure she has no part in it; she is too wise for that." But not wise enough to match the wisdom of the serpent; for into her Garden of Eden came the serpent in the person of the King. Louis XIV chanced to visit Blois when he was on the way to the frontier to claim the hand of the Infanta who had been chosen to marry him. The stop at Blois was a bore to him, and he and his party ridiculed the rough hospitality. He was, of course, not even conscious of the existence of the young maid of honor to whom he seemed like a being from another world. Even the Grande Mademoiselle said of him, "He is the handsomest man and the best made in his kingdom and assuredly in all other kingdoms." Needless to say, the young Louise fell in love immediately with the beautiful young god who never deigned to look at her, but, to give her due credit, she did not even guess that she was in love with him, the mighty king so far above her. All she would say was, "What a pity he is king!" It was but the awakening of a girl's life to the realization that there was

beyond her horizon a big world which made the erst-
while Paradise now but a lonely prison as the heroic
Louis passed on to claim his Infanta.

When the Duke of Orleans died, his widow and
daughters moved to the palace of the Luxembourg. As
a consequence of the removal the Marquis de St. Remi
lost his position, but in spite of that Louise continued
to live at the court of the Duchess. It was about this
time that Henrietta of England was married to the
King's brother, Philip of Orleans. Louise's dearest
friend, Mademoiselle de Montalais, had received the
coveted appointment of maid of honor to the Princess
and Louise wept at the thought of losing this dear companion, perhaps with a little feeling of jealousy that
she herself was not selected to enter the great world of
the court of Louis XIV. One day a distant kinswoman,
Madame de Choisy, wife of the Chancellor, found her
in tears and discovering the reason asked her if she also
would like to enter the household of the Princess.
Louise was overcome with joy; she smiled through her
tears as she manifested her desires. "In that case," said
Madame, "wipe your eyes, for all the arrangements are
not yet made and there will be room for you."

At the end of the fortnight the coveted appointment
arrived, and Louise, filled with joy, hastened to take her
position as maid of honor to Henrietta, who had joined
the royal court at Fontainebleau. Then she thought
that day the happiest of her life; but she lived to curse
it. She was at that time a very lovely girl of seventeen, of the same age as Henrietta, of a pure complex-

ion, large blue eyes, flaxen hair, beautiful in every way but quite unconscious of it since she possessed an unaffected modesty and was timid and retiring; in a word Louise was a simple, innocent, religious girl in love with life. But now this innocent, charming girl was suddenly thrown into a world of splendor, dissipation and intrigue; intrigue, indeed, that was her undoing. It has been said by many that Louise would have resisted the seductions of the court if she had had the right kind of mother, wise and virtuous. But all the Memoirs of the time admit that she was an intriguing, ambitious woman who was willing to use her daughter for the advancement of the family. But if she did scheme in this manner, her plans came to little, for Louise once in power sought nothing from the king for her relations.

Louis was already giving scandal to a court not easily scandalized by his marked attention to Henrietta, the wife of his brother. It was believed he was in love with her, and in order to put down the scandal his mentors decided that his attention should be diverted elsewhere, and consequently Louise de la Vallière was the chosen scapegoat. The whole thing is so nauseous it is hard to believe it. Indeed, it is hard oftentimes to get at the truth in the courts of the Bourbons. Louis XIV was vile. It is said that people forget what he did for France and remember only that he was a great lover. At any rate, love in those days was quite the *bel air;* it was a kind of religion, and the nation rather demanded that the king should be a lover as well as a warrior. Henry IV had set his seal upon it, and he was especially vile. Whether Louis XIV was the debauched thing he is represented to be we will never know. Much of it may be considered legendary. The Protestants hated him on account of the revocation of the Edict of Nantes, and the pamphleteers of Germany, England and Holland encouraged the legend of debauchery. But allowing for all possible legend the truth is bad enough. Fénelon said once, "God will have compassion upon a prince beset from his youth up by flatterers." However that may be, it was not at all necessary to turn the attention of the King to the beautiful Louise. He was then twenty-two, a fine dancer, a polished talker; in a word the cleverest man in his kingdom. He had been reared in the conviction that he would be the handsomest man at court and the most idolized there, and therefore he disliked and distrusted all those who competed with him in beauty, wit or intellect. Against such a man the little girl from the country did not have much of a chance. At one of the ballets given at Fontainebleau he appeared as Ceres—the Grand Monarch as a female impersonator!—and he prided himself on his achievement. To Louise he again appeared as a young god, one whom she loved to admire from a distance, never dreaming that he would ever condescend to notice her. If she had ever guessed the danger, she might have fled from it, for she was a deeply religious girl. But the damage was done before she even suspected the danger. The King chanced to meet her on one of his visits to the apartments of

Henrietta. Perhaps he fell in with the plot to use the simple girl as a blind for his unholy affection, but whatever the reason for the regard it soon developed into a real passion. Thenceforward he had eyes only for the poor little provincial who was scarcely more than a servant to Henrietta. It was the prince and Cinderella. Naturally the girl's head was turned by the realization that she was the chosen one. At one of the royal lotteries Louis won a priceless pair of bracelets. All the courtiers suspected that he would present them to Henrietta, but to their surprise he boldly gave them to the little nobody, Louise de la Vallière. The Queen who was present affected not to notice it. She retained her self-possession—it was an old story with her—and smiled sweetly, perhaps after all gratified that Henrietta was not the recipient of the King's favor. Louise wrote afterwards: "That confidence was a sad misfortune for us all. One tear from her would have saved me." There is no doubt that the girl was sincere and innocent. She had repulsed the Count de Guiche, she had repulsed Fouquet the superintendent of finance, but the King actually swept her off her feet. She had been at court scarcely two months when she became his victim. Immediately she was overwhelmed with remorse; the shame of her position prostrated her and she hid herself from the court as much as possible, fearing that her sin would be discovered. Somehow even at that gossipy court the liaison was concealed a long time. The disgrace of the famous Fouquet is said to be due to the fact that he sought to pry into the affair. The same Fouquet died in prison a true penitent. His mother, who was a very holy woman, threw herself on her knees the moment she heard of his arrest and said, "I thank Thee, God; I have always prayed for his salvation, and here is the way to it."

It should be said of La Vallière that all during the course of her sinful life she never succeeded in stifling her conscience. She was always awake to the horror of her position. And when in 1662 she refused to tell the King what she knew of the alleged relations between Henrietta and the Count de Guiche she took advantage of the storm that followed to flee to an obscure convent at Chaillot, eager to be rid of the intriguing court, and more eager, very likely, to regain her peace of soul. But the King followed her and insisted upon her returning to court. Mademoiselle de Montpensier described the affair thus: "All that winter (1661-2) there were many bickerings; the Queen Mother was very much disturbed over the love of the King (for La Vallière). Monsieur and Madame had the girl living with them; they were glad of it, although they had scarcely any part in it. I do not know what chagrin one day took hold of La Vallière. One fine morning she went away; no one knew where; it was Lent. The Queen Mother was so disturbed before going to the sermon, there was fear the Queen would notice something. The King was not at the sermon. The Queen went afterwards to Chaillot and the King went all alone, wearing a mask, to St. Cloud, where he knew she was in an obscure convent. The portress did not wish to speak to him. Finally La Vallière was induced to see him and he brought her back." The girl's enemies suspecting her great influence with the King sought to ruin her publicly by telling the Queen, Maria Theresa. Among these enemies was a niece of Mazarin, Olympia Mancini, whose sister Marie was the only one that the King had ever really loved; he had wanted to marry her—better if he had—but affairs of state had prevented the union. As a consequence of the publicity La Vallière was removed from the service of Henrietta and was lodged in a small apartment in the Palais Royal, where in December, 1663, she gave birth to a son, Charles, who was immediately taken by Colbert and given to two of his friends to bring up. The child, however, only lived ten months. Even though the secret was known to only a few, La Vallière knew that she was paying dearly for her supposed love.

But a change had gradually come over the girl. On her return to court concealment of the liaison was practically abandoned. She was now willing to brave all scandal, she who was by nature so timid and reserved. The reason for it was that she was consumed with love for the King. Within a week after the death of the Queen Mother, Anne of Austria, January, 1666, she appeared at Mass side by side with Maria Theresa, the queen. What a mixture of lust and religion! One finds it everywhere in the history of the Bourbons. Yet somehow with her the thought of religion was the dominant one, far as she was then from the thought of a true conversion to God. Even now the favor of the King was waning, all due, strange to say, to her inclination to penitence. She was not hardened sinner enough to please Louis. He resented her tears, her expressed regrets for her fall; she was getting to be something of a kill-joy. During the same month that the Queen Mother died she gave birth to a second child, the future Mademoiselle de Blois. Perhaps the death of the Queen Mother, Anne of Austria, had stirred up the religious sentiments of La Vallière. Anne had died of cancer. She suffered greatly but with Christian patience, trusting that by her sufferings she would expiate her sins. When dying she dismissed everybody saying that now she wanted to think only of God.

The King now recognized his daughter, Mademoiselle de Blois, by having her legitimated by act of Parliament; he also made La Vallière a duchess and conferred on her the estates of Vaujours. Again a son was born, Louis de Bourbon, afterwards the Count of Vermandois, who was also legitimated by act of Parliament. Though the children were brought up secretly under the direction of the Colberts, there was now indeed no secrecy about the whole horrible affair. The King idolized the children, but—the same old story of such unions—his affection for their mother was getting very cold. The unfortunate girl was never meant to be a grand courtesan like Pompadour or du Barry. She had, in spite of her wickedness, too much of the sense of sin. She could never forget her sin. It is said by some historians, in opposition to most of the memoirs, that her mother was a good woman and despised her for her

fall and was filled with bitterness toward her. Anyway
the King was tired of this recurring remorse. She
was not a politician; she cared little for affairs of state;
she cared nothing for literature and art; she was no help
to him as a ruler. She was rather a reproach to him
with her lamentations and he turned his attention elsewhere for a more companionable sinner. Even at the
time of the birth of her last son her place was already
filled by the notorious Montespan, who was continually
plotting to oust her. It was an unbearable position to
La Vallière, who did not seem to realize that she had
served the queen in the same manner. She was the
official mistress—what a title to take glory in!—but she
even had to share the apartments of Montespan at the
Tuileries where there was continual bickering and misunderstanding between the two women. La Vallière
thought she would die of grief. The discarded woman
saw her position in its true light, saw her horrible disgrace, saw that she had sacrificed her youth, her conscience, her fame, her peace, her mother's respect, and
all for nothing. The curse was upon her; she was
discarded. It broke her heart. The King found her
in tears. "Let there be an end of this, Madame," he
said; "I love you and you know it, but I will not be
constrained." And he even reproached her for not
being friendly with Montespan!

And then she turned to God with her broken heart,
not so much from sorrow at having lost God as at
having lost the King. Whether from pique or from
remorse, she determined to leave the court for good.

She left a note for the King: "I should have left the court sooner, after having lost the honor of your good graces, if I could have prevailed upon myself never to see you again; that weakness was so strong in me that hardly now am I capable of making a sacrifice of it to God: after having given you all my youth, the rest of my life is not too much for the care of my salvation." She left at six o'clock in the morning after having embraced her children. It was late in the evening when she arrived at the convent at Chaillot. She exclaimed to the abbess, who was a friend of hers, "Madame, I have no longer a home in the palace. May I hope to find one in the cloister?" She was conducted to a cell. But there was no peace in her heart, no rest. She could not pray. It was all a bit of hypocrisy. She still loved the King, and she still hoped that he would come for her a second time and lead her back to court in triumph. But Louis was no longer her gallant lover, much as he resented her retirement from court, which he regarded as a blow to his pride. Instead of going for her himself he sent Colbert and De Lauzun to fetch her. The King received her in the presence of Montespan and both wept over her and conversed with her an hour or two. The degradation of all three could hardly have been greater. "It is all incomprehensible," wrote Madame de Sevigné; "some say that she will remain at Versailles, and at court, others that she will return to Chaillot; we shall see." Indeed, everybody declared that she had acted foolishly, knowing that even though the King had wept over the return of the prodigal he would be very glad from that time on to get rid of her so long as he could save his own face in the matter. So she remained at court, "half penitent," as she said, but practically a prisoner of the King. She was detained there by his orders. He would not stand for any public penitents since such a course would be a reflection upon him and a humiliation to Montespan, who was now all in all with him. So La Vallière dragged out two years of this miserable existence, knowing that she was ousted and forgotten, yet hoping, hoping for a return of the love which had been all in all to her but only a mere pastime to the King. Even when her mother advised her to withdraw to her duchy of Vaujours, offering to bear her company and assist in the education of her children, the King opposed the program. She sighed for the convent cell of Chaillot, but he opposed that, too. He wanted no public scandal; she must remain at court and at least make believe that she was happy.

One day La Vallière accompanied the Queen to the Carmelite convent, and so deeply was she impressed with the life that she consulted her confessor as to the wisdom of her entering there. He urged her not to resist the grace. From that time on she took advantage of every opportunity to visit the convent. The sisters, unaware of the identity of the grand lady of the court, received her kindly. She shuddered, however, at the thought of entering the religious life. The world was a pleasant place and life was sweet. She was still young, she was very beautiful, she had her beloved children. To sacrifice all these was more than she could bear. On one of her visits to the convent she was accompanied by a friend who unthinkingly called her by name. Immediately every eye was averted and every lip closed, making the courtly sinner in her purple and fine linen feel herself an object to be avoided. It was another grace from God.

The more she thought about it the more she saw that she was called to a life of penance. One of her biographers, Madame de Genlis, describing the penitent life of La Vallière in the introduction to the *Reflections on the Mercy of God,* that simple and beautiful treatise which La Vallière was writing during these days when she was trying to make up her mind to go to the limits of the penitential life, calls her vocation sublime. She asserts that the humiliations and sorrows of abandonment never gave her the idea of embracing the religious life; that she wished to give a great example of atonement, to make to God a voluntary sacrifice, not merely to give herself to God out of despair. Her heart had been soiled by criminal passion and for that reason she desired to go into solitude, but she was humble enough to believe that she was unworthy to be admitted to the number of the wise virgins who had dedicated themselves in Carmel. She knew the need of purifying herself first. When she felt that she had succeeded in conquering her resentment toward Montespan she resolved upon dedicating her life to God. She confided her design to Bossuet and to the Marshal de Bellefonds, the latter of whom was very instrumental in fostering her vocation and to whom she wrote some of the most beautiful spiritual letters in existence. Her friends, as soon as they discovered her intention, tried to dissuade her. The King of course opposed her going to Carmel. He refused to believe in the reality of her vocation, and again he felt it a reflection upon his mode of life. Her children were also induced to oppose her going. She felt all the opposition keenly but it did not break down her resolve, even though she still clung to the world. Bossuet feared for her, and showed her the sin of her position and its great danger. But even Bossuet when he saw that she was determined to leave the court bade her wait a year, since he feared it was but another impulse similar to her former flights from the court.

The year was nearly over when she became very ill, so ill that she believed herself near to death, and was therefore full of regrets that she had not devoted her life to penance. During the sickness the King visited her and she realized that her soul was still exposed to terrible danger. It made her determined to break with the world once and for all. Again the King opposed her. He represented to her the austerity of the life in Carmel. He bade her choose a rich abbey, but she refused, saying that she could not govern others when she had not been able to govern herself. Even Madame Scarron, who as Madame de Maintenon later on married Louis, thought she was foolish. "Madame," she said to La Vallière, "here you are one blaze of gold— have you really considered that at the Carmelites before long you will have to wear serge?"

But she persisted in her endeavor. This time she

would not resist the grace. Already she was practicing in secret the austerities of the convent. It was no easy task, surrounded as she was by every manner of scandal, and even insulted on every occasion for her wish to rise above her sordid surroundings. During those months she arranged her business affairs quietly and devoted her leisure to the study of Latin, always reciting the praises of God in that tongue.

At last, on the twentieth of April, 1674, she left the court for good, and without a regret. The night before she went to take leave of the Queen and threw herself on her knees and begged pardon for all the sorrow she had caused her. The Queen embraced her tenderly and wept. Evidently Maria Theresa was a very forgiving woman. La Vallière then took leave of her children, a trial which put her desire for penance to a hard test. She had given her jewels to her children and to some of her dearest friends. She arranged for a pension for her mother and gave presents of money to her sisters and to her faithful servants.

She left Versailles in the morning after the High Mass, amid the tears of all. She embraced even her persecutors. "She seemed touched," wrote Mademoiselle de Montpensier; and then she added laconically, "She is not the first sinner to be converted." The King then bade her farewell. He watched her as with tottering step she entered her carriage, but he manifested no emotion. He was not keen about the whole proceeding. He considered that there was too much ado about the whole affair, creating as it did a public scandal, and he always had a horror of public scandals as injuring his royal dignity. He felt too that she was not in earnest, that she had been moved only by jealousy, that she was starring herself, and he could not forgive her for her public penance at the knees of the queen. Mademoiselle de Montpensier could write that the King came to Mass with his eyes red, and could quote Monsieur as saying that "We have wept very much," but it is hard to believe that there was any tenderness left in the heart of Louis for the woman whom he had destroyed.

The carriage of the penitent was followed by a great crowd, some admiring her for her courage in leaving a life of luxury for the cloister, others prophesying that she would never be able to bear the austerities of Carmel. But their fear did not frighten her; she felt only a deep spiritual joy. After all Carmel could bring her no greater suffering than that she had been enduring at court. "When I am in trouble at the Carmelites," she had said, "I will think of what those people have made me suffer." But while others might question her steadfastness, the great mind of Bossuet believed in her. "God has laid in this heart the foundation of great things," he said; "the world puts great hindrances in her way and God great mercies; I have hopes that God will prevail; the uprightness of her heart will carry everything."

On arriving at the grate where the superioress, Mother Clare was awaiting her, she threw herself on her knees and said, "My mother, I have always made such a bad use of my will that I have come to put it in your hands never to take it back." She was immediately conducted before the Blessed Sacrament where she spent some time in prayer. Her hair was then cut off at once and she was permitted to follow all the practices of the religious life. She begged permission to wear the habit even during her novitiate and did not shrink from any of the austerities of the convent. Even the hardest, most menial work was a joy to her. After such an earnest preparation she made her profession June 3, 1674, the Monday after Pentecost. She received the veil from the hands of the queen herself and sat in a tribune next to the queen while Bossuet preached the sermon. It was one of his greatest sermons and is always found among the choicest selections from his works. He said in part: "The world itself makes us sick of the world; its attractions have enough of illusion, its favors enough of inconstancy, its rebuffs enough of bitterness, there is enough of injustice and perfidy in the dealings of men, enough of unevenness and capriciousness in their intractable and contradictory humors—there is enough of it all without doubt to disgust us."

A year later she took her vows. Louise became Sister Louise of Mercy. Her life was always an exemplary one in the convent. Even Mademoiselle de Montpensier, who never seemed to care a lot for her, admits that "she is a very good religious." She was from thence on extremely pious and took to the life of penance courageously. The hard and narrow pallet, the fasting, the silence, all such a tremendous change from the luxurious life which had always been her lot, all these she bore with never a complaint. She felt herself unworthy of the high dignity to which she had been admitted. She had even wanted to be professed as a lay sister, but her superiors did not think she was strong enough for that life and so refused her the honor which her humility had desired. She was content to leave all the world behind her. Out of respect for the convent she did not even wish to have her children visit her, but the King over-ruled her scruples and made her see them. But their visits did not turn her aside from her vocation. She was consumed with zeal. She arose two hours before the rest of the community and passed that time in the chapel. She suffered from the cold, she fasted most of the time on bread and water, while the gentle hands that had once been adorned with jewels devoted themselves to the most menial tasks. It was a penance for her to go to the parlor when some of her friends came to see her. Even the Queen would come sometimes to talk with her, surely a humiliation to both of them. Even Montespan who had ousted her came with Madame de Maintenon to visit her. The former Duchess de la Vallière was calm during that trying interview. "I reflected," said Madame de Maintenon, "on Magdalen the sinner and Magdalen the penitent." When Montespan in turn was rejected by the King it was to her former enemy she came looking for consolation. No doubt it was the example of La Vallière in her penitential convent that later on brought the humiliated Montespan to make her peace with God and seek to undo some of the harm she had done. A more acceptable visitor to the converted woman was the famous Abbot de Rancé, himself a converted sinner and a great penitent, who came to the convent to encourage the new penitent in the hard life she had chosen.

La Vallière had left the world, but the trials of the world followed her even into the convent. First of all her brother died, and then seven years later her son, the Count de Vermandois, grand admiral of France. The young count, after the departure of his mother for the convent, became haughty and presumptuous and dissipated. The King finally had to banish him from the court. He repented, due no doubt to the prayers of his mother for him. He died suddenly while serving in the army, in 1683. Some writers maintain that he had struck the dauphin in a fit of temper and had been imprisoned for life, being the famous Man in the Iron Mask. Bossuet was chosen to break the news of his death to the mother. When he had told her the sad news she stood motionless for a while, her hands clasped, her head bowed. Then she rallied, and said, "It would ill become me to weep over the death of a son whose birth I have not yet ceased to mourn."

When in 1680 her daughter married the Prince of Conti, Armand de Bourbon, Madame de Sevigné wrote: "Everybody has been to pay compliments to this saintly Carmelite. I was there, too, with Mademoiselle. The Prince of Conti detained her in the parlor. What an angel appeared to me at last! She had to my eyes all the charms we had seen heretofore. I did not find her either puffed or sallow; she is less thin though and more happy looking. She has those same eyes of hers and the same expression; austerity, bad living and little sleep have not made them hollow or dull; that singular dress takes away nothing of the easy grace and easy bearing. As for modesty, she is no grander than when she presented to the world a princess of Conti, but that is enough for a Carmelite. In real truth this dress and this retirement are a great dignity for her."

Bossuet had said, "This soul will be a miracle of grace." It was a miracle of grace to herself that she who belonged to one of the most luxurious courts could live this life of hard penance for thirty-six years. And she lived it to the full. It was a life of work; working for the poor, night after night in the infirmary tending to the sick, lacerating her once pampered body, and above all praying. Every humiliation and fatigue brought her only joy. She was dead to her former world. As the King once said—he never saw her after she had left the court—"She was dead to me the day she entered Carmel"; and it might be said that she was likewise dead to everything else she had known in the world.

Madame de Genlis very touchingly describes her last days. "During the long succession of years which she passed in the cloister," she writes, "one always saw in her the same equality of disposition, the same sweetness; one never perceived in her conduct any effort, any struggle; nothing troubled the interior peace in which she rejoiced; sometimes melancholy but without depression, recollected and submissive without affectation, perfection seemed in her but a gift of nature, and such is the perfection that produces true piety; it is the fruit of a Divine grace. So many virtues ought to obtain the happiness which crowns them, that of a holy death. God prepared her for this last sacrifice by an increase of infirmities. She suffered in silence. Far from being tempted to complain, she smiled at the suffering; it was for her the presage of undying happiness ardently desired for thirty-six years! Erysipelas having attacked her leg it incommoded her a great deal, otherwise she would have said nothing; it was noticed at last and she was ordered to go to the infirmary. The mother superior reproaching her for this kind of excess, Sister Louise replied, 'I did not know what it was, I have not even noticed it." A few days afterwards she wished to leave the infirmary and resume her exercises of piety and her ordinary tasks; but one could see easily from her extreme weakness that she was nearing the end of her career. On the fourth of June, two days before her death, a sister who found her very much exhausted could not refrain from expressing her pain at seeing her in such a state. The holy penitent, lifting her hands and her eyes to Heaven, replied only in a Latin verse of a psalm that expressed the resignation of hope. The next day she arose at three o'clock in the morning as usual, but she was not able to go to the choir. A sister came upon her; she was not able to stand or to speak. She was brought at once to the infirmary. The doctors asserted that they would cure her, but she felt and declared that all remedies would be useless. She accepted death with a humble and peaceful submission, although it was accompanied by the most cruel sufferings. She repeated many times these words: 'To expire in the most excruciating pains, that is what is due to a sinful woman.' She passed all the day in this state without making a single complaint. The disease having made considerable progress during the night she herself asked for the last Sacraments. 'God has done all for me,' she said; 'He received formerly the sacrifice of my profession, I hope that He will receive again the sacrifice of justice which I am ready to offer to Him.' She confessed and received the holy Viaticum with the greatest presence of mind and all the most touching marks of piety. A little after she asked for Extreme Unction which she received with full consciousness. Madame the Princess of Conti was sent for and she arrived soon after to receive the last embraces of her mother and to taste the consolation of admiring the pure and perfect tranquillity she enjoyed. Several hours before her death the pains left her entirely and she expired gently at noon, June 6, 1710, aged sixty-five years, ten months, after having passed thirty-six years in the practices of the religious life and of an austere penance."

So passed the great penitent whom Madame de Sevigné had once called "the little violet which hid itself amid the grass." She was referring then to the La Vallière who had sold her soul for the love of a fickle king. But she was a better prophet than she knew. It was a poor withered violet that was transplanted to the garden of Carmel, but withered as it was, the dews of Heaven and the river of penitential tears made it at last throw forth a fragrance as beautiful as that which came from the alabaster box which another Magdalen once broke for the anointing of the Lord.

Chapter 15

MADAME DE MONTESPAN

THERE is very little of the lovable in the character of the notorious Madame de Montespan. One can almost weep over the wreck that La Vallière, the young girl of seventeen, made of her life—the little violet, as Madame de Sevigné called her, destined for the shade of the woodlands but torn up from its native soil and transplanted to the barrenness of Versailles, with its noxious vapors and its pitiless glare of blasting sunlight. La Vallière was a victim of circumstances. Montespan was a scheming woman, who sacrificed all the fine things in life, even a devoted husband, for a mean ambition. Her ambition eventually destroyed her, and we justly feel that she got all she deserved. Yet, we hesitate to condemn her without a hearing. Why cast the stone? Montespan sinned, sinned greatly and brazenly; some of the iniquity attributed to her is as incredible as the *La Bas* of Huysmans, which seems to have drawn on certain facts or legends in her life. But, incredible as her crimes may be, there is at the happy ending the story of the grace of God, the passion, so characteristic of Bourbon days, to die well. History says a lot about Montespan the sinner; it does not stress the point of Montespan the penitent.

Again, it is not always easy to get at the exact truth in Bourbon history. It has been said that under Louis XIV there was a "passion for personal narrative," when "princesses, warriors, statesmen, courtiers and beauties vied with each other in recording not only passing events, but also the individual passions, interests and prejudices by which they were influenced." But, eliminate the prejudices that describe Montespan as little short of a fiend, a sorceress, an addict to the iniquities of the Black Mass, and she is indeed bad enough; bad enough to be a shining example of the limitless mercy of God. To understand how a Montespan could die well, you must understand the heart of Christ—a thing that is easy and at the same time impossible.

Françoise Athenais de Pardaillan, Marquise de Montespan, was born in 1641 at the chateau of Tournay-Charente, the daughter of Gabriel de Rochechouart, duke of Mortemart. Little is told of her girlhood days except that she was educated at the convent of St. Mary at Saintes. At the age of twenty she was appointed maid of honor to Queen Maria Theresa, and soon attracted attention even in that brilliant court of Louis XIV. Madame de Sevigné says that she was surprisingly beautiful, highly cultivated and with all the proverbial wit of the Mortemarts. She was a brilliant beauty, blonde, with blue eyes and a perfect face; she was a cultivated and amusing talker, haughty and passionate, "with hair dressed in a thousand ringlets, a majestic beauty to show off to the ambassadors." Even the supercilious Saint Simon admired her.

In January, 1663, she married the Marquis de Montespan, who was a year younger than herself. There is
no doubt that it was a love match as far as he was
concerned, although much of his admiration was pride
in winning the beauty of the court. Anyway she did
not love him, and married him simply because she
was compelled to do so by her family. Even the birth
of two children did not bring her any affection for her
husband. It is said by some biographers that the fault
of her defection was due to him; that she feared the
influence of the King and begged the Marquis to take
her away from the court to his estates and that he
refused. But that is not true. She was not the kind to
run away from danger and from the possibility of
wearing a crown.

La Vallière was at that time the mistress of the King.
She and Madame Montespan had been girl friends, and
La Vallière, who felt that she failed sometimes to amuse
Louis, encouraged the visits of the dashing beauty, who
was all too soon to become her rival. Montespan evidently envied her old girlhood friend the doubtful honor
that had been conferred upon her, and in order to
attract the notice of the King put herself out to be very
nice to her. She sensed the situation at once; she
saw that La Vallière was not able to amuse the King
in his tedium and she determined to benefit by the
weakness. She played her cards well. The King
remarked how attentive she was to La Vallière, and his
visits to his mistress were always more agreeable when
the witty Montespan was there; while, on the other

hand, the apparent religious sentiments and strict virtue of the Marquise captivated the Queen, who was delighted that there was a good woman to hold the interest of the King against the La Vallière whom she despised.

The Marquis himself, who when all is said seems to have been a man of high honor, was disgusted with the position of La Vallière. Perhaps he sensed the danger to the mother of his children, and he warned her. But she was not the kind to listen to warnings, she who was devoted to the pleasures in a court that made pleasure its god. The Marquis succeeded to an inheritance in Provençe and begged her to go there with him, but she refused. It was too late now, for she had come to realize that the Grand Monarch was par-ticularly fond of her.

The King was then in the midst of military affairs. At the time he was thirty, brave and brilliant, handsome as a god, but wallowing in brutal lusts. In the Flemish campaign all the ladies of the court, including the Queen herself, accompanied him, and in this summer of 1667 his passion for Madame de Montespan began. During the campaign she was quick to ingratiate her-self, conciliating the Queen and gradually undermining her friend La Vallière.

But the Marquis was not fooled as easily as the Queen. He knew what had happened, and he wrote his wife a blasting letter, ordering her to confide their son to the guardianship of his messenger that he might not be contaminated by contact with a mother who had thrown off all restraint. He came to Paris and cited her before the courts, while at the same time he wrote a firm and reproachful letter to Louis. But the King could afford to laugh at the miserable husband. Was he not the King? The injured husband put on mourning, hung the carriage entrance to his house with black, put black livery on his servants, drove about the country in a mourning-coach, declaring that his wife had died of an attack of levity and ambition. All this of course much to the annoyance of the King. He even had the Marquis arrested but released him after a few days' imprisonment. We might have more pity for the Marquis if we did not know that he later accepted forty thousand dollars from the King to pay his debts. There were queer notions of honor in those days that were always boasting about honor.

Meanwhile a child was born of the adulterous union in March, 1669, and entrusted to the care of Madame Scarron, who was afterwards Madame de Maintenon, the morganatic wife of Louis. This child, the Duc de Maine, was for state reasons of succession declared legitimate by act of Parliament in 1673. Seven children in all were born, and the two who survived with the Duc de Maine, Mademoiselle de Nantes and the Count de Vexin, were also legitimized, and all three installed eventually at Versailles. The shame of the Grand Monarch could go no further. And the Marquis finally gave up the fight for his honor and retired to Spain, where he got an official separation in 1674.

But the haughty woman cared little about that. She

felt secure of her position. She paraded her favor, superintended the household of the Queen and even openly insulted her. "Pray consider that she is your mistress," said Louis reproachfully to her, but nevertheless he was madly in love with her, sought to please her in every way possible, made her gifts of money, jewels and even the glories of Versailles. She gambled inveterately. She lost and won four millions in one night's gambling. Louis paid her debts. One of her dresses was worth a fortune, but Louis would beggar his kingdom to pay for it. The wise monarch lost all fear of scandal. "La Belle Madame" was the real queen. She permitted herself liberties which displeased him; high-tempered, she quarreled with him time and time again and gave him such tongue lashings that the courtiers wondered how he could tolerate it. But nevertheless he loved her, or at least was her slave.

It was an epoch of brutal instincts, licentious writings, loose morals, gross language. The court and the city were dissolute and profligate. The very history of the times is soiling. And on the surface all was polish. Louis kept his sins as secret as possible. Even the Queen received the King's mistresses. It was all a game of bluff. She was not supposed to know officially of his misdeeds, while she ate her heart out in secret at the horror of it all. Hence the saying that Louis on the Flemish campaign was accompanied by three queens. Degradation could go no further, even though we are obliged to allow for all the Huguenot calumnies. Whatever decent instincts Louis may have once had, all were gone now. Montespan was the shame of his life. She tyrannized over him, she exasperated him with demands for money and places; he even had suspicions of her fidelity to himself. It was a degrading scandal.

Meanwhile the decent people at court were trying to stop the scandal. The Huguenots and the Jansenists condemned the King, and the Catholics resented his notorious life as a reflection upon their Church. Among the Catholics who sought to clean the Augean stables were Père la Chaise, the King's confessor, and Bossuet, the preceptor of the Dauphin; while Madame de Maintenon and others seconded their efforts. But Madame de Montespan affected to laugh at them all, feeling that she had the King in her power. But when the time of the Jubilee arrived, the very first sermon before the court was evidently directed against her. It was followed by other sermons, some of them so plain and pointed that the King was mortified at these public accusations against him. One must marvel at the courage of Father Bourdaloue. He took as topics for his sermons before the court, Impurity, Final Impenitence, Hell—all of which made even the Grand Monarch tremble.

The story goes that one day the King met a priest carrying the Blessed Sacrament to a dying officer. Louis, who, strange to say, always had a great devotion to the Blessed Sacrament—one always finds strange contradictions in the Bourbons—turned and accompanied the Host and was so impressed that he was immediately converted and resolved forthwith to separate from

Montespan. Whatever truth there may be in the story,
all the decent people tried to make him promise never
to see her again. Bossuet, who knew that Louis had
not lost all religious feeling, wrote many letters to
him urging him to the break. "Pluck this sin from
your heart," he wrote, "and not only this sin but the
cause of it; go even to the root. In your triumphant
march amongst people whom you constrain to recognize your might, would you consider yourself secure
of a rebel fortress if your enemy still had influence
there? We hear of nothing but the magnificence of
your troops, of what they are capable under your lead-
ership! And as for me, Sir, I think in my secret heart
of a war far more important, of a far more difficult
victory which God holds out before you. What would
it avail you to be dreaded and victorious without when
you are vanquished and captive within?"

It was a hard task for Bossuet. "Pray God for me,"
he wrote to the Marshal Bellefonds, "pray Him to
deliver me from the greatest burden men can have to
bear, or to quench all that is man in me that I may
act for Him only. Thank God, I have never yet
thought, during the whole course of this business, of
my belonging to the world; but that is not all; what is
wanted is to be a St. Ambrose, a true man of God, a
man of that other life, a man in whom everything should
speak, with whom all his words should be oracles of
the Holy Spirit, all his conduct celestial; pray, pray, I
do beseech you."

Finally the courageous curé of Versailles forbade the

King to approach the Sacraments, and Louis, beaten, full of remorse, succumbed, and, April 13, 1675, made his Easter duty. Bossuet triumphed by sending away Montespan and by obtaining the entrance of La Vallière into the Carmelites. Louis had given orders to Montespan to retire to her chateau at Clagny. There Bossuet paid her a visit and begged her never to see the King again, but she practically insulted him. Bossuet was not sure of the King's repentance. He knew that he still corresponded with her. But he wrote to him: "Your Majesty has given your promise to God and the world. I have been to see her. I find her pretty calm; she occupies herself a great deal in good works. I spoke to her as well as to you the words in which God commands us to give Him our whole heart; they caused her to shed many tears; may it please God to fix these truths in the bottom of both your hearts and accomplish His work, in order that so many tears, so much violence, so many strains that you have put upon yourselves may not be fruitless."

But the hypocritical King was not yet ready to be converted. When he returned to Versailles after several months in the army he arranged that Montespan would be there to receive him. Again Bossuet pleaded with him, but Louis angrily told him to mind his own business. "Say nothing to me, monsieur; I have given my orders, they must be obeyed." And Bossuet obeyed. "He had tried every thrust," says Saint Simon, "had acted like a pontiff of the earliest times, with a freedom worthy of the earliest ages and the earliest bishops of the Church. He saw the futility of his efforts; henceforth prudence and courtly behavior put a seal upon his lips."

How long the iniquity would have continued it is hard to say. Some writers think it would have gone on to the end only for the so-called Poison Affair. Montespan is presumed to have been a believer in witchcraft as early as 1666 when she had a Black Mass said over her, and it is asserted that when the affection of the King began to wane she resorted to magic and love potions. When another of the victims of the King, Angelique de Fontanges, died in childbirth it was hinted that she had been poisoned. Montespan was even charged with being associated with the notorious La Voisine who was addicted to the worst kind of witchcraft, but the affair was hushed up and the trial discontinued because, it is said, Louis found it was all coming too near home. She is even accused of having tried to poison La Vallière and others and of having planned to have the King repudiate the Queen and marry herself. Louis was horrified, as it was even insinuated that she had tried to poison himself. But he did not prosecute her. He even allowed her to remain at court, where she stayed, hoping against hope to recover the affection of the sovereign. Louis, it is said, might have reinstated her but for the indecent joy she had exhibited on the death of her rival Fontanges.

Madame de Sevigné wrote: "The star of Quanto (Montespan) is paling; there are tears, affected gayeties, poutings—in fact, my dear, all is coming to an end. People look, observe, imagine, believe there are to be seen, as it were, rays of light upon faces which a month ago were thought to be unworthy of comparison with others. If Quanto had hidden her face with her cap at Easter in the year she returned to Paris, she would not be in the agitated state in which she now is. The spirit indeed was willing but great is human weakness; one likes to make the most of a remnant of beauty. This is an economy which ruins rather than enriches."

"Madame de Montespan asks advice of me," said Madame de Maintenon. "I speak to her of God, and she thinks I have some understanding with the King; I was present yesterday at a very animated conversation between them. I wondered at the King's patience and at the rage of that vain creature. It all ended with these terrible words—'I have told you already, Madame, I will not be interfered with.'"

Whatever one may believe about the Poison Affair, it is certain that Louis himself became a sincere convert shortly after. His conversion was due to Père la Chaise and to Madame Scarron, and they succeeded in making him break with Montespan. Strange circumstance, it was Montespan who had brought the widow Scarron to the notice of the King when she engaged her to care for her children. A convert from the Huguenots, she became a sincere Catholic, and we can well believe that she was honest in her assertion that her mission in life was the salvation of the King. "The King passed two hours in my closet," she wrote; "he is the most amiable man in his kingdom. I spoke to him of

Father Bourdaloue. He listened to me attentively. Perhaps he is not so far from thinking of his salvation as the court supposes. He has good sentiments and frequent reactions towards God." It was she who restored Louis to the Queen, who had been compelled to bear with the degraded Montespan for twenty years. Gradually Madame Scarron's wholesome influence displaced that of Montespan. The King grew to admire her sterling worth, and when a few years later the Queen died, July 30, 1683, he made her his wife. He did not love her. Did he ever love anything but his own glory? "This is the first sorrow she ever caused me," he said of his pious Queen. Very little sorrow at that, we can well believe. Madame Scarron, or Madame de Maintenon, was now in the ascendant; Montespan was humiliated, but she bore this humiliation seven years before she could be prevailed upon to leave the court. It was Louis who at last ordered her to go, and to add to the bitterness of the humiliation, he sent the message by their son, the Duc de Maine. There was nothing for her to do but to leave.

Some time before that, when she saw that her influence was declining, she decided to build and endow a convent. As soon as the work was started the rumor went about that she was going to imitate La Vallière, but she smiled at the absurdity of it, for she was contemplating a retreat rather than a place of serious penance. She left the court in tears and fury, and with animosity toward her son, the Duc de Maine, whom she never forgave for his part in her dismissal. She retired to the Community of St. Joseph, the convent she had built, but it was a long time before she could accustom herself to it. She was forever on the go, to Bourbon, to Fontrevrault, where her sister was abbess of a convent, and to other places. She could not content herself any place, for she had no mastery over herself. But at last the grace of God touched her. Montespan, great sinner though she was, had never been able to crush all religious feeling in her soul. Even in the days of her glory and her shame it was said that she would leave the King in order to go and pray in her cabinet, and that she continued her austerity in fasting even during her dissipation. Added to that, she was always very kind to the poor. All of this won for her the grace of repentance, and at last she put herself under the care of Father de la Tour, the general of the Oratory, as her confesssor. From that time on her conversion was assured and her penance increased. But through it all there remained the hope that now that her husband was dead the King, if Madame de Maintenon should die, would take her back and marry her on account of the children. Before the death of her husband her confessor had made her write a letter to him begging him to take her back and be reconciled with her, but the injured husband wrote that he never wanted to see her again. "Little by little," writes Saint Simon, "she gave almost all she had to the poor. She worked for them several hours a day making strong shirts and such things for them. Her table that she had loved to excess, became the most frugal; her fasts multiplied; she would interrupt her meals in order to go and pray. Her mortifications were continued; her chemises and her sheets were of rough linen, of the hardest and thickest kind, but hidden under others of ordinary kind. She unceasingly wore bracelets, garters, and a girdle, all armed with iron points, which oftentimes inflicted wounds upon her; and her tongue, formerly so dangerous, had also its peculiar penance imposed on it."

For twenty-two years this life of penance continued. No penance was too hard for her to endure for her sins. The hair shirts with iron points that lacerated her once dainty body were not so much a penance as a reminder of the crimes she had to expiate. She spent vast sums on hospitals and other charities and even sewed for the sick in those charitable institutions.

When she quitted Paris for the last time for Bourbon she had a presentiment that she would never return, and therefore she paid all her pensioners and doubled her alms. She had been at Bourbon only a few days when she felt that her end was near. She called all her servants into her room, made a public confession of her public sins and begged their pardon for all the scandal she had given by her wicked life. She then sent for her confessor and received the last Sacraments. The fear of death which all her life had haunted her now disappeared, and she awaited the end calmly and trusting in the mercy of God. She died in 1707, at the age of sixty-six, still retaining the marvelous beauty which had made the name of the Grand Monarch a byword in civilization.

Paris and Versailles received the information of her death with the greatest indifference. The King forbade her children to wear mourning for her, and their disgraceful want of feeling was the only thing in the whole episode that attracted attention. The King was about to set out on a shooting excursion when he was told the news.

"Ah, indeed," he said, "so the marchioness is dead! I should have thought she would have lasted longer. Are you ready, Monsieur de la Rochefoucauld? I have no doubt that after this last shower the scent will lie well for the dogs. Let us be off at once!"

So passed from the world where she had once ruled as queen the haughty, passionate, ambitious, sinful De Montespan. Her whole life is a commentary upon the folly of sin; yet the historians who have exhausted every detail of her crimes, who have held up their hands in horror at her shamelessness, have curtly dismissed her penitence. Some have even sneered at it as insincere, but to do such penance as this woman did for twenty-two years requires a great deal of sincerity and a great supply of the grace of God. It was God alone Who could turn the brazen De Montespan into a weeping Magdalen. She atoned long and well for her sins. Who knows what part her penances had in winning for Louis the grace of a happy death? He came to the day when he wept bitterly over the sins of his youth, his scandalous profligacy. When he was dying the parish priest of Versailles said to him, "Prayers are offered in all the churches for Your Majesty's life."

Louis replied, "That is not the question; it is my salvation that much needs praying for." And the memory of Montespan and other associates of his crimes must have been before the eyes of the so-called Grand Monarch when he wrote, "In the last moment where we arrive sooner than we think perhaps, God will not ask if we have lived honest men, but if we have kept His Commandments."

Chapter 16

MADAME DE LA SABLIÈRE

It has been said of Madame de la Sablière that her chief claim to immortality rests upon her kindness toward the poet La Fontaine for a quarter of a century. Poor, foolish, sinful La Fontaine owed her much. She made possible much of his genius. But more than all it was she after the grace of God who saved his soul at the end. As long as the name of the poet is remembered, just as long is the name of his protectress glorified.

But apart from her association with La Fontaine, an association that was always pure and above suspicion, Madame de la Sablière occupies her own place in history. A woman of great intellectuality and of vast erudition, she may be regarded as the personification of that great charm which characterized the women of letters of the second half of the seventeenth century. To my mind none was superior to her, not even the celebrated Madame de Sevigné.

Yet Madame de la Sablière made no pretense of being a writer. What we have from her pen is chiefly her correspondence with her spiritual director, the famous Abbot de Rancé of La Trappe. But in that writing her soul shines out, the soul of a woman who had loved and suffered and sinned, and finally by conversion to the faith became one of the most sincere penitents that ever lived, and devoted her life to the care of the incurables. To study the life of this poor sinner is to get a new grasp on hope. If she found the way back to God, no one need ever despair.

Marguerite Hessein, such was her maiden name, was born in Paris, 1640. She was the oldest of four children of Gilbert Hessein and his wife, Margaret Menjot. Gilbert Hessein was a banker, and also dealt in diamonds and other precious stones, and soon acquired a considerable fortune. He was a staunch Huguenot, as was his wife, and of course they brought up their children in the reformed religion. It was a very pious family. This is especially noted in Antoine Menjot, an uncle of Madame de la Sablière. He was a noted doctor, doctor to the King, a philosopher and a theologian, and enjoyed a certain fame among his literary friends. He was an ardent defender of Protestantism, and such a religious man that he would pray for eight hours at a stretch. Of all his niece's associates he was the one who exercised the greatest influence upon her. He was her adviser, her confidant, all through her life.

When the girl was only nine her mother died. No doubt she suffered much from that great loss, but it only meant an increase of vigilance on the part of her father and her uncle Antoine. The father doted on her; the uncle also. The latter saw to it that she was well instructed. He taught her a great deal himself, and employed learned professors to teach her Greek and

Latin and mathematics. To this book learning was added her instruction as a grand lady of the world. A first cousin of hers had married a count. The countess took the motherless girl under her wing and introduced her to all the amenities of the social life. Thus the girl had the double advantage of being learned and socially fitted for the grand manner of the court.

The whole world was open before her. She was beautiful, rich, talented. Needless to say, with all these qualifications she had many suitors as soon as it was known that she was in the market. For, market it was and nothing else; and to this way of disposing of the lives of girls may be attributed much of the marital unhappiness and unfaithfulness which was the scandal of Bourbon times. For Marguerite Hessein was but fourteen when her father decided that she ought to marry. One reason for his haste was that he himself wanted to get married again, for, ten days before the marriage of his daughter, he took a second wife, who, by the way, brought him little happiness.

The husband chosen for Marguerite was a cousin of hers, Antoine de Rambouillet, Seigneur de la Sablière. He belonged to a very wealthy family and was considered one of the finest catches in France. He, too, was highly educated, having completed his course of studies in Rome, and was something of a popular poet besides. Even Madame de Sevigné found his verses "the prettiest in the world." But, polished gentleman that he was, his morals did not amount to much. He made no objection to marrying his beautiful cousin, and so the ceremony took place, March 15, 1654. It was a great wedding. All the wealth of Paris was present, and much of the glory of the court. The wedding bells were merry. Why not? A bride beautiful, clever, learned, rich; a bridegroom handsome, clever, learned, rich. A fine home was provided them; they lived in opulence and the best houses in France were eager to receive them. What more could be desired? The young couple did not believe that anything was lacking to their happiness, for happy they were, indeed, during those first years. True, there was no great love uniting them; perhaps they did not regard love as essential to their marriage. But they were at least good friends, blood relations, and with plenty of money and friends. That helped a great deal. Their home was the center of all the culture and wealth of Paris.

The young Madame de la Sablière was but fifteen when her daughter Anne was born; the next year came a son, Nicolas, and two years later a daughter, Marguerite. To every evidence a happy, united home. Yet all the while tragedy was approaching. Why the rift in the lute ever came, or why it did not come sooner are two questions, one as impossible to answer as the other. It is hard to get at the truth. To all appearances it was a happy family for thirteen years. As far as we can see there was no fault on the part of the wife. She was good and faithful and loyal, and seemingly much in love with her husband. Very likely it was a matter of money that caused the trouble. Madame de la Sablière's father died in 1661, and the estate which she inherited from him was much less than her husband had expected. This was one reason for complaint on his part, and as far as we know the only reason. Anyway he could make no other charges against her. But the real cause was deeper than that of money. He was a man of very little morality, and he had grown tired of the wife whom he had never really loved. His fancies wandered elsewhere and he determined to break the bonds which united him to the mother of his children. Life for both of them became hard. Bickering was the order of the day, and he openly declared that it was impossible for them to live together any longer. Finally things became so unbearable for the wife that, March 1, 1667, she sought refuge in a Catholic convent, rather a humiliation to one who prided herself on her Protestantism. Perhaps it was the kindness of the good sisters to her in her sorrow that helped toward her conversion. But she had little thought of conversion then; her mind was too full of family troubles. She was a proud woman, and she felt crushed by the open avowal of her husband that he wanted to get rid of her. He even urged her to ask for a legal separation, but, fearing that it was a ruse to deprive her of her children, she refused to take action. Then, too, she still had hopes that she might regain his love, love which it is plain she never had. But so discouraged did she become that she finally sought and obtained a separation on the grounds of his abuse of her. That did not end it. He was essentially a tyrant. He persecuted her in petty things, and broke down her spirit to such an extent that she blindly signed everything he asked her to sign, and in this way took away her children from her to be under his sole direction.

Abandoned by her husband, deprived of her children and her home, the young wife gathered up the broken bits of her life as best she could. She established a little home of her own and took her brother Pierre to live with her. Pierre was a friend of Racine, La Fontaine, Boileau, and all the other writers of the day. Madame de la Sablière was then in the prime of her beauty, and of a fascination so irresistible that it was the marvel to all her friends how her husband could have treated her so badly and dismissed her so ignominiously. With her blond curls and great intelligent eyes she made a striking picture that won the admiration of even her women friends. The "beautiful Sablière," Madame de Sevigné called her, and Ninon de Lenclos referred to her as "a pretty parterre that charms the eye." And again, one of the writers of the time called her "one of the prettiest and most singular women of the world."

Madame de la Sablière always had had an abundance of friends in the days of her prosperity; she did not lack them in the days of her misfortune. They all rallied about her and scathingly condemned her husband for his unappreciation of the jewel he had cast away. Her modest home became the most important salon of the day. The old salons, like that of Rambouillet, had disappeared. New ones had sprung up, many of them filled with the précieuses of the type that Molière ridiculed. But Molière did not ridicule Madame de la Sablière. He knew her for what she was, a simple, modest woman, thoroughly educated but making no vain display of her culture. It was this unassuming learning that drew about her all the noted writers of the time, as well as the best—and sometimes the worst—of Parisian society. Here one met Molière, Racine, Fontenelle, La Fontaine, Madame de Sevigné, all great personages, but all happy to be considered friends and admirers of Madame de la Sablière. The great Fouquet and his family were her intimate friends. She in her turn was loyal to them in the time of his disgrace when he was condemned by the King. In a word, it was said that no science, no art was stranger to her. All in all, the woman must have had a wonderful charm to attract and hold so many friends and of such varying temperaments.

The real nature of Madame de la Sablière, showing not only her love for the makers of literature, but her kind heart as well, is seen in her association with La Fontaine. La Fontaine, who, by the way, had once entered a seminary with the intention of becoming a priest, had acquired an enviable fame with his poems. The Duchess of Orleans had made things easy for him and freed him from financial worry, but as soon as she died he found himself in rather a precarious position, a poor poet without a roof over his head. It was then that Madame de la Sablière invited him to come and live with her and her brother Pierre. The invitation was a God-send to the needy poet. He accepted it and remained her guest for more than twenty years. La Fontaine, with all his wicked living, was very much of a child, improvident, incapable of looking after himself. Much of his glory, then, can be attributed to Madame de Sablière, since by looking after his temporal needs during all those years she gave him the inspiration and the leisure to do the work which is one of the glories of French literature.

Meanwhile, amid all this acclaim of her salon, there is question if the woman was happy. She could not be. She still had hopes of reconciliation with her husband, still had hopes of having her children restored to her. La Sablière himself was very prosperous. But his life was as wicked as ever. He died as he had lived, in 1679, at the age of sixty-five, making no mention of his wife and leaving her nothing. As a result of his death, however, she recovered the friendship of her children.

No matter how guilty the man was at the beginning of the trouble between him and his wife, it is not surprising that he refused to mention her name, for at the time of his death the abandoned wife had already brought disgrace upon her name and that of La Sablière. He cared little, perhaps, but it gave him the chance to justify himself with the world.

Madame de la Sablière through all her misfortune had kept her fair name unsullied for years. It was her greatest curse ever to meet the Marquis de la Fare. He, too, was a poet, a brilliant cavalier, a fine soldier, and of an old family. At one time he had vainly aspired to the affections of the notorious Madame de Montespan. He was thirty-two when in 1676 Madame de la Sablière, then thirty-six, first met him. It became a great passion for them both, a liaison that lasted six years. It was one of the loves that both assured themselves would last forever, but like all sinful loves it was doomed to end in sorrow and disappointment after having destroyed the souls of the lovers. Some say it was La Fare's craze for gambling that lured him from her; others, that he had found a new love. Whatever the cause, La Fare abandoned the woman who had sacrificed all for him, and he left her crushed and brokenhearted.

Madame de Sevigné wrote about the matter to her daughter: "You ask me what has caused the break between La Fare and Madame de la Sablière; it is bassette (a new gambling game then much in vogue); would you have believed it? It is under this name that the infidelity is declared; it is for this mistress of bassette that he has left this religious adoration. The moment came when this passion had to cease and pass to another object; would anyone believe that bassette was a way of salvation for anyone? Ah, it is well said that there are a hundred thousand routes that lead us there. She regards at first this distraction, this desertion; she examined the bad excuses, the reasons so little sincere, the pretexts, the embarrassed justifications, the conversations so little natural, the impatience to leave her, the journeys to Saint Germain where he played, the ennuis, the know not what more to say; at last when she had well observed the eclipse which had come upon her and the foreign body that little by little concealed all that love so brilliant, she took her resolution. I do not know what it has cost her, but at last without any quarrel, without reproaches, without any noise, without dismissing him, without any understanding with him, without wishing to confound him, she let herself be eclipsed; and without abandoning her home, where she still returns sometimes, without saying that she was renouncing everything, she finds herself so much at home at the Incurables that she goes there as if she were there all her life, feeling with pleasure that her trouble was not as bad as that of the invalids she tends. The superiors of this house are charmed with her spirit; she rules them all; her friends go to see her, she is always in very enjoyable company. La Fare plays at bassette.

'And the combat ends for lack of combatants' (*Le Cid*). Behold the end of this grand affair which attracted the attention of everybody; behold the route which God had marked out for this pretty woman; she did not say with arms crossed, 'I will wait for the grace'; all serves, and all is set to work by this Great Workman Who always infallibly does that which pleases Him."

And again: "Madame de la Sablière is in her Incurables, well cured of an evil which all believed incurable for a long time, and whose cure gives more joy than any other. She is in this blessed state; she is pious and truly so; she makes a good use of her free-will, but is it not God Who makes her do it? is it not God Who has delivered her from the empire of the devil? is it not God Who has changed her heart? is it not God Who directs her and sustains her? is it not God Who gives her sight and the desire to belong to Him?"

Madame de la Sablière was not, perhaps, cured as quickly as all that. She was crushed and broken-hearted at being so betrayed, but she kept silence. She would not let the world know her secret. Her heart needed consolation and she had sense enough to know that God alone could give her that. She thought first of shutting herself up in some convent—Protestant though she was—but her wise friends advised her against this course, knowing how unfitted she was for such a life. She needed active work to take up her mind, and nothing appealed to her so much as the care of the Incurables.

About this time her husband died and as there was nothing more in the world for her to hope for, she was strengthened in her resolution to devote herself to the care of the sick. It was at this time she decided to become a Catholic. Protestantism held no consolation for her. The Catholic faith alone could give her courage to live. How long was her preparation we do not know, but in 1685 she abjured Protestantism and was received into the Church by Father Rapin, a Jesuit, a well-known writer of his day, and an excellent, cultured priest who was especially interested in the conversion of Calvinists. With new ardor the convert,

convert and penitent, threw herself into the work at the Hospital for Incurables.

She had her own little house near the hospital, but she was seldom at home. Most of the time she was deep in her work for the afflicted. Her uncle, her friends, pleaded with her against her determination to give all her time to the work. But she heeded them not. Her life was to do penance for her sins. She had in Father Rapin a prudent director, but when he died she knew not where to turn. The thought came to her that the Abbot de Rancé, whom she had known well in his worldly days before his striking conversion to the most austere of lives, was the one best fitted to guide her soul. She wrote to him asking him to direct her, but he designated another priest as confessor and forbade her to have recourse to La Trappe save in the case of absolute necessity.

But she persisted. "I cannot give myself to God," she wrote, "without giving myself absolutely." De Rancé wrote her letters of advice, but at last she won the day and he agreed to direct her conscience by letter. She was then a woman of forty-six, already afflicted with an incurable disease, and able to take no other food than milk.

Then began a correspondence between de Rancé and Madame de la Sablière which continued to the time of her death. In her letters, which are spiritual classics, she makes a complete revelation of herself, enthusiastic, mystic, energetic, and a fervent, sorrowing penitent.

She profited much from De Rancé's letters. "Your words," she wrote, "are burning arrows that carry into my heart heat and light." But it was not all letter-writing. Her penance was the practical kind. She consecrated long hours to the service of the sick and to the reading of pious books. She wrote down the result of her meditations in Christian thoughts—or Pensées—which make admirable spiritual reading today.

Her life was thus divided between her little home and the hospital; she had no time for anything else. So engrossed was she in working out her own salvation and in atoning for her sins that gradually her friends dropped away. She cared little. God and the sick were friends enough.

Even La Fontaine, who had for so many years made her house his home, was not there so often now. He adored her, always respected her, and she was ever first in his thoughts. When in 1684 he had been admitted to the Academy, his discourse, in verse, had been addressed to her. But even when her new work carried her away from him, and even when he had become somewhat indifferent to her, she still kept a motherly eye upon him. It was she, indeed, who made him destroy some of his licentious writings and express his regret for others that had been published. She even tried to get him to go to La Trappe. But, "I find," she wrote to Father Maisne, de Rancé's secretary, "the desire La Fontaine had to go and see you has become chilled. He has shown me the letter you wrote him giving him permission. Men take all that which concerns their end as a fable; there are souls over whom the realities flow without stopping or penetrating." But she did not give up the work of winning him to God. Canon Maucroix had written to her: "I know the too prolonged weaknesses of M. de La Fontaine. Besides the fact that they offend God, they do not become an old man, and if they continue longer they will be decidedly troublesome. But nevertheless I do not despair of his salvation. His soul is the most sincere and the most candid I have ever known. Only, Madame, you must speak to him, you must absolutely."

Madame de la Sablière was very much disturbed by that letter. She knew her duty was to act on it. One night when the sinful old poet returned from some of his evil associates, he found his hostess waiting for him in the hall-way.

"My friend," said she, "I am here to ask pardon of you."

"For what, my good friend," said he.

"For having appeared to forget you, and for having neglected your friendship for cares I believed more important."

"It is true," said he, "I thought that you no longer cared for me. That embarrassed me, and if I had money I would have left your house."

"Think of eternal things," she said. "I wish it. I wish it. Listen! if you make no effort to live better I will impose upon myself the hardest penances. And wait—I will put on a hair shirt on your account; and for you I will take the discipline. I swear it, and you know I have never failed to keep my word."

La Fontaine was so impressed that he began to cry.

"I will do all you wish," he said. And he was as good as his word. Two years later he, too, was wearing a hair shirt. When he fell ill in December, 1692, the Abbé Pouget succeeded in converting him. When the poet regained his health his true friend Madame de la Sablière was no more. La Fontaine's faithful friends, Racine, Boileau and Canon Maucroix did much to bring him back to God.

Toward the end he centered his thoughts on eternity and used his poetic talent in writing pious hymns. He wrote to the Canon: "The best of your friends has not a fortnight to live. O my dear friend, to die is nothing, but think you that I am about to appear before God. You know how I have lived. Before you have this letter the gates of Eternity will perchance be opened for me." And we can well believe that La Fontaine owed his conversion, under God, to the good friend who threatened to wear a hair shirt in his behalf.

La Fontaine was not the only one who was impressed by the penitence of Madame de la Sablière. Her example of charity and penance accomplished more good among her former associates in the world than she ever knew. Madame de La Fayette, the noted writer and friend of Rochefoucauld, turned more and more to religion after his death. One day she visited Madame de la Sablière at the Incurables and was deeply impressed with the self-sacrifice of the former belle of the literary and social salons. Madame de La Fayette died in true repentance after horrible sufferings. Who knows how much she owed to the prayers of her friend at the Incurables?

So, too, with the notorious Ninon de Lenclos. One reads so much of her evil life, but little of her repentance at the end. Somehow, although Ninon sounded the depths of iniquity, there was always something of religion tugging at her heart. When her mother died, Ninon's health broke down. She begged to be admitted as a penitent to a Convent. In those days many women of the world had their own apartments in convents, especially the Carmelites. The nuns were always kind to these penitents. But Ninon soon changed her mind. She rejected the grace of God. She was a quiet and saddened girl, but faith and innocence had fled. So she went back to her evil life, and grew old in iniquity, preserving her beauty even into old age. She was at the height of her fame, or infamy, when she used to visit the salon of Madame de la Sablière before the latter's conversion.

The two women were great friends in those days and we may believe that the penance of the nurse at the Incurables was not forgotten by Ninon when she came to the end of her wild career. When she felt death near she had herself brought to the Church of St. Paul where she made a general confession. She received Holy Communion, the first time since she was a little girl. She was eighty-five when she died in 1705.

But to return to Madame de la Sablière's threat to

La Fontaine that she would do penance for him. She had no need to make the threat. She was already doing penance. She withdrew from the world more and more every day. She realized its nothingness. She wrote to De Rancé, "If my bad health did not seem to me a sacrifice worthy of God, I would desire death with ardor."

But death was coming nevertheless. Day after day her health was getting worse. She herself, while pitying the incurables was an incurable, afflicted with a malignant growth. Her visits to the hospital became fewer, she could scarcely leave the house. Gradually she withdrew into the solitude she had so long desired. "I am happier than I could ever tell you," she wrote to De Rancé. "I am with God and the sufferings which I regard as continual marks of His goodness to me." She was slowly dying. From her bed of pain she contemplated the poor cemetery of St. Sulpice. "How happy I am," she wrote to de Rancé, "I see only Eternity. When one has given her soul to God, all is done. I see here every day the place where I will be buried, and I find the sight so tranquil that I quite love it."

She could face death even more calmly than her friend Madame de Sevigné, who had always been a good woman. "Alas!" writes Madame de Sevigné, "how this death goes running about and striking on all sides. . . . I am embarked in life without my consent. I must go out of it—that overwhelms me. And how shall I go? Whence? by what door? When will it be? in what disposition? how shall I be with God?

what have I to present to him? What can I hope? Am I worthy of Paradise? Am I worthy of Hell? What an alternative! What a complication! I would like better to have died in the arms of my nurse."

With Madame de la Sablière penitent love had cast out fear. Life at the end was calm after the years of austerity and self-sacrifice. She died in her little home January 5, 1693, aged fifty-three, and was buried quietly the next day in St. Sulpice Cemetery—"so tranquil that I quite love it." So died the woman who had been a shining light in her social world. What a difference between the grand lady of the salon and this poor emaciated body that had spent itself in atoning to God for its sins? "We must hope for everything from God when we have sincere recourse to Him however unworthy we are of His graces."

That is one of her maxims, and it may be taken as expressive of her whole penitential life. Madame de la Sablière is one of the great heroines of penance because of her simple trust in the mercy of God.

Chapter 17

MADAME POMPADOUR

LOUIS XV, King of France, stood looking out the window in the palace at Versailles. It was raining hard. On such a day there was not much else to do but watch the rain. But to the tired, yawning monarch, there was a spectacle being staged out there in the storm that served to give a little interest to the dreary morning. For Louis was watching for the passing of the funeral cortège of her who had ruled him and France for twenty years, her for whom he had sacrificed everything decent in life, Pompadour the vampire. Surely the King with the old memories of the favorite crowding upon him must feel the tug at his heart-strings, surely he must mingle his tears with the rain. But if you knew Louis, the lackadaisical, cold-hearted sensualist, you would know that it was beyond his powers to manifest any grief. Pompadour had ruled him and ruined him, but he had never really loved her. He had not loved her living; he could waste no sympathy on her dead. The rain continued to sound its *Dies Irae* against the pane. Through the blurring water Louis at last saw the funeral procession bearing his dead mistress to her grave in Paris. The horses clattered over the stones, the winds sighed, the rains swirled, the King yawned. Idly he watched the last exit of the actress Pompadour, and then, as the last of the procession was seen, he turned away from the window and rang down the curtain on the tragi-comedy with the insipid remark, "The Marchioness has a wet day for her journey." And then Louis yawned again.

In all history I know of no better commentary upon the vanity of earthly glory and the folly of sin than the unwept passing of the ambitious, scheming Pompadour. It is one of the many lessons of the kind we are continually finding in the history of the Bourbons. Today religion, tomorrow lust; today the fear of God, tomorrow a defiance of God's law. Sin after sin that would have shamed the pagans, yet running through it all the intention to die well at least. Tempting God was the chief recreation of the court of the Bourbons. His Most Christian Majesty! What a farce! Brunetière says of the eighteenth century that it was the least Christian and the least French in all history. One must of course be a Catholic—what else, indeed?—but Catholicity to the multitude meant only the last sacraments. The monarch's conviction that he was the state meant also that he was above the restraints of the commandments of God. It was all a travesty on religion; hypocrisy was the real king in those days.

Blame Pompadour as much as you will, and she deserves it all, but the real criminal in this nefarious liaison was Louis XV. He had the makings of a good man, of a great king even. Whatever is said against his preceptor, Cardinal de Fleury, by his enemies—and is it always hard to get at the exact truth in Bourbon history, where every liar wrote memoirs—it is certain that he gave his pupil a solid religious training, warned him against sin, and filled him with the fear of Hell. High hopes for the young Louis to be a great king. That is the feeling one gets in looking at Rigaud's painting of the King in his young years. He was "beautiful as an angel," of imposing presence, every inch a king. But beneath all the royal trappings there was a weakness. Blood tells. And Louis had inherited some pretty rotten blood. A sickly child, and therefore brought up with extraordinary care, his education was rather toward the effeminate, in spite of Fleury. He was encouraged in laziness for the sake of his poor health, encouraged in selfishness for the sake of his poor health, encouraged in self-gratification for the sake of his poor health. The whole aim seemed to be just to keep him alive and to permit him no exertion. Louis was born tired and he did not want to make the effort to wake up. Said one of the courtiers, "I cannot conceive a man who is able to be everything and who prefers to remain a cypher." And again, "He signs everything that is put before him." But in spite of that congenital ennui Louis might have amounted to something had he lived in a different court. It is certain, at any rate, that the moral wrecking of his soul can be laid at the door of his courtiers, who found a virtuous king the most ridiculous of mortals. When Louis at the age of seventeen married Marie Leczinska, the daughter of the dethroned king of Poland, it seemed as if the courtiers were to lose out in their efforts to corrupt the King and thus bring him under their sway. Marie was seven years older than her boy husband. She was no beauty, indeed, but was of charming character and very pious. Louis up to the day of her death had the highest admiration for her and even wept for her—more than he did for Pompadour—but though she idolized him even when he had humiliated her and broken her heart, he never really loved her. Still for several years he was faithful to her, and she bore him two sons and five daughters. But she soon palled upon him. Louis was the victim of his vanity rather than of his lust. It was expected of a Bourbon to be a free liver. He was too virtuous to be popular; virtue was too bourgeois. So at length Louis fell for the court flatterers. They got him to drink too much, then to gamble for large stakes, and then to flirt. He manifested his kingship by forming a liaison with the Countess de Mailly, the eldest of the five daughters of the Marquis de Nesle. It was a secret amour for three years; then came the open rupture with the Queen, and the Countess was openly acknowledged as the mistress of the King. Louis soon made up for the time he had lost in virtue. He went to the bad rapidly. A son was born to him by the sister of the Countess. She died soon after, and Louis broke his heart crying after her. He became penitent, religious, but the attack of goodness soon wore out. He took another sister, then the fourth—all from the same family. Indecency could go no further. It is only among the Bourbons one finds such horrible things.

The Countess got her deserts. She was dismissed, banished from court. She was certainly an unlovely character, a depraved, scheming woman, yet—the same old story of the grace of God, the same old story of the Magdalen—her disgrace was the greatest boon that ever could be given her. The Countess became a sincere penitent. Thenceforth until the day of her death she devoted herself to charity. She kept for herself only enough for the bare necessities of life and devoted the rest of her income to charity. Her downfall had humbled her, and very likely had saved her soul. One day she came to church and the crowds were pushed aside to make room for her to enter her pew. One of the bystanders, who resented any consideration for a woman with such a history, cried out sneeringly, "Here's a fine fuss for a wanton." And the humbled Countess merely replied, "Since you know her, pray to God for her." Even the Bourbon court could produce its Mary of Egypt.

The cold sensualist must find other hearts to break. There were plenty ready for him waiting to be broken. The favored one was Madame de la Tournelle. An ambitious, calculating woman, she made the King pay for the honor. He settled an income on her and made her the Duchess of Chateauroux. But the craven Louis soon had to pay the price. He was stricken ill and priests refused to give him the Sacraments unless he first dismissed the scandalous woman from the court.

Louis, perhaps really penitent and afraid of the judgment of God, agreed to the terms. The Duchess drove
back to Paris and was almost torn to pieces by the
rabble who hated her. The populace had a higher ideal
of morals than had the court. Louis expressed his
penance publicly; if he were going to die, he wanted to
die well. To him and to all the court it seemed that
the end was near. The prayers for the dying were said.
But—unluckily—he recovered. In the first fervor of
gratitude he was reconciled with the Queen, but the
reconciliation and the good resolves lasted only for a
while. Louis wanted the Duchess back, and he gave
orders for her to return to court. But God had other
designs. The Duchess died before she had a chance
to go back to her sin. And—the same old story of
the grace of God—she too died well. Feeling that her
end was near, she sent for a priest. Father Segaud
came and gave her the last Sacraments. During her
illness the King was greatly distressed, and, with his
usual mixture of lust and religion, had several Masses
said for her. She died December 8, and was buried
very early on the morning of the eleventh, lest the
people who hated her even in death would maltreat
her poor corpse. There is a very striking thing told
about the Duchess. She always wore a medal of the
Blessed Virgin. On her deathbed she told the priest
that she had always prayed for two things—that she
would not die without the Sacraments and that she
would die on a feast of the Blessed Virgin. Somehow
her prayers were answered. Many of the moralizing

historians sneer at what they consider her hypocritical deathbed. Somehow they always reckon without the mercy of God. Rather late, of course, to wait till one is in the shadow of death to do penance, but one may also say, better late than never. Knowing the story of the penitent thief, it is not in our province to decide just at what moment it is too late for penance.

But Louis soon dried his tears, soon forgot the Divine warning in the death of the Duchess, the only woman he ever really loved. The King must be amused lest time should hang too heavy on his hands. You may be sure that there was great rivalry for the shoes of the dead Duchess. What an honor to strive for! Other times, other morals, we are smugly told; as if the prevalence of laxness excused it. This time Louis had a real shock in store for his courtiers and the people of France, choosing for his "left-handed queen" a woman from the bourgeoisie. What a terrible disgrace! Let the King commit adultery, if he will—kings can do no wrong— but at least let him observe good form in his sin. It was unheard of for a Bourbon to ignore the ladies of noble birth in choosing a mistress. That was their prerogative. But this time they had to swallow their pride. Louis was king, at least in regard to his sins. And so the Duchess was hardly cold in her grave when Louis elevated to her place a woman from the common people.

This woman, who was afterwards created Marchioness de Pompadour, was less surprised than anyone else. She had set out to win the coveted honor and nothing could stop her when she determined to gain her point.

She was a born manager, a born schemer. Born Jeanne Antoinette Poisson, the daughter of a man who held a responsible position in a banking house in Paris, she was far removed from courtly circles. Her father was a drunkard, coarse in the extreme, with no moral sense, so dishonest that very soon he was obliged to flee the country and remain in exile fifteen years; her mother, who had the reputation of being rather loose, seemed to have but one ambition in life, and that was to have her beautiful and talented daughter honored as the mistress of the King. When Poisson fled the country, a rich man named De Tournehen became the protector of Madame Poisson and her son and daughter. He was very fond of Jeanne—some hinted that she was his own daughter—and he spared nothing on her education. She spent one year with the Ursulines of Poissy, where two of her aunts were religious. But the mother considered she was much too pretty to be left there, fearing perhaps that she might develop a vocation, and so, much to the disappointment of the nuns, she was taken from the convent when she was but nine years of age. I like to think of what the course of French history might have been had the little Poisson girl been permitted to remain in the convent. At least France would have been spared the ignominy of a Pompadour. As soon as she was taken from the convent there was immediate concern to polish her to the limit. She had masters in singing, dancing, elocution, the playing of the harp, and became adept in all these arts. She had a fine mind, was well read, had a clever wit, rode to perfection, dressed in the most exquisite taste, and, more than all, possessed a beauty that was extraordinary. So at the age of eighteen she was one of the most accomplished women of her time, perhaps of all time. And the incentive to it all was her desire that one day the King would look favorably upon her. When she was a young girl, her mother took her to a fortune-teller. Imagine their delight when the seeress prophesied that one day the child would be the mistress of Louis.

In order to prepare the way, a husband first of all had to be found for her. De Tournehen, the complaisant protector, arranged all that. He succeeded in marrying her at the age of twenty to his nephew, Lenormant d'Etioles, who was very rich but far from prepossessing, since he was short, plain and red-headed. De Tournehen settled a considerable fortune upon the young couple, and the marriage bells rang joyfully. D'Etioles was the happiest man on earth; he was madly in love with his beautiful, talented wife, and he surrounded her with every luxury, gave her a town house in Paris and a country house near the royal chateau of Choisy. At once she started a salon which became the meeting-place of all the wits and men of letters. Voltaire, Fontenelle, Montesquieu and others considered it an honor to be invited by the beautiful and clever Madame. A daughter, Alexandrine, was born. To the mere observer the woman seemed to have all that makes for happiness. But in truth she was far from being happy. She wanted the King, she wanted the throne, and she would not be happy until these wishes were gratified. And yet, what vain hopes, for she knew that the King could only choose from the nobility—God save the mark!

But she immediately set her cap for him. She followed him on the hunt. Louis openly snubbed her and gave strict orders that this brazen woman should be kept from the hunting grounds. Snubbed, she nevertheless bided her time and hoped. The wonderful opportunity came at the time of the marriage of the Dauphin with the Spanish Infanta. The chief feature of the celebration was a great masked ball and she determined that there she would make her last attempt to captivate the King. No need to go into all the details of the story of that masked ball; it suffices to say that the ambitious woman succeded in making the King her slave and was soon installed as his royal mistress, while, to make her position more respectable, she obtained a divorce, or rather a judicial separation, from her broken-hearted husband.

After the victory of Fontenoy, which somehow takes some of the curse off the vile Louis, the King sought to make things a bit more honorable, in a court that loved etiquette more than anything else, by giving her the title of Marchioness de Pompadour. He returned to court, and the Marquise, now that she was a noble and no longer a plebeian, was formally presented at court and to the Queen, who, though sick of the whole rotten business, had royal dignity enough to conceal her chagrin. When she was presented to the Dauphin, he, despising her and bitterly resenting her usurpation of his mother's place, covertly stuck out his tongue at her. Rather undignified, perhaps, but the Dauphin after all was like a clean breath of wind in that stifling court. It has been said sneeringly of him that "Not to save France would he forego a Mass, were the country in flames at her four corners." It was a curse to France that he did not live to succeed to the throne.

Pompadour, however, cared little about the feelings of the Queen and the Dauphin. She was a child of destiny. She was victorious. Yet even at that she had many a heartache. The court ladies resented her presence as a woman from the common people; they ridiculed her, discredited her, spied on her; and on the other hand the public hated her and lampooned her. She minded the opposition very little in so far as it hurt her own feelings, but she chafed under it, fearing that the unpopularity would in time discredit her with Louis and thus cut short her career. She knew that she was skating on very thin ice, but it is a tribute to her powers that she was able to circumvent all her enemies. She succeeded even in ingratiating herself with the Queen by being nice to her, and the poor Queen in order to avoid open scandal let her be nice to her. It was no glory to be queen of France in those days.

Pompadour was fighting alone against all France, but her colossal ambition was enough to fight the whole world. She planned her campaign carefully. She chose her allies. She made a treaty with the Paris Brothers, the great financiers of the day, to use her influence with the King for them in the matter of loans if they would in turn use their influence for her. But her great work was with Louis himself, and she set out to make herself indispensable to his happiness, his freedom from being bored. Her one great game was to amuse the King, to keep him on the move, to save him from the worry of state affairs. "Louis," said the Abbé Goliani, "had made the trade of king the most ignoble one in the whole world." Pompadour was determined that the dead monarch should have no resurrection. "Do what Madame wishes," said Louis to the Minister Maurepas. He was not to be bothered; she would see to that. Amuse the King at any cost; keep him from his conscience, from the thoughts of Hell that used to trouble him in the old days.

A fine actress, singer and dancer, she had a private theater set up at court, where she succeeded in getting many of the nobility to act, she herself being the star of the company; but one can well believe that she gave herself to this work not so much for her personal enjoyment of it as for the pleasure it gave the King, to please whom was her whole aim in life in order to make her own position secure. She worked hard for her doubtful honor. Woe to those who sneered at her now. Maurepas was her enemy. She knew it, and she determined to get rid of him. "You set small store by the King's mistresses," she said to him one day. "I have always respected them, Madame," he replied, "for something which they once were." Only a Frenchman could make such a retort.

But Maurepas had to go. Louis dismissed him, no matter how valuable he was to the state, just because Pompadour wished it. She was victorious. She was not only queen, she was also king. She let her power be felt in every department of the state. She hesitated at nothing. It was said that she sold commissions, a thing easy enough to believe, for Pompadour who had come to court a poor woman was soon noted for her wealth. Even the foreign ambassadors felt obliged, at the expressed wish of the King of course, to pay homage to her as they did to the Queen herself. Pompadour was indeed as regal as the Queen; she had her fifty or sixty servants, living with no limit to her prodigality, building mansion after mansion wherever her fancy suggested. Her relatives could well glory in her shame. She was lady bountiful to all of them, no matter how distantly they were related to her, one of the very few things that can be said in her favor. She idolized her brother and set no limit to her ambition for him, but to do him justice he was not keen about advancement at such a horrible price as his sister was paying. Even when in 1754 her little daughter Alexandrine died, she spared a little while to shed a few tears, but life was too short for such a useless thing as mourning. She dried her eyes and went back with more zeal to her work of pleasing Louis and ruling France. "My life," she said, "is that of a Christian, a perpetual conflict." A blasphemous kind of Christian, indeed. But conflict it was, for till the day she died she could not sit back and say that her position was secure. But always that

ambition of hers won, cost what it might, even when
she pandered to the lowest instincts of the lecherous
Louis.

Never sure of the King, she could not know just when
his dead conscience would rise again. Louis had known
better; he still knew better. He had stifled his conscience, but always there was that fear of Hell. Pompadour herself had little fear of Hell, but then she had
not the antecedents of a Louis. If she feared Hell it
was for the effect it would have in distressing the King.
And just now there was reason to fear Hell. In the
March of 1751 Father Griffet had thundered against the
morals of the court in a Lenten sermon, choosing as his
text the woman taken in adultery. It took a courageous
man to preach on that topic to such a congregation.
Meanwhile prayers were printed and circulated everywhere begging God to convert the King from his scandalous amours, while the Jesuits made no secret of the
fact that they were having said fifteen Masses every
day for his conversion. Pompadour was wise enough
to sense it all. She decided to get religion, to be converted before she would be turned out. Trust her
always to know the psychological moment. She made
it evident that she had broken the liaison with the King,
and that henceforth her association with him would be
solely one of Platonic friendship. We can well believe
all that, for her power over Louis was more over his
mind than his heart. He had never really loved her.
But the liaison broken, her power over him was even
stronger. All that being so, it was easy enough for her

to get religion. Anyway, she became reconciled to the Church outwardly, attended Mass regularly, spent a great deal of time in prayer, fasted often and even got up during the night for her spiritual devotions. The general impression at court was that she was really sincere. Nevertheless her sincerity was not such as to include in her penance the renunciation of the position which her sin had purchased. The Jesuits at any rate were not so sure of her repentance, and they demanded that if she were sincerely converted she should give proof of it and repair the scandal as much as she could by leaving the court and becoming reconciled to her husband. After all, that was the common sense of repentance. Pompadour did not demur, but deep in her heart she hated the Jesuits, and their suppression in France can be attributed in a great measure to the animosity of this supposed penitent. But for the time she bowed to the will of the Jesuits. She wrote to her husband and asked him to take her back, but at the same time took good care to send a messenger to him to tell him not to take her at her word or he would incur the displeasure of the King. She did not need to worry. The fooled husband had long ceased to love her and was now busy with his own love affairs. He refused to take her back. But the grand gesture of self-renunciation had been made by Pompadour, and as usual she won. She even went so far as to write a long letter to the Pope, Benedict XIV, explaining her position and striving to exonerate herself, but the Holy Father took the letter for what it was worth and of course decided in favor of the Jesuits. Needless to say, Pompadour was wrathy with the Pope, the Jesuits, and with everyone else who saw through her hypocrisy. She succeeded, however, in finding, or rather dragooning, a confessor who gave it as his opinion that it was all right for her to remain at court. So she remained, and now that she was outwardly a respectable Catholic the Queen allowed her to be appointed *dame du palais,* and Pompadour, no doubt with her tongue in her cheek, continued to rule France.

There was no department where she did not excel. With a fine taste for literature, she surrounded herself with the poets, the historians, the philosophers. Up to that time literature had been a poor enough trade. She saw to it that it was made a remunerative one, and she succeeded in getting many of the writers pensions. So, too, with painters and engravers, she encouraged them and made herself their patroness. It is to her that is due the beginning of the manufacturing of Sèvres porcelain, and much of the credit of the establishment of the Ecole Militaire is given by historians to her, all proofs of the universality of her genius.

What her guilt was in causing the disasters of the Seven Years' War it is hard to say. The alliance with Austria was an evil thing for France, and that alliance is laid at the door of Pompadour. Said one of the Austrian statesmen, "It is to Madame de Pompadour that we owe everything." To her, yes, or rather to her wounded vanity. One day she had sent her regards to Frederick the Great. Ungallantly he replied to the messenger, "I do not know the woman." From that day on she hated Frederick. On such petty personalities international wars often depend. Just as she hated others, so she was hated in return. The French people despised her, for they blamed her for all the evils of the terrible war. So great was the animosity to her and to the King that an attempt was made on the life of the latter. Louis was only slightly injured but he was sure that he was going to die, and as usual he prepared himself for death. The populace was threatening Pompadour with death. She was in an agony of suspense. Was this the end of her reign? The King gave orders for her to leave the court. Her trunks were all packed and she was about to go when Louis again recovered, and again was reconciled with her. But then came the defeat of the French at the battle of Rossbach, and the resentment of the people was revived against the woman who was blamed for the war and the appalling financial condition of the country.

But if the war crushed the people of France, it surely crushed Pompadour. It humiliated her, gave her the death blow. She had never been of robust health, and her late hours, her loose living, had exacted its toll. Even in 1757 she felt that she was near her end and she made her will. She rallied, however, from that attack and returned to her task of pleasing the King, now indifferent to her, yet for all that depending entirely upon her. Louis was always the victim of habit. A strange habit, indeed, for as he admitted he never really loved the woman but kept her so long "because to have sent her away would have killed her." No doubt she realized that, and felt that Louis would not be a bit sorry for her death. The glory of life had passed, indeed. The vivacious, versatile, regal Pompadour was actually dying of melancholy.

She broke down finally in February, 1764, but once again she tried to flatter herself that she was getting better. When she returned to Versailles, the scene of so many of her triumphs, she was told that her end was not very far off. She took it philosophically if not coldly. And again the grand gesture to the King; she sent to him to ask him whether he wished her to die penitent or impenitent, that is, would she send for a confessor, or would she out of deference to him refuse the consolations of religion. The King, who had a little more faith, told her to be reconciled to God. It all sounds as if they thought they were conferring a favor on the Almighty. Pompadour read over again the will which she had made, and added a codicil. The preamble of the will sounds pious enough: It runs: "I recommend my soul to God, beseeching Him to have mercy on it, and to accord me grace to repent, and to die in a state worthy of His clemency, hoping to satisfy His justice through the merits of the precious blood of Christ my Savior and through the powerful intercession of the Holy Virgin and of all the saints of Paradise." Then she ordered her women attendants to dress her and to put rouge on her cheeks so that her cadaverous look might not frighten anyone. She discussed certain business details and then lay back to wait for the end. One of the priests from La Madeleine came and heard her confession and remained a long time by her bed of death. As he finally rose to leave she said, "One moment, Monsieur le Curé, we will take our departure together." And so a few moments later she died, at the age of forty-two. She was buried in the Church of the Capuchins in the tomb which she had had erected, side by side with the little Alexandrine, who had at least been spared the knowledge of the shame of her mother. The priest who was appointed to preach the customary eulogy was rather nonplussed. What could be say in praise of this woman who had so scandalized the whole of France? He solved the problem by preaching a panegyric of the good Queen.

As one of Pompadour's biographers writes, she retained her empire intact to her last hour, but no sooner had she closed her eyes than she was forgotten. The Queen a few days later wrote to one of her confidants, "Finally there is no more talk of her who is no longer, than if she had never existed. Such is the way of the world; it is very hard to love it."

So passed the great Pompadour. "She made and unmade ministers, she selected ambassadors, she appointed generals, she conferred pensions and places"; for twenty years she was "paramount in all matters from politics to porcelain," the real ruler of France. It has been said by some of her apologists that she was no worse than her contemporaries. If so, God help her contemporaries!

Yet all was not rotten at the court of Louis. The

life of Queen Marie takes away much of the bad taste left by Pompadour. Marie was a woman deeply religious. It was at her request that Pope Clement XIII instituted the Feast of the Sacred Heart. She was filled with charity for the poor and used to scatter money lavishly to the beggars who surrounded her carriage. Some wag called them the "Queen's Regiment." She needed to be religious, indeed, for her heart was broken. In her later years she was much attracted to the religious life, and spent a great deal of time at the Carmelites of Compiègne, which later on during the Revolution gave so many martyrs to the faith. When leaving the convent she would say, "You remain in the ante-chamber of God, I depart for Babylon." Even Pompadour knew the glory of Marie. "The Queen is a saint," she would say, "the grandeurs of earth touch her no more. I wish I could say as much." And again, "The Queen is without doubt a brave woman; she bears her old age, her infirmities, her sorrows (for she has them) with a courage I admire. I see by her example that true devotion is some good."

It was the same with the Dauphin. He died the year after Pompadour. When he was dying he said to his weeping mother, "What, mother! You don't doubt that the Kingdom of Heaven is worth more than an earthly one. I see you always sad and in tears since it has become plain that I shall leave the earth." "Alas, my son," she replied, "I don't know whether I am weeping for sorrow at your condition or for joy at the resignation with which you bear it." "All in good time," said he; "let it be for joy, for it is a joy to me not to grow old in this world." And surely it was a consolation to the Queen to be able to say, "How happy he is; he dies like a saint; it is we who are to be commiserated."

It is almost a desecration to put the Pompadour in the company of converted women, of those heroines who by the road of pain and through the flood of tears came to final sanctity. Pompadour became converted because there was nothing else to do. Had she lived a thousand years she would have still gloried in her shame, would have clutched the scepter still for which she had sold her soul. And yet who can tell? Pompadour was penitent at the end, sincerely penitent we believe, in spite of the theatricalness of her end. And that is no slight grace. But, apart from all that, her story is worth reviewing for the very reason that it points the lesson so hard for all of us to learn, that the wages of sin is death and that the whole world and its glory is poor enough exchange for peace of soul. Louis and Pompadour know the difference now. God grant they did face their God with truly contrite hearts. But whether they did or not, the one great message their poor ghosts are trying to send from eternity is the folly of sin, the worthlessness of a life that seeks to get along without God.

Chapter 18

MADAME TIQUET

When the lady of high society, Madame Tiquet, was forced by the law, which had convicted her of the attempt to murder her husband, to lay her beautiful head on the block, there were not wanting many among her contemporaries who were eager to cast the stone of derision upon her grave in the cemetery of Saint Sulpice. It had been said that she died a true penitent. But how could they believe that? A woman of sin, a hypocrite, a murderess at heart,—why bring odium upon religion by associating her name with anything sacred? It was too speedy a change, they believed, to be sincere. She was a hypocrite all her life; she must be one at her death. They measured penance by length of years. La Vallière at that time had already served twenty-five long years of atonement for her wicked life at court. They could grasp that idea of penance, but to speak in the same breath of this murderous Madame Tiquet who yesterday was convicted of sin was almost blasphemous. Anyway, supposing that she was sorry at the end, what else could she do? She might as well make the best of it and at least die well.

I can imagine these Pharisees saying the same thing on Calvary on Good Friday if anyone had suggested that one of the two thieves was good. A good thief, indeed! His conversion was too sudden, of too short duration to be other than hypocritical. He would be just as bad again if he could come down from his cross of shame. Nailed to the cross, what else could he do but repent? Pharisees are always so wise. Thieves are thieves to the end. And it is a sure way to argue if you leave out of the equation that strange thing, the mercy of God. The Good Thief, if he had escaped the cross, might have gone on being a bad thief until the end. But somehow he took advantage of the mercy that was offered him and became a true penitent although his heart was to bear the burden of its grief but one hour or less. Not a long penance, but an intensive one, its perfection attested by the pronouncement of the Divine Sufferer, "This day shalt thou be with me in Paradise."

After that example of deathbed penance, who can say of any sinner that his sorrow at the end was hypocritical? Penance is not measured by the sordidness of the life preceding it. I dare say the details of the life of the Good Thief would make rather disgusting reading. And so with Madame Tiquet. A high-born lady of the salons, she was morally of the scum of the earth, just such a woman as our yellowest of journals features in the latest murder case in these our own civilized times.

It is the year 1699. All Paris, from Louis XIV down —Louis the Grand Monarch, who has had his fill of sin and is now leading a virtuous life—is filled with excitement. Society, high and low, is talking of but one thing, the fact that Madame Tiquet must be beheaded for the crime of having attempted to murder her husband. A woman of position, of wealth, of culture, a noted beauty in her own circle, "perfectly beautiful," we are told, yet a breaker of her vows, a woman of sin, a murderess—no wonder her fate held the whole attention of the world of her day. Yet it is not because she was the central character in a *cause célèbre* that her story deserves telling, for your daily paper will furnish you tales far more lurid, but because, wretched, abandoned thing that she was, she was not too far beneath the mercy of God. Grievously she sinned, but heroically she atoned. And if Madame Tiquet could find her way back to God, surely there is hope for the rest of us.

She was born Angelique Nicole Carlier, at Metz, in 1657, and was left an orphan at the age of seven by the death of her father, a man of considerable importance in his world. Her mother had died some time before. It was all a dreadful calamity to the child, for her father had unwisely committed her to the care of an aunt who had little affection for her, but rather was envious of the girl who was destined to be rich some day, for Carlier had left to his daughter and to his son, Philip Auguste, a considerable fortune. Angelique developed into a girl of extraordinary beauty, and this, combined with her wealth, her noble blood, justified her in her conviction that she would soon make a stir in the world. The jealous aunt was to blame for the mistake that started the girl on her way to the block.

Angelique had hardly arrived in Paris, where she had determined to make a great contest, when she allowed herself to be persuaded by her aunt to marry Claude Tiquet, who held a government position as counselor. Tiquet was very much of a bluff. He pretended to be richer than he really was; he had in fact squandered much of the fortune left him by his father in vicious pleasures. He proceeded at once to dazzle the simple girl from the country with his magnificent presents. And, ambitious as she was to shine in the great world, she believed that marriage with him would give her all that her heart desired—wealth, position, social success. So she married him in haste and repented almost immediately. She soon discovered that she had married a jealous, domineering tyrant. He was so close to financial ruin that he obliged her to pay the expenses of the menage. Debts crowded upon him, he was pressed by his creditors, and he was insistent that she use her money to save him. Imagine the dismay of the ambitious woman when the conviction was brought home to her that she had been duped into a sordid marriage with a ruined roué. When she refused to let him squander her fortune, he showed his anger in no mistakable manner. He took vengeance in petty persecution and curtailed her liberty as much as he could. But she refused to let him break her spirit, and still resisted his demands on her money. She had never loved the man; now she scorned him. Proud and imperious, conscious of her beauty and her brilliant talents, she determined to ignore him and queen it in her own home, finding a refuge from her loveless marriage in lavish entertaining. Her self-possession galled him, and he threatened to isolate her from her social world which was the be-all and end-all of her existence. She retaliated by threatening to go to law to prevent him from using her money. It was a mean, sordid family squabble.

And the irritation increased with the years. In spite of the fact that she had two lovely children, she deplored her marriage more and more. There could be no resignation. But splendid actress that she was, and with the pride of her noble blood, she kept her irritation concealed from the world. She radiated peace. No one could show more esprit, humor, talent, culture, and she took her place in the salons of Paris as if she were the happiest wife in the world.

Things might have gone on in this cold, hypocritical way had she never met the man for love of whom she was finally willing to do murder. It was in 1696 she first met Gilbert Galmyn, Count of Montgeorges. He was then thirty-nine, captain of a company of Grenadiers in a regiment of French Guards, the typical soldier with a fine reputation for bravery and honor. While on a furlough at Paris between two campaigns he was unfortunate enough to meet the beautiful Madame Tiquet, very likely through her brother who was also an officer in the Guards. He proceeded to fall in love with her at once, and she with him. What a contrast this fine, noble officer was to the tyrannical husband whom she loathed. It is all reminiscent of the traditional story of Mary Magdalen. The Talmud tells us that Mary was married to a rich lawyer named Pappas who was so insanely jealous of her that whenever he went out he locked her up at home. Proud and imperious, just like Madame Tiquet, she resented bitterly this tyranny, and at last in order to get away from it ran off with a gay young officer named Pandera and lived with him in the gay and fashionable town of Magdala, scandalizing everybody by the reckless extravagance of her life and her free love.

The only difference is that Madame Tiquet did not run away but played the Magdalen at home. Tiquet himself concealed his jealousy as much as he could, and exercised surveillance over his wife though manifesting no knowledge of her liaison with Montgeorges. His jealousy got a respite when the Count returned to the army, but the jealousy broke out in earnest when the handsome Captain was back in Paris soon again. Tiquet, in order to prevent his wife from seeing her lover, hired a servant, a certain Jeanneton, a hypocritical woman, to spy upon her and report to him all she saw, while he himself, like Mary Magdalen's husband of old, kept the key of the house. Madame Tiquet, realizing that half of her fortune had disappeared in paying the debts of her husband, obtained from the courts a decree of separation of goods, and this being made public so humiliated Tiquet that he publicly accused her in regard to her associations with Montgeorges, and succeeded in getting a letter of cachet from the King permitting him to shut her up in a religious house of refuge. The

Madame had sense enough to know that she was beaten, so feigning submission as a dutiful wife, she wept and swore that though appearances were against her the accusations of infidelity were vile calumnies. She promised, however, that she would never again see the Captain, and Tiquet, satisfied with the submission, handed over to her the letter of cachet, which at once she proceeded to throw into the fire. Tiquet was enraged. He saw that he had been duped and he immediately sought a second letter of cachet, only to be dismissed by royalty as a nuisance. Then he entered complaints against Montgeorges, but the dashing Captain had such a host of friends that the only result of Tiquet's animosity was to cover himself with ridicule. And of course his wife had to suffer for it. Tiquet, knowing that the servants in the house were in favor of his wife, naturally distrusted them, and in order to control her every action hired as his butler a certain Jacques Moura, a man of thirty-five, a somber, morose, silent individual, who was to contribute so much to the destruction of Madame Tiquet, body and soul. He had his orders never to open the door except at the command of the master of the house, and even then he was sent to see that Madame never went out save in the company of the spy Jeanneton. The humiliated wife, shut up in this prison, became desperate. Montgeorges, entirely ignorant of the real situation, sent her messages imploring her to see him, but she could not escape from her prison. She hated Moura, but in spite of that she pleaded with him. All to no avail. Moura in turn hated her because she was a grand lady so far above his station, and then the woman realized that in spite of his hate real or pretended, this servant was actually enamored of her. Thereupon she sought to be delivered from her prison by flattering him. She succeeded. He relaxed his espionage, but he became so insane in his passion that in the end she submitted to a liaison with him that continued for a long time. In all history there are found few viler women than this same Madame Tiquet. But her sin was soon to bring its punishment.

Tiquet, suspicious of everybody, soon suspected that Moura was not working solely for his interests and he summarily dismissed him, alleging some negligence of duty. Moura, however, soon succeeded in getting back his position, but this time he brought back to it a bitterness against his employer. Madame thus found him a ready ally in her plot to get rid of her husband, a desire that possessed her more and more every day.

She herself conceived the idea of murdering her husband, and Moura agreed to it so heartily that he took it upon himself to execute it. To this end he hired an adventurer named Cattelain, who got some of his friends to help him with the murder. But Cattelain was a clever criminal. He refused to deal solely with a servant. He knew that Madame was interested and he insisted on seeing her in order to be sure of his wages. She fixed the price, gave him a big sum, and also promised to double that again as soon as he had accomplished the crime. This action of Madame Tiquet finally brought her to the block. It was planned that Cattelain and his gang should attack Tiquet just as he was entering his home on return from Parliament. It was winter, and night fell early. Cattelain bungled the job. For some reason he delayed. Tiquet had the key in his door when he was attacked. It was too late. The plot failed. Tiquet entered the house and Moura received him as usual, listening sympathetically as his master dilated on his escape from some murderers.

Cattelain, though he had failed, knew what a weapon he held over the head of the woman who had hired him. He demanded blackmail from her and she kept on paying it. And Tiquet, more suspicious, became more tyrannical than ever. But by the help of Moura Madame still continued to see Montgeorges, who never suspected to what crime her love for him was impelling her. Her love for him was an obsession, so that every meeting with him meant a new and greater hate against her husband, who continued to lock the door at night and keep the key under his pillow, raging with jealousy and hate against her even though he suffered her to pay the debts of his old debaucheries. She could have escaped the house forever, just as Magdalen had escaped hers, but by some strange sense of perverted loyalty she feared that such an open scandal would injure the career of her lover.

There was only one way out; Tiquet must be murdered. She tried poison. She dropped a powder into the soup which a servant was bringing to her husband who was confined to his room, but the servant, noting the strange action, and knowing the animosity of the woman, feigned to stumble and broke the cup. So she gave up the idea of poison and determined to bide her time.

Two years thus passed, years of hate during which she and her husband scarcely spoke to each other. She decided at last to manage the affair herself with the assistance of Moura who was still a slave to her charms. He brought to her a sergeant in the regiment of Montgeorges, Grandmaison by name, who agreed to commit the crime of murder for a price on condition that Montgeorges should know nothing about it, a condition to which she readily assented, since her lover was the last man in the world she would want to know of the horrible plot that was being hatched out of love for him. Grandmaison in turn got his aids, and she enlisted the help of her own servants. All was arranged. Tiquet, returning home one night, was shot. Five different wounds were inflicted on him, none of them, however, fatal. He was carried into the home of a neighbor where he remained until his recovery, indignantly refusing to see his wife, and stating that he knew of no other enemy save her. He suspected her of being the prime mover in the plot. But through it all she retained her sangfroid and even went to the police to lodge complaint of the attempted murder. She displayed the utmost indignation at the crime. She had no fear. Nobody could accuse her. She was safe. She held her head higher than usual. She frequented the salons, especially that of her friend, Madame d'Aulnay, the novelist, and was something of a heroine in the social set where her fine talents always made her a favorite. Nevertheless there was an undercurrent of suspicion against her, even though the general belief was that Moura, incensed at his discharge, had attempted to kill his employer. The upshot was that Moura was arrested, and shortly afterwards Madame Tiquet herself. Moura denied all and of course she did the same, with that cold indifference which considered it a joke that she should be charged with anything criminal, she the refined, cultured, noble lady. Of course they could prove nothing—of course! She was plainly innocent, and then by some freak of justice Cattelain, whom she had quite forgotten, reappeared on the scene. He was a coward, and, fearing that his former attempt would be discovered, confessed everything about his complicity in the first attempt at murder three years before.

But Madame was still unbroken, still self-possessed. She sneered at Cattelain; it was but a plot on the part of her husband, she said. But sneer as she might, her defense was useless. She and Moura were both found guilty of the attempt to murder Tiquet, and, according to the penal code of that time, were both condemned to death. Montgeorges, who was the prime cause of the crime, was astounded at the revelations. Out of his love for the woman, he besought all who had influence at court to seek a pardon for her. But in vain. Even Tiquet himself, who had recovered from his wounds, begged the King to commute the sentence, and in the next breath asked to have her property confiscated in his own favor. But the King refused to interfere with the course of justice, and Parliament reaffirmed the sentence.

During all the appeals the condemned woman was still as calm as if she were queening it in her own salon. Even when she was told that her appeal had been rejected, she never lost color. She was ever mistress of herself. "I am not frightened at my punishment," she said with dignity; "the day that ends my life ends my miseries. Without defying death, I shall bear it with fortitude. I have answered on the judgment seat without being troubled; I have listened to the sentence of my arrest without a shudder; I shall not be untrue to myself on the scaffold, even to the last sigh of my life."

According to the barbarous custom of the time, she was put to the torture in order to make her confess the crime of which she still declared herself innocent. The torture was horrible and she broke down under it, confessing the two attempts on the life of her husband and naming her accomplices, Moura, Cattelain and Grandmaison. The execution was set for that very afternoon of the torture, June 18, but it chanced to be the Feast of Corpus Christi, and on account of the religious processions, the end of the tragedy was deferred till the following day. The delay gave her a chance to make her peace with God, and she availed herself of that opportunity.

Her hauteur, her pride, had disappeared, and instead

had come a strength of soul that prepared her to meet death. There were many who doubted her repentance. They saw a proud, sinful, imperious woman, and they were asked to believe that within twenty-four hours this same criminal had turned wholly to God. They refused to believe it. Again, they reckoned without the grace of God. She was still the strong-willed, courageous woman, still the polished, refined lady of the world. She was as calm in preparing for death as if planning some social diversion. She wrote to her children, and even interested herself in the white garments she was to wear to the scaffold in expiation of her crime. She sought instruction as to the route she was to take to the block, and then with her accustomed sweetness thanked her fellow prisoners who had done her any service.

The curé of Saint Sulpice, Father Trotti de la Chetardie, came to bring her the consolations of religion. He had already visited her when she was in prison before her condemnation. At that time, still the haughty woman who was convinced that she would be found innocent, she received him kindly but with very little fervor. Now, however, things were different. She was facing death, and in spite of her past wickedness wanted to die well.

"Can I still hope for the mercy of God?" she asked him.

The priest assured her that God wished to save her soul and was infinitely merciful. But to test her contrition he exacted that she should seek forgiveness from her husband. She did this by writing a letter to the man she had so despised. There are still extant some verses which she is said have written during her last night on earth, verses of repentance and sincere piety. They may be translated as follows: "In this place of bitterness, great God, refuge of sinners, I, humbly prostrate, implore Thy aid against so many evils with which my soul is poisoned. My days are full of iniquity, but Thy clemency surpasses them. Come, by the effects of Thy grace to restore calm to my disturbed soul. Under the weight of my chains, every moment of my life presents itself against me, happy in my misfortune to lose it in Thee if it must be that it be taken away from me. The arrow that pierces my heart is not at seeing myself in chains. The keenest of my pains comes from the fear of Thy just rigor."

The day of the execution dawned, June 19, 1699. She dressed herself in her white garment with as much care as if she were going to the salon of Madame d'Aulnay. Before the door of the prison a cart drew up. Moura was there, and she was assisted to a place beside him. The priest took his place at her side while another priest sat beside Moura. Moura tried to excuse himself to her for his avowals under torture, but she calmly assured him that she herself had confessed all, and that anyway at this time there was nothing for them to do but to finish courageously.

But calm as she was she paled at the sight of the multitude that filled the streets. All Paris was there to behold her march to death. Stands had been built to accommodate the curious, and some of these stands had broken beneath the weight of the load of humanity. At the place of execution there was a "frightful multitude of people." It was all in all a gala day. The sight of so many eyes upon her burned into the soul of the proud woman. She turned in mute appeal to her confessor.

"Madame," said he, "look up to Heaven which you desire to enter. Drink this bitter chalice with the same courage with which Jesus Christ, Who was as innocent as you are guilty, drank His."

She lowered her head in shame as she realized there were so many witnesses to her disgrace. "Let the objects which you see with the eyes of faith," said the priest, "take from you those you see with the eyes of the body." Up to that time she had covered her face with her sleeve. Now she let the sleeve drop, careless as to the gaze of the gaping crowd. There was deep silence. The sight of the beautiful woman going to her doom struck pity into the hearts of all. Arrived at the scaffold, she regarded it without trembling. Then she turned to Moura and exhorted him to be resigned and to share her confidence in the mercy of God.

The ending was dramatic in the extreme. There was a sudden rumbling of thunder, the rain began to fall, soon developing into a regular deluge. The crowd rushed to shelter. Even the executioners hid from the storm, while Madame Tiquet and Moura stood in the cart heedless of the deluge. The rain ceased; the heavens cleared, and a ray of sunlight fell upon the criminals once more. The executioners returned to their place ready to go on with the work that had been interrupted. In a moment Moura was swinging from the gibbet. This was of little interest to the people, however; they had come to see the great lady die.

The woman watched the execution of her accomplice without a tremor. She joined her hands and breathed a prayer for his soul. A moment more and it was her own turn. That mattered little. She was already done with earth and had centered her heart on Heaven. There is no other way to explain the serenity of her death. She bade adieu to the priest and thanked him for the hope he had given her for the pardon of God. She begged the prayers of those about her, and then knelt and kissed the block before putting her head upon it. Tears were in the eyes of all the onlookers. There was genuine pity, which became horror when the executioner, a novice at the work, so bungled the affair that no less than five strokes were required to sever the beautiful head from the body. And in that horrible manner ended the criminal career of the beautiful Madame Tiquet. The severed head was exposed for several hours according to the requirements of the law, and then the remains were buried in the cemetery of Saint Sulpice.

There is an interesting letter concerning this celebrated case from the pen of Charlotte Elizabeth, the Princess Palatine, who was married to the Duke of Orleans. "Everyone," she writes, "is talking here of the woman who had her husband, the counselor, assassinated, and of the courageous fashion in which she bore her frightful death, for the executioner struck her five or six times before her head became separated from her body. So many people wished to assist at the sight, that windows were let at fifty pieces of gold. She was called Madame Tiquet, and had had her fortune told some years ago. It predicted that she would live to an extraordinary old age, and would lead a happy life if she avoided a man bearing her own name. Her maiden name was Carlier, and it happened that the executioner who beheaded her had the same name. This is really a curious thing."

For a long time the affair of Madame Tiquet held the attention of the public. Some pitied her; some loathed her very memory; some regarded her as a true penitent, some as a hypocrite to the end. It is always so easy to judge, so easy to condemn. Hypocrite she may have been, playing the part of the grand dame to the end. But we who know what the grace of God can do prefer to regard her as she appeared on that June day, a sincerely penitent woman who came by the way of sorrow to the pardon of God. Happy the sinner who gets the one instant in which to make his peace with God.

Chapter 19*

FRANCES, SISTER OF
ST. VINCENT FERRER

On another day, while he celebrated Mass at Valencia, on his return from one of his apostolic journeys, St. Vincent Ferrer saw appear before him, and as it were over the altar, a woman surrounded with flames and holding in her arms a little disfigured child. Astonished at such a vision, he adjured the woman, in the Name of the Lord, to tell him who she was and what she wanted.

She was one of his own sisters, named Frances, who had been dead some time. She had married a rich merchant. The latter having been obliged to undertake a long journey, the chief servant of his house profited by his absence to constrain the merchant's wife to commit sin with him, under the threat of death unless she consented. She was weak enough to yield; but recovering from her fright, and being covered with shame in her own eyes, she poi-

---

* This chapter has been added by the Publisher to the 2006 edition of this book. It is taken from *St. Vincent Ferrer*, by Fr. Andrew Pradel, O.P. (London: R. Washbourne, 1875; Rockford, Illinois: TAN, 2000), Imprimatur, pp. 144-145.
—*Publisher*, 2006.

soned the man to rid herself of his foul presence; and as she had conceived, she destroyed the off-spring before it was born. To complete her misery, she dared not avow these crimes in Confession and so she added to these murders numerous sacrileges.

At length, remorse filled her soul. She made her Confession to an unknown priest, with the greatest sorrow for her crimes, and died three days afterward. God having condemned her to an expiation of terrible duration [in Purgatory], she addressed herself to her brother to abridge its length. She indeed appeared again to St. Vincent three days afterward in glory, crowned with flowers, surrounded by Angels and ascending to Heaven; thus did she disappear from his sight.

Chapter 20*

EVE LAVALLIERE

"Eve Lavalliere" was the stage name of Eugenie Fenoglio, famous Parisian actress of the early 20th century. Born in 1866, Eve had risen to stardom after a tragic childhood. After years of family problems, at age 18 the young girl had witnessed her violent, alcoholic father fatally shoot her mother, then point his gun at Eugenie—but for some reason he instead turned his gun on himself, committing suicide.

After this ordeal, the orphan struggled with loneliness and thoughts of suicide. A turning point came, however, when she was introduced to a traveling theatrical group. It was discovered that Eugenie had talent, and her rise to fame began.

Eve Lavalliere "reigned as undisputed queen of the light-comedy stage" in Paris from 1901-1917. She had a great power to fascinate, being witty, enigmatic and full of life. Many famous people, including members of European royalty, paid her homage.

---

* This chapter has been added by the Publisher to the 2006 edition of this book. It is adapted, with permission, from Chapter 37 of *Modern Saints, Book Two*, by Ann Ball (TAN, 1990), Imprimatur, pp. 386-391. —*Publisher*, 2006.

The actress's personal life was disordered. She had several affairs with wealthy men, who supplied her with money, furs and jewels. Her most serious liaison was with a promoter and director, by whom she bore a daughter—who disliked her mother, pursued a perverse way of life, and would cause her mother many trials, even purposely addicting Eve to cocaine as she lay ill near the end of her life.

Eve's success left her unhappy, and on at least three occasions she came close to suicide.

However, in a little French village where she had gone to relax, grace was to touch the heart of the worldly French actress. Through the help of a good priest, Eve returned to the Sacraments of her childhood Faith. She gave up acting immediately, leaving journalists to speculate over her disappearance from the stage.

Eve saw her conversion as her birth to true life; she wrote off her former years as years of death. Henceforth she considered her real birthday to be the day on which, after much preparation and contrition, she had returned to Holy Communion.

The former actress's conversion was sincere and entire. She spent about three years attempting to find a convent that would accept her, but she was always turned down. Eve had especially wanted to enter Carmel. At the last convent she applied to, the Mother Superior was very impressed by Eve's purity of heart and ability to love, but in the final analysis the community felt they could not accept her because of her poor health, her child, and her fame. Eve accepted this as God's will.

Having returned to the Catholic Faith, Eve had finally found God—and happiness. She would spend the remaining 12 years of her life in prayer, reparatory suffering, and some mission work. Despite much physical and spiritual suffering, which included bouts of depression, Eve described herself as "indeed, the most perfectly happy of women."

At the end of her life, Eve's once-beautiful face was attacked by illness and swellings; the doctor even had to sew her eyelids shut. Yet Eve thanked Our Lord for permitting her thus to expiate the sins she had committed through these faculties. When she died in 1929, her body was buried near the small church in Thuillieres where she had spent her last days. Eve's motto was "Abandonment, love, trust."

If you have enjoyed this book, consider making your next selection from among the following . . .

Prices subject to change.

Prices subject to change.

Prices subject to change.

Prices subject to change.

At your Bookdealer or direct from the Publisher.
Toll-Free 1-800-437-5876   **Fax 815-226-7770**
Tel. 815-226-7777   **www.tanbooks.com**
Prices subject to change.

RIGHT REV.
HUGH FRANCIS BLUNT
1877-1957

Msgr. Blunt was a priest of the Archdiocese of Boston. The son of Irish-born parents, he had developed a love of books in his youth through grammar-school exposure to and memorization of poems by "the New England poets."

Msgr. Blunt traced his desire for the priesthood back to his days as an altar boy. Ordained in 1901, he was the chief editorial writer for the *Boston Pilot* from 1911-1919; then, beginning in 1919, he served as pastor of St. John's Church in Cambridge. There he had a parish school (including both elementary and high school) of 1,900 pupils. The title of "Monsignor" was conferred on Father Blunt by Pope Pius XII in 1944.

A prolific writer, Msgr. Blunt is said to have contributed to "almost every Catholic magazine here and abroad." He also wrote many Catholic books, including books of poetry. His prose books include *Great Wives and Mothers, Great Penitents, Witnesses to the Eucharist, Seven Swords* and *The Quality of Mercy.*

Over a period of years, Msgr. Blunt collected almost 1,000 books about Cardinal Newman. He eventually donated the collection to Regis College.

Msgr. Hugh Francis Blunt went to his reward in 1957.

The above information and photo have been taken from the book *Catholic Authors: Contemporary Biographical Sketches 1930-1947*, edited by Matthew Hoehn, O.S.B., B.L.S., St. Mary's Abbey, Newark, 1948.